THE LOST DECADE
2008–18

THE
LOST
DECADE
2008–18

How India's Growth Story Devolved
into Growth without a Story

PUJA MEHRA

EBURY
PRESS

An imprint of Penguin Random House

EBURY PRESS

USA | Canada | UK | Ireland | Australia
New Zealand | India | South Africa | China | Singapore

Ebury Press is part of the Penguin Random House group of companies
whose addresses can be found at global.penguinrandomhouse.com

Published by Penguin Random House India Pvt. Ltd
4th Floor, Capital Tower 1, MG Road,
Gurugram 122 002, Haryana, India

First published in Ebury Press by Penguin Random House India 2019

ISBN 9780670091836

Typeset in Bembo Std by Manipal Digital Systems, Manipal
Printed at Replika Press Pvt. Ltd.

www.penguin.co.in

This is a legitimate digitally printed version of the book and therefore might not
have certain extra finishing on the cover.

For my Praandhan Shri Radharaman Dev Ju

Contents

Introduction

In 2017, I was approached to co-author a book on India's economic policy in the Narendra Modi years. Researching for that proposal convinced me that to understand the apparent crises today—agrarian, rural, investments, banking, manufacturing, stagnation in exports, jobs, informal sector, institutions—requires grappling with the developments of the last ten years. Not just the Modi years.

What this backward glance reveals is that India was booming, cruising at 8.8 per cent plus economic growth before the start of the worst phase of the global financial crisis in September 2008.[1] This was the first time after Independence that the economy had sustained high growth for three consecutive years. It was an economic boom that lifted living standards of a large section of Indians, even if unequally. Per capita income was growing by 7.4 per cent annually.[2]

Big business and, later, even mid-sized firms acquired iconic companies overseas. Demand and wages for construction labour shot up. Project books overflowed. Increments, salaries and hiring went up. If companies set up new offices, factories and businesses, then young Indians bought new houses, all funded by debt. Real estate prices soared.

The needs of cities grew. Many more house helps, watchmen, drivers and cooks were required, which rural India supplied. City demographics changed. Lifestyles changed. Consumption baskets changed. The middle class started travelling by air instead of rail. The protein intake among poor families improved.

It was as if India's turn to claim the global spotlight had come. It was finally going to take off. With sustained high growth over an extended period, India could have approached what economists call a 'take-off', which means rapid and self-sustained GDP growth.

This momentum was called the 'India Growth Story'.

It was this unfolding 'story' that the global financial crisis disrupted ten years ago, in September 2008.

The immediate task of economic policy changed overnight. It now had to make sure that the 'India Growth Story' was not destroyed completely and the impact of the crisis was minimized.

The Indian authorities managed this well, but a series of policy failures followed 2009 onwards, almost as soon as the economy rebounded after the initial impact. The ten years from 2008 to 2018—the wasted decade as I call it—saw waning political will for reforms. The end result is that ten years have been lost but the pre-global financial crisis growth momentum has still not been regained.

Today, India's GDP is growing at a world-beating rate, but little on the ground suggests that people are actually feeling better off. There's no exuberance like before. Economic discontent and insecurity are on the rise, Dalits and farmers are restive, and traditionally land-owning classes are demanding quotas in government jobs. The middle class is palpably disaffected, the informal economy is struggling, and big businesses are no longer aggressively expanding. Balance sheets of the corporate sector and bad-loans-afflicted banks remain stressed. Debt is still not getting repaid. Finding a job is not easy, setting up a business is still difficult, savings earn little. To the average person, the GDP growth showing in the estimates put out by the official statistical apparatus seems out of sync with the day-to-day experience. The insufficiency of sustainable livelihoods threatens the demographic dividend. It may turn into a demographic nightmare.

The 'India Growth Story' has devolved into 'Growth without a Story'.

This book, organized into four chapters, reconstructs this slide.

'The Shock (2008–09)', the opening chapter of the book, revisits the seriousness of the global financial shock. In 2008, as one storied institution after another crashed on Wall Street under impact of the knock-on effect set off by the sub-prime crisis, shock and panic paralysed the global financial system. The US Federal Reserve and the US Treasury announced they were ready to print and pump as much money into the financial system as would be necessary to revive frozen credit markets and prevent the crisis from bringing down the US economy. But billions of dollars of bailouts and the unorthodox liquidity infusion programme, Quantitative Easing, could not prevent the crisis from turning into the worst global economic downturn since the Great Depression of the 1930s. Even ten years later, the world economy has still not recovered from it fully.

The authorities in India responded to the unfolding global crisis with alacrity, though. The crisis managers in the Reserve Bank of India (RBI) and the Manmohan Singh-led government administered timely emergency measures, averting a growth collapse and making sure no Indian bank or financial institution buckled under the impact of the domino effect spreading through the global financial system.

These initial monetary and fiscal responses were designed by economic experts, with little interference of politics, in contrast with the way economic policy was formulated in the decade that followed.

The global financial shock in September 2008 disrupted the pre-crisis momentum and slowed the economy for a year. The growth rate responded well to the emergency measures instituted and quickly rebounded by mid-2009.

The second chapter, 'A Recovery Destroyed (2009–12)', discusses the destruction of this 'V'-shaped recovery by developments essentially political in nature.

The Mumbai terror attacks in November 2008—two months after the collapse of the iconic Wall Street firm Lehman Brothers that marked the beginning of the worst phase of the global crisis—and the coronary bypass surgery Manmohan Singh underwent in January 2009 proved more significant determinants than the global crisis of how economic policy shaped up in the second term of the UPA government.

For changes in portfolios these unfortunate developments forced brought a politician locked in the 1970s dirigiste mindset, Pranab Mukherjee, to the finance ministry—the key portfolio for economic policy formulation. If the emergency measures were guided by economics, Mukherjee mostly acted in defiance of the advice he received from economists, including Manmohan Singh.

Driven largely by ideology and politics, he loosened the purse strings to step up public spending as if there were no tomorrow and ended up overstimulating the economy between 2009 and 2012.

This chapter discusses Mukherjee's policies and attitude towards the RBI that complicated the fiscal–monetary policy mix with disastrous consequences for both inflation and growth rates, a matter that featured routinely in Governor D. Subbarao's deliberations with Dr Singh. But the prime minister did not seem to have used his authority to press his finance minister to give up the profligacy. Its coordination with New Delhi less smooth now, the RBI, which had handled the immediate aftermath of the global financial crisis well, muffed its monetary policy.

If a monetary–fiscal policy fumble was not enough, a body blow to policymaking soon followed in the shape of a Comptroller and Auditor General of India (CAG) report on the 2G spectrum allotments by the telecom ministry headed by A. Raja. Its release—first in bits and pieces leaked to the media and then through the official channel in Parliament—in November 2010 kicked up a political maelstrom.

By 2012, a spate of scam, and corruption charges, Anna Hazare's Lokpal movement, and what is called the 3Cs—Courts,

Central Vigilance Commission (CVC) and CAG—plunged the UPA government into a policy paralysis. Parliament was not allowed to function, officials paused decisions, files stopped moving and projects stalled, leading to defaults on loan repayments and financial stress in companies and banks. Business confidence dipped. Mukherjee's 'retrospective tax terror' further soured the investment climate.

The chapter details how the seeds of the non-performing assets (NPAs) crisis in the banking system were in fact sown in this phase with the illustration of the IDBI Bank's controversial loan to the now-defunct Kingfisher Airlines. There was complete failure of oversight in the banking department and an obdurate stalling of reforms by forces both in and outside the government. The Opposition obstructed the UPA government's plans for rolling out the Goods and Services Tax (GST).

By the time Mukherjee was elected President of India in mid-2012, the economic recovery of 2009 had been completely derailed and food inflation was proving hard to control. I argue in the book that India needs to revisit its opinion of Pranab Mukherjee's tenure as finance minister, which has largely escaped critical examination, although, after Arun Jaitley (four years), it is he who held the portfolio most crucial to economic policy for the longest duration (three-and-a-half years) of the wasted decade.

The cocktail of politics, structural issues crying for reforms and policy failures brewed a full-blown macroeconomic crisis which is chronicled in the third chapter, 'A Slow Recovery Again (2012–15)'. For the RBI, the battle against the decade-high inflation segued into a defence of the rupee with the onset of the 'taper tantrums' triggered by decisions taken by the US Federal Reserve that landed India—christened a miracle economy just a few years earlier—into the ignoble 'Fragile Five' grouping of economies.

Singh's efforts at damage control immediately after the exit of Mukherjee from the UPA government in 2012 made only a small difference to the narrative and the reforms record of the

UPA. A National Food Security law and amendments to the law governing land acquisitions were passed in 2013–14 despite the policy paralysis, which shows the UPA government could push its way where it wanted in Parliament. But this was often not the case. The problem, it seems, was a political one in which the populists and status quoists in Singh's cabinet were able to veto the reformers and call the shots.

With eighteen months to go before the 2014 Lok Sabha elections, Singh brought back like-minded reformer P. Chidambaram— regarded well by the investor community and the bureaucracy for his 'dream budget' record—to the finance ministry in August 2012. A year later, Raghuram Rajan was appointed RBI governor. The two firefighters ensured the inflation rate, fiscal deficit and current account deficit were contained and, as the International Monetary Fund's Paul Cashin had told me in an interview back in 2014, India was no longer counted among the 'Fragile Five'.

Food inflation remained a problem area, though. The UPA government's minimum support prices policy is often blamed for its food inflation record, but the fault lay with the management of the procured stocks. Offloading food grains in the open market could have dampened prices, but there was an overbearing reluctance to take decisions.

With inflation burning holes in household budgets, economic discontentment turned into an angry political backlash against the UPA government, creating the conditions conducive for a 'Modi Wave'.

Briefly, in 2014, with Narendra Modi's arrival in New Delhi, there was tremendous hope and aspiration for the economy recovering its lost fizz, but the energy did not translate into any coherent plan. Instead, more misguided politics, dressed up as economics, followed. The modest but steady economic recovery Modi had inherited from the previous government was disrupted, even as the investment slowdown on since 2011–12 kept deepening.

The story of the replacement of the Nehruvian relic, Planning Commission, with NITI Aayog in this chapter gives insights into Modi's approach to prime ministership and institution building.

Chapter four, 'Another Recovery Destroyed (2016–18)', retraces the major economic policies of the Modi government. Political calculations were central to the decisions taken.

A political call was taken to go slow on tackling the banking system's growing problems, especially infusion of public money to provide for losses on account of loans gone bad. The Modi government dithered on the banking crisis despite a detailed presentation from Modi's trusted bureaucrat Hasmukh Adhia and advice from a number of officials in the finance ministry on the measures that were needed. Neglected, the banking problems escalated into a full-blown NPAs crisis.

Initiatives for land, labour and other reforms were announced but were soon abandoned. The loss of direction was a result of political calculus. The electoral losses the BJP suffered in the state assembly polls held in 2015, in Delhi and Bihar, and the less-than-modest success of the initial measures aimed at downsizing the black economy threatened to end the Modi Wave. Demonetization was announced to regain control of the political narrative and reinvent Modi's image. The poor design of the GST system was similarly an outcome of political compulsions.

In all these decisions, economic advice, just as had been the case in Singh's government, was sidelined. A key difference, however, was that busybodies were able to create rifts and controversies so serious that one after the other economists decamped from the government and the RBI. Finally, decades of neglect by successive governments together with policy mistakes made by the Modi government resulted in a farm crisis.

This chapter also lays out the paradox of India being the fastest-growing economy in the world, but without a world-beating sector. Indeed, no segment of the economy—exports, manufacturing, agriculture or investments—is a winner at the moment. Success

stories of the previous decades—telecom and manufacturing—
have unravelled. And amidst all this, a sense that things 'could have
been so much better' continues to linger. Little progress has been
notched up on the list of pending big reforms and it remains nearly
unchanged in ten years.

Argument of the Book

Overall, this book tells the story of an economy enervated by
politics. The argument of the book is that the growth potential
of the economy is not being realized because of the constraints
placed on it by a decrepit political system. The key characters are
all charged, a few acquitted. This book is not a study in contrasts
between the two regimes that occupied office in this decade. Nor is
it about politics per se. It is about the impact of politics on policies
and the economy.

Many would argue that India has done rather well in the last ten
years—if every third Indian lived in poverty ten years back,[3] today
one in five Indians is living in poverty.[4] The per capita income has
improved from $1090 to $1942.[5] India is feted, especially at home,
as the fastest-growing major economy in the world.

But how much progress has been notched up on resolving
chronic problems in the ten years gone by? Urbanization? Education
reforms? Agrarian reforms? Administrative reforms? Banking
reforms? Land and labour reforms? Generation of sustainable
livelihoods? Generation of black money?

High growth momentum cannot be sustained without reforms.
The last decade, therefore, represents a missed opportunity—for
radically reforming India's economic systems, sustaining high
growth rates and improving lives meaningfully. The cost of these
failures is further delay in realizing our collective and individual
potentials.

'There is no time to lose,' Manmohan Singh had told Parliament
on 24 July 1991, presenting the epochal budget.[6]

If 1991 marked the rise of good economics in India, politics struck back with a vengeance in the past decade. Our present and future could have been better if policymakers had greater resolve, the kind Singh exuded during the balance of payments crisis in 1991.

The developments in the last decade that ended up pushing away the economic future that was nearly within our reach are discussed and argued with the aid of facts and official data available in the public domain. These are presented alongside the reflections of several of the dramatis personae based on their conversations with me. I have respected the privacy of the conversations I have had with various public figures. Only those willing to go on record are named.

The book uses the Central Statistical Office's (CSO) 2004–05 base year series for national income data before 2011–12. For the years after 2011–12, the CSO's updated series data (with base year 2011–12) is used. The reason being that the much-delayed and controversial back casted series was released literally hours after the manuscript was completed and submitted to the publisher. Only minor updates were possible thereafter. In any case, as I have written elsewhere, the back series is too flawed for any significant meaningful analysis to be possible using it.

1

The Shock (2008–09)

In the summer of 2006, Y.V. Reddy, the twenty-first governor of the RBI started preparing for growing imbalances in the global economy.[1] The RBI's 25 July 2006 statement flagged the risks from the emerging global scenario.[2]

The RBI began speaking in specifics about the risks a year later. There were imminent threats to the economy from the 're-pricing of risks by [global] financial markets and the danger of downturn in some asset classes', it warned on 31 July 2007, and added that the impact of these developments and the policy responses of the major central banks to these developments around the world now constituted the most important influence on the economy and the RBI's policies.[3]

These statements are among the earliest recorded warnings—and preparation for minimizing the impact—of the global financial meltdown in the world.

The meltdown would go on to become a full-blown crisis, the worst since the Great Depression of the 1930s. But the antennae of the authorities in the United States, where the crisis originated, hadn't caught the warning signals of it even till as late as May 2007. Even though sharp increases in sub-prime mortgage loan delinquencies had been noticed in the United States and an alarming number of homes were entering foreclosure.

And yet, the US Federal Reserve foresaw no broader economic impact from the defaults its Chairman, Ben S. Bernanke, said on 17

May 2007 in a scheduled speech on the phenomenon.[4] He ruled out heavy-handed regulation of lenders or of the troubled housing market.[5]

Barely three months later, the US financial system was quaking from the sub-prime[6] market collapse, and the Fed, as the Federal Reserve is colloquially known, was scrambling to ready its very first response to the crisis.

'The market is not operating in a normal way,' Bernanke announced in a hastily convened conference call at 8.45 a.m. on 10 August.[7]

To facilitate the market's orderly functioning, he said, the Fed would stream liquidity. Funding issues at two large US financial entities had unnerved the markets. Washington Mutual and Countrywide had, in statutory filings, reported unprecedented disruptions in the credit market and liquidity difficulties.

In the weeks that followed, it became clear that small releases of liquidity would not be enough. The crisis spread like wildfire. As it unfolded, there was hardly a storied financial institution on Wall Street that remained untouched. The ferocity of the crisis dried up liquidity, setting off solvency cascades.

The Fed was now desperate to somehow stop the turmoil in the housing and finance markets from bringing down the entire US economy. For the first time in four years, it began cutting interest rates.[8] It dropped its benchmark rate by an unusually large one-half percentage point, thereby employing the most powerful weapon in its armoury.

The deepening crisis forced the central bank to become a sort of lending bank itself, even as institution after institution crumbled under losses because of their exposure to sub-prime loans and because of liquidity issues. The Fed invoked its emergency powers to throw a $30 billion credit line to JPMorgan Chase to take over Bear Stearns, and to announce an open-ended lending programme for the biggest firms on Wall Street in March 2008.[9]

The US Treasury bailed out mortgage giants Fannie Mae and Freddie Mac.[10] In the days after the two went into conservatorship,[11] Washington Mutual was closed down by regulators. Merrill Lynch vanished. Wachovia appeared to be sinking. Insurance behemoth American International Group (AIG) teetered.[12]

14 September 2008, a Sunday, will go down in Wall Street history as the day the world grew disillusioned with American capitalism.[13] In a deal brokered by the US government, Merrill Lynch agreed to sell itself to Bank of America.[14] But similar efforts to prevent the bankruptcy of Lehman Brothers failed. The same day, AIG sought a $40 billion lifeline from the Fed to escape a credit rating downgrade that was slated for Monday. It was provided one, the first in a series of US taxpayer-funded bailouts, for $80 billion.

Lehman Collapses

The iconic securities firm, Lehman Brothers, filed for bankruptcy protection later that Sunday, at 1.45 a.m.[15] This was the biggest bankruptcy in American history, with losses of $2.8 billion that quarter, over $600 billion in debt, hardly any collateral, and 25,000 employees who lost their jobs.[16]

On Wall Street, the Dow Jones plunged 500 points, the largest drop since the 9/11 terror attacks.[17] Fear and panic gripped financial markets around the world. Images of traders exiting the Lehman building on Times Square carrying boxes of their belongings became a symbol of the global financial crisis. Which idolized institution would go down next? The entire global banking sector seemed poised to tumble like a row of dominoes. A full-blown crisis of confidence froze money markets globally.

In the months that followed, one free-market dogma after another crashed and burnt. One of the loudest cheerleaders of free markets, former Federal Reserve Chair, Alan Greenspan, once dubbed the 'Oracle' and the 'Maestro,' a single sentence from whom could send the markets up or down, was gobsmacked. In 2003, he had confidently asserted, 'Not only have individual financial institutions become less vulnerable to shocks from underlying risk factors but also the financial system as a whole has become more resilient.'[18] When Greenspan retired in 2006, everyone assumed he would be immortalized in history's financial hall of fame. Two years later, in a House Committee hearing,[19] a little over a month after Lehman's collapse, the broken banker admitted that he was 'in a state of shocked disbelief'. Greenspan's faith in capitalism had taken a severe beating. 'I have found a flaw. I don't know how significant or permanent it is. But I have been very distressed by that fact.' When a Congressman asked him if he had been misled by his own ideas, Greenspan replied, 'That's precisely the reason I was shocked because I'd been going for 40 years or so with considerable evidence that it was working exceptionally well.'[20]

Bernanke and Henry M. Paulson Jr., treasury secretary under then President George W. Bush, began discussions on 18 September 2008 with congressional leaders on what would go on to become the biggest bailout in United States history.[21] The financial system, they warned, was imploding, and the Fed could not be relied upon to prevent the collapse on its own.

The same day, the Fed streamed almost $300 billion into global credit markets through lending programmes operated by the European Central Bank and the central banks of Canada, Japan, Britain and Switzerland. But this could not unfreeze the global credit markets. The US crisis was rapidly turning into a global liquidity frost.

The US Treasury was selling new treasury bills at an unprecedented pace—$200 billion in the week the four once-proud financial institutions were bailed out—and parking the liquidity thus raised at the Fed for unencumbered use in its campaign to save Wall Street.

Having exhausted everything that was imaginable, the Fed turned to the unconventional. On 16 December 2008 it dropped its benchmark interest rate to almost zero and started lending overnight federal funds at 0 per cent to 0.25 per cent.[22] Through unorthodox lending programmes, it pumped vast quantities of money into the system and announced that it stood ready to print as much money as was necessary to revive the paralysed credit markets and fight the worst economic downturn since World War II.[23]

'We are running out of the traditional ammunition that's used in a recession, which is to lower interest rates . . . It is critical that the other branches of government step up, and that's why the economic recovery plan is so essential,' President Barack Obama told a news conference on the same day.

The Fed's balance sheet expanded from $900 billion to more than $2 trillion between September and December 2008 as it flooded the financial system with liquidity.[24] Early 2009, the Fed pledged to pump an extra $1 trillion into the financial system through a programme of buying treasury bonds and mortgage securities that became known as 'quantitative easing' or 'QE'. In the second round of QE eighteen months later, it added $600 billion.

By 2015, three phases of QE had streamed $4.5 trillion into the international financial markets.[25]

Following the collapse from a distance of about 7700 miles, the RBI was prepared for possible contagion spread to India. It could spread through Indian companies and financial institutions' exposure to the toxic financial assets overseas and the linkages with the money and foreign exchange markets. On 30 October 2007, Reddy said, 'The immediate task for public policy in India . . . is to manage the possible financial contagion which is in an incipient stage with highly uncertain prospects of being resolved soon.'[26] Reddy retired on 5 September 2008, just ten days before the collapse of Lehman Brothers.

The collapse of Lehman Brothers on 15 September 2008 marked the beginning of the worst phase of the global crisis. But within hours of Lehman Brothers filing for bankruptcy, the Indian authorities had swung into crisis management.

First Aid

Many of the dramatis personae in the government during the crisis were new in their hot seats.[27] India's chief financial bureaucrat, Union Finance Secretary Arun Ramanathan, was appointed barely a week after Lehman's collapse. The Union economic affairs secretary, Ashok Chawla, was appointed on the day the news broke of Lehman's collapse, on 15 September. The central bank governor, Subbarao, was appointed eleven days before the Lehman collapse. The two key crisis managers in those early days were Finance Minister P. Chidambaram and Planning Commission Deputy Chairman Montek Singh Ahluwalia.

The worry for India was that the credit squeeze around the world meant credit would dry up, irrespective of the underlying credit worthiness of Indian companies and financial institutions. Chidambaram's instructions to the crisis managers at the RBI and the government were precise. He wanted measures that could ensure three objectives: enough liquidity in the market; no run on banks; and no bank collapses resulting from asset-liability mismatch.

The day Lehman collapsed, the RBI and the other Indian regulators ring-fenced its Indian subsidiaries.[28] Restrictions were placed on their operations, and they were prohibited from remitting funds out of the country. The quarantine prevented the spillover of any direct knock-on impact of the happenings on Wall Street into the Indian financial system.

In India, all financial markets—equity, bond, forex and credit—were left stunned by what was happening in the US. Fear took over: Could fissures from the quaking Wall Street spread to some Indian institution and take it down?

'When Lehman Brothers collapsed, India was affected, as was virtually every country in the world. However there was dismay and disbelief in India, especially as the Indian financial sector was cautiously regulated, and also our banks did not have exposure to the toxic assets which were at the root of the crisis. "We were not affected by the Asian financial crisis of the late 1990s. Why should we then be affected by this crisis?" was the question most people, including analysts, were asking. What people neglected to see was that in the ten years between the Asian crisis and the Lehman crisis, India had integrated deeply into the global financial system. Any disruption anywhere was going to have a knock-on impact on us,' recalls Subbarao.[29]

'The speed and ferocity of the crisis unnerved not just global financial markets but even policy makers. There was anxiety in advanced economies about how the crisis might spread and which institution might be the next one to fall,' he adds.

In a panic, banks, other financial institutions and traders were hoarding liquidity. The flow of credit, thus, choked, and the entire system became paralysed. During a crisis of the magnitude that was unfolding in the US, the fear that money once parted with will not return drives banks, market participants, traders and financial institutions to hoard liquidity. This locks down the system, bringing trading, lending, payment transfers and other financial activities to a halt. In such a situation, restoring confidence in the markets becomes the primary objective of crisis managers.

The RBI showed due urgency. Within hours of Lehman's collapse, it instituted emergency measures for easing liquidity in the money and forex markets to ensure their orderly functioning and to neutralize the impact of the global squeeze. But the deficit persisted. The dates of Lehman's collapse coincided with the date for advance tax payment in India. Companies redeemed the money they had parked with short-term mutual funds for making these payments. About a third of the full year's tax dues had to be furnished to the authorities. Rs 48,000 crore was sucked out of the system for meeting tax obligations.[30] This outgo added to the crisis-induced shortage of cash.

Credit markets drying up can spell destruction for vulnerable institutions. Credit shortage can increase risk of payment defaults. A single failure to fulfil an obligation can set off a cascade of defaults.

The worry in the government was that any signs of stress would most certainly be read as related to the happenings on Wall Street, even if they were in no way connected, leading to tremendous fear.

Lehman's operations were ring-fenced, and none of the toxicity could spill into the Indian financial system. Indian authorities moved with alacrity in addressing liquidity issues as and when they arose, and there were no insolvency-type situations. But there was fearful apprehension of the possibility that there might be some.

The country's second largest bank, ICICI, said it might have to set aside an additional $28 million (Rs 131 crore) to cover losses on investments in Lehman securities in the UK.[31] The exposure was small and did not constitute a risk to the bank's solvency. Its Indian operations were insulated.

'The size of the exposure is very, very small related to the size of our balance sheet,' joint managing director Chanda Kochhar said on a business news channel.[32]

Mumbai-based brokerage houses put out varying estimates of the extent of the bank's exposure to Wall Street. One said ICICI would lose up to $200 million on bonds, including debt issued by Lehman.[33] Another said that if any other global institution fell, the bank's losses would rise further.[34] Trouble started brewing for the bank when investors, worried by the analysts' notes, rushed to sell their shares in the bank, dragging its stock down.

Financial Stability Worries

The then RBI Governor D. Subbarao says he had begun to be concerned by growing speculation about the health of ICICI Bank. Newspapers were writing stories, he says, that the bank was about to collapse. TV news showed queues forming outside branches of ICICI Bank, especially from second-tier cities and towns. His view at the time was that at a time when public confidence in the financial sector was already broken, reports like this, even if they were fake news,[35] could trigger bank runs and wreck financial stability . . .[36]

The perception of heightened risk had sent up overnight borrowing rates for ICICI Bank to 20 per cent. There were fears now of a run on ICICI Bank deposits.

The bank made use of a massive communication campaign to send out messages and emails to its 27 million customers, saying,

Dear customer, your deposits with ICICI Bank are safe. Your bank is well capitalized with good liquidity. Please do not listen to baseless rumours . . .[37]

CEO K.V. Kamath said the rumours were 'baseless and malicious', but they refused to die down.[38]

The governor consulted his senior advisers on how RBI should respond to the reports about ICICI.[39] Opinion was divided on what, if anything, RBI must do. One view was that RBI should just keep quiet since it was not the standard practice for the regulator to issue a statement regarding a specific financial institution. In fact, such an assurance might have made even previously unsuspecting people suspicious and exaggerate the fear. The other view was that this was an extraordinary situation with fear and panic rapidly spreading. The RBI could not sit back and let the events unfold. An assurance from RBI would have stemmed the anxiety about the health of ICICI. This was a situation which demanded that RBI leverage on its credibility to guard financial stability, says Subbarao.

In the event, the governor decided to go with the latter option. A statement was issued, saying that ICICI had enough liquidity, and RBI was ready to make more cash available to the bank, should it run short.

A bland statement like this might seem banal from this distance of time, but in real time, it proved remarkably effective in calming the anxiety around ICICI.

'ICICI's leadership was, if I may say, a little nervous, and rather closed. That itself was feeding rumours about ICICI,' recalls

Chidambaram.[40] He insisted that Kamath go on television and say that the bank was sound and that there was no need for any apprehensions about it.

'It took a little persuasion. But I told him, "I'm very clear in my mind, you have to go on television and make this statement. Once you make this statement, I will come and support you,"' recalls Chidambaram.

The markets too wanted a more drastic approach to resolution of the crisis. ICICI Bank was being hammered on the stock markets. It traded at Rs 364 per share on 10 October 2008, down from Rs 1231 per share at the beginning of the year.[41]

Kamath was convinced that manipulators and rumour-mongers were behind the crash. He called up the Securities and Exchange Board of India (SEBI) chief, C.B. Bhave, seeking restrictive action against market speculators, at least against those going after financial companies.[42] He dialled the finance minister demanding a ban on speculative trades. Chidambaram asked him to speak to his customers to reassure them.

Chidambaram then asked his ministry officials, 'Why shouldn't we implement the ban?'

The joint secretary in charge of the capital markets division, K.P. Krishnan, explained that banning speculation wasn't going to resolve the problem.[43]

'You have very high fever. There are two options. One, take a paracetamol and sleep it through. Two, break the thermometer, and do not acknowledge that you have fever,' Krishnan told Chidambaram.

The phone rang. It was the Prime Minister's Office (PMO) calling Chidambaram over for a discussion on 'banning speculation'. Chidambaram asked his ministry officials to accompany him to the meeting.

'You can use all the mumbo-jumbo of finance with the PM; he understands,' Chidambaram told them.

The officials briefed the prime minister. A decision was taken to not give in to the pressure for trading restrictions and to protect market freedom.

'What is speculative trading? These are all contextual fears. Every other day you want people to speculate in the market because that keeps the market alive and active, produces volumes. When you face a crisis, then you come to the other end and you say, "speculative trading" [accusatively, as if it were a destructive market activity]. We refused to take any decision in panic. Because we did not have the subprime problem,' recalls Chidambaram.[44]

Finally, after about a day or so, Kamath went live on television and said, 'Hand on my heart, the deposits are safe.'[45]

Says Chidambaram, 'Immediately, I responded by saying, "Yes, I fully endorse what Mr Kamath said."[46] Both the RBI and the ministry were advised to continue to keep that narrative going: that there's nothing wrong with ICICI Bank.'

It worked. The markets believed Kamath. ICICI shares recovered.

Liquidity Squeeze

The call rate in the money market was 13.1 per cent on 16 September 2008. By 10 October, it had shot up to 18.5 per cent.[47] (Call rate is the interest rate on bank loans to brokerage firms for transactions in their client accounts.) Even well-established companies were being denied credit. Flow of working capital was affected. The government was of the view that the liquidity released by the RBI was well short of the financial system's requirements. Chidambaram, in particular, believed that the crisis demanded a more aggressive response from the RBI.[48]

At the time, Subbarao was all set to fly to Washington DC as the leader of an Indian delegation to the annual meetings of the International Monetary Fund (IMF).[49] Hours before he was to leave, Montek Singh Ahluwalia, who would go on to become the government's main crisis manager, urged the governor to further ease liquidity. The governor responded positively the next day.

A day later, Chidambaram suo moto constituted a nodal crisis management body, essentially a committee on liquidity management, with Finance Secretary Arun Ramanathan as the chairman. The RBI saw the committee, to which it asked to nominate a representative, as the government's trespass on its turf. Subbarao was upset.[50] He called Chidambaram to let the latter know in unequivocal terms that his action was totally inappropriate, and urged him firmly to dissolve the committee. The call ended with Subbarao telling the finance minister that the Reserve Bank would not participate in the committee.[51]

Two days later Chidambaram reasserted himself on the crisis. He wanted to avert a situation where, say, a mutual fund might collapse under redemption pressures,[52] for the fall of even one fund could have a domino effect on the rest.

He asked the SEBI chief C.B. Bhave and U.K. Sinha, chairman and managing director of UTI Mutual Funds, to make it to the RBI headquarters on Mint Street, Mumbai, the next morning, on 14 October. Bhave and Sinha were in by 8 a.m. The two officials met the RBI top brass—the governor was still in Washington—and the central bank announced a special funding facility for mutual funds before the stock markets opened that day. That announcement eased much of the stress in the markets.

The contagion from the building global crisis could have entered India through three possible channels: the finance channel, the real economy (mainly global demand for Indian exports) channel, and the confidence channel.[53]

In the first few weeks after the Lehman collapse, the finance channel seemed to be by far the most vulnerable to bringing in the contagion. The external developments touched domestic vulnerabilities, triggering complex and pernicious loops.

With global liquidity having dried up, corporates started turning to domestic banks for their credit needs. Simultaneously, corporates also started liquidating their investments in domestic money market mutual funds. These mutual funds, in turn, started withdrawing their investments from NBFCs (non-banking financial companies), which, reeling under the pressure of sudden substantial withdrawals, turned to banks. This heightened the stress on banks as they were already struggling to cope with the additional credit demand from the corporates.

The government and the RBI agreed that confidence would return to the financial markets if the liquidity stress was not allowed to trigger any insolvency. Because even a single case of insolvency would be seen by the public as linked to Wall Street and would hurt public trust in the financial system, complicating crisis management for the government. It was, therefore, important that the domestic financial markets go on functioning normally.

And so, maintaining comfortable domestic and forex liquidity was the best form of crisis management. This meant the RBI would have to ensure that the system was flush with rupee liquidity; it also had to augment foreign-exchange liquidity and drive a policy framework aimed at keeping credit operations functional, which was crucial for preventing the global turmoil from hurting India's GDP growth.

The RBI established dedicated lines of credit for augmenting the liquidity of NBFCs and mutual funds to provide them the cash they needed to pay off their investors.

Even as RBI was responding to the rapidly evolving situation, often in anticipation of potential developments, the fear and uncertainty in financial markets was so intense that there were always calls for even more action, says Subbarao.[54] The government too often joined this chorus, believing that in a crisis situation, it was important to be seen to be doing something all the time to instil confidence in market participants.[55]

All this was in the context of central banks around the world, having exhausted their traditional tool kits, resorting to unorthodox measures. Every time any central bank, especially from an advanced country, initiated an unorthodox measure, there were demands that the RBI should do the same regardless of whether our situation required it or not. For example, the UK, fearing a run on its banks, had made deposit insurance universal. There were calls that we must do so in India too, recalls Subbarao. The RBI view was that any such measure would not be credible, and might in fact exacerbate the panic.

Central banks around the world are given to agonizing over every move they make. They measure every word they utter, finesse every punctuation, calibrate every nuance, all out of anxiety that failure of their actions to deliver the intended impact would erode their creditability and, therefore, policy effectiveness down the line.

In times of crises though, timeliness of action should get greater consideration. On 20 October, just four days ahead of a scheduled monetary policy review, Governor Subbarao reduced the policy repo rate—the rate at which commercial banks borrow overnight from the Reserve Bank—by 1 percentage point. That the announcement was made off-schedule sent out the signal of it being extraordinary. Plus, this represented a change of regime. The pre-crisis fight against persistently high inflation was being paused, and the tightening monetary stance was being reversed.

The governor covered the government's concerns in his off-schedule policy statement. The signal was: 'Financial stability has overtaken inflation as the overriding concern.'[56]

A cut in the repo rate of 1 full percentage point that Subbarao effected in October 2008 was a non-standard action from the perspective of a central bank used to cutting the interest rate by a maximum of half a percentage point (50 basis points in the jargon) when it wanted to signal strong action. Within RBI, there was serious deliberation on the advisability of going into uncharted waters and how it might set expectations for the future. There were concerns that in the future, the market may discount a 50 basis-point cut as too tame. But considering the uncertain and unpredictable global environment and the imperative to improve the flow of credit in a stressed situation, Subbarao bit the bullet again and decided on a full percentage-point cut.[57]

'In hindsight, I can say it was a good decision,' says Subbarao.

The RBI began pumping in liquidity aggressively thereafter, trying to douse the ferocity of the crisis. Quite like the Fed in the

US, the RBI would take its policy interest rates down to historically low levels, wading further into unconventional territory.[58] At the lowest level, reached three years later in October 2011, the RBI's policy rate, at 3.25 per cent, was not zero in nominal terms, but given the inflation rate it was practically zero lower bound. There was no room for further cuts after that.

The global crisis had increased the volatility of capital flows. The flight of dollars created pressures in the Indian forex market. First, there was a stampede of forex out of the Indian equity and debt markets on the part of foreign institutional investors (FIIs), as part of their global deleveraging process. These investors had put billions of dollars into global markets in the pre-crisis years. Adding to those pressures, as external financing dried up, Indian corporates raised funds locally and began converting those into foreign currency to meet their overseas obligations.

The exchange rupee-dollar rate plunged, falling from 46.63 on 16 September to a low of 50.52 on 2 December because of the outflow of dollars.[59]

To attract forex inflows, the RBI instituted a number of measures.[60] It raised the cap on the interest rate that banks could offer to foreign currency deposits by NRIs. Norms for external commercial borrowing by corporates were relaxed substantially, and NBFCs and housing finance companies were allowed to access foreign borrowings. To mitigate the dent on export prospects, credit and refinance facility for exports were enhanced. The lendable resources available to apex institutions like the Small Industries Development Bank of India, the Export Import Bank of India and the National Housing Bank were expanded so as to increase the flow of credit to productive sectors.

The Mumbai Terror Attacks

On 26 November 2008, dastardly terrorist attacks struck Mumbai. The city shut down, but the terrorist attack was not allowed to impact the financial system.

Chidambaram was on the phone several times with Subbarao, asking when the markets would reopen.[61] He was particular that the regulators demonstrate to the world that India would not be cowed by terrorists and that our financial markets were too resilient to be hit by anything, even something of the magnitude of the 26/11 terror attacks.

The payment and settlement systems for financial transactions, the real-time gross settlement (RTGS) and national electronic funds transfer (NEFT), recommenced on 27 November, the day after the attack. A breakdown could have brought commercial activity to a standstill, which would have sapped the confidence of an already shaken public. The potential for panic was frightening. The day after, the government securities, the foreign exchange and money markets, the stock markets and clearing houses, all returned to normal functioning.

On 30 November, Chidambaram, who'd had a stint as minister for internal security in Prime Minister Rajiv Gandhi's government in the late 1980s, was appointed the Union home minister after the incumbent, Shivraj V. Patil, resigned, owning moral responsibility for the terror attacks.

Prime Minister Manmohan Singh, a distinguished economist, decided to keep the finance portfolio with himself. Montek Singh Ahluwalia and the chairman of the Economic Advisory Council, C. Rangarajan, would assist him. Singh's intention was to retain the charge till the 2009 elections at least[62], but he could not for reasons that will become clear in the next chapter. The string of events set into motion with the terror attacks in Mumbai would, thus, turn out to have an impact greater than even the global financial crisis on India's economic policy approach and the state of the economy over the course of the decade 2008–18.

Right from the beginning of the global financial crisis, the prime minister would hold frequent meetings, involving the finance minister and the RBI governor. Occasionally the finance secretary would be called in too. Rangarajan and Ahluwalia would invariably be present. On occasion, cabinet ministers and secretaries to the government were invited too, to discuss the government's response to the crisis.

As Chidambaram got busy with putting in place new legal and operational provisions for strengthening the country's security framework, his involvement in matters of the economy reduced. Prime Minister Singh continued to seek his assistance and inputs on finance and the economy. Singh drafted Ahluwalia, a lightweight as far as the power equations in the government were concerned, for the main firefighting required to deal with the crisis.

The government's assessment was that the global crisis had the potential of inflicting a debilitating impact on the real economy. RBI's liquidity measures and policy rate cuts were not bringing down banks' lending rates, and therefore not compensating adequately for the global liquidity crunch and demand collapse.

The Rescue Plan

Emergency fiscal measures were needed to stave off a GDP growth collapse. Ahluwalia and the team of economists entrusted with the job of crafting a rescue plan for the economy settled on a two-part fiscal response, supplementing the monetary measures being taken by the RBI.

In the beginning of 2008, before the Lehman collapse, Chidambaram had already announced loan waivers for farmers. At the time of the announcement, the move was motivated by political considerations ahead of the impending 2009 Lok Sabha elections, rather than sound economics. Most of the government's economists, as well as the RBI governor at the time, Reddy, had objected to the waiver, pointing out its weakness in addressing rural stress and its pernicious impact on the credit culture.[63] Waivers penalize farmers who repay loans on time and benefit only borrowers from banks. But, with the financial crisis striking the economy unexpectedly, having a farm loans package in the pipeline proved felicitous—a case of getting a policy response right by fluke due to changed circumstances; not well-grounded policymaking.

Recalls Arvind Virmani, then chief economic adviser: 'In a public meeting, I had politely said I don't agree with that [farm loans waivers], but [on the breakout of the global financial crisis] it turned out to be a very timely thing. In the sense that that was that thing which actually I proposed be implemented immediately because it was injecting purchasing power into the economy.'[64]

Quickly pushing out the farm loan waivers became the first element of the response plan the government's economists devised. The finance ministry processed the scheme with urgency. Natural stabilizers formed the second set of responses. An economic collapse naturally reduces tax collections, but expenditures adjust slowly. It was decided to maintain the expenditures, which implied that the fiscal deficit could be expected to automatically expand. Expenditure heads, technically called automatic stabilizers, were left untouched.

The government's detractors, and eventually urban voters even, were critical of this focus on rural spending, in particular the MGNREGA (Mahatma Gandhi National Rural Employment Guarantee Act). But to arrest the dampening effects of the global financial crisis, an immediate pickup in consumption was needed, without which, projections showed, a drastic fall in GDP would be near certain. Among the choices available, MGNREGA was the fastest and easiest way of putting money in people's pockets. Infrastructure would have been too long-gestation.

The third element was an active one: a temporary reduction in taxes.

All in all, the downtrend in fiscal deficits achieved in the first four years of the UPA government, these decisions implied, would have to be disrupted.

In the absence of a stimulus, it was estimated, GDP growth would slow down to 5 per cent, but with the stimulus would be more likely closer to 7 per cent.[65]

Ahluwalia announced a ten-point fiscal stimulus package, a mini-budget of sorts, on 7 December.[66] It included an across-the-board tax cut to bring down the prices of cars, cement, textiles and other products. An additional Rs 20,000 crore was proposed to be spent on infrastructure that year.[67]

Soon there was more evidence of economic activity slowing down. Exports had shown negative growth for two consecutive months. Manufacturing had shown negative growth for the first time since 1994. Business confidence had been dented significantly.[68]

Worried that the package announced may prove insufficient for lessening the impact of the global financial crisis on the economy, the government prepared a second, more comprehensive set of measures.

Exactly a month after the announcement of the first stimulus package, Ahluwalia announced this subsidiary package,[69] in January 2009, this time in tandem with the RBI. The coordinated plan focused on higher public spending, additional liquidity for onward lending at lower interest rates, boosting sagging sales of commercial vehicles and making easier credit availability for the export sector, housing and small industries.

In Mumbai, the RBI, to arrest moderation in GDP growth, provided monetary stimulus. It slashed its repo rate to 5.5 per cent from 6.5 per cent. It reduced the reverse repo rate from 5 per cent to 4 per cent.[70] And it reduced the cash reserve ratio (CRR) of scheduled commercial banks from 5.5 per cent to 5 per cent to pour an additional Rs 20,000 crore into the system to facilitate the flow of funds from the financial system to meet the needs of productive sectors.[71]

This was over and above the over Rs 3,00,000 crore the RBI had pumped into the monetary system since mid-November 2008.[72]

Simultaneously, in Delhi, the government directed public-sector banks (PSBs) to step up their lending with the additional liquidity that had been made available to them at cheaper rates. The second fiscal package provided Rs 20,000 crore for recapitalizing the state-controlled banks over the next two years, apart from other measures.[73]

Much of the 7 December package had been prepared when Chidambaram was in the finance ministry, but it was finalized and announced after he was asked to move to the home ministry, which he joined on 1 December 2008.[74]

On account of the two-part stimulus that fiscal year, 2008–09, the government agreed to a revenue loss of Rs 40,000 crore and an expansion of the fiscal deficit to about 6 per cent of the GDP, more than 3 percentage points in excess of the original target that was set before the crisis.[75]

The two Chidambaram-Ahluwalia-Singh stimulus packages sought to balance the fiscal giveaways for industry and urban consumption with the spending focused on rural Indians that was already in place. No more fiscal loosening was expected that financial year, Ahluwalia made it clear, at the announcement of the second package.[76]

Growth Story Interrupted

This rescue plan had an economic logic, a goal and a road map. It was grounded in sophisticated technical economic analysis. It ensured that the Indian economy had shock absorbers in place for facilitating early revival of growth, and that Indian banks were financially sound and well capitalized. Government recapitalized PSBs over two years to maintain CRAR (capital to risk weighted assets ratio, a standard metric to measure balance sheet strength of banks) of 12 per cent; NPAs for these banks declined from 7.8 per cent as on 31 March 2004 to 2.3 per cent as on 31 March 2008.[77]

Bank credit growth fell from 22.3 per cent in 2007–08 to 17.3 per cent in 2008–09.[78] Domestic demand moderated, as was projected. But the payout of a part of the arrears to government employees, in keeping with the Sixth Pay Commission award, in the second half of 2008–09, along with the farm loan waiver, helped to sustain domestic demand.

The global financial shock of September 2008 was a turning point for India. It had disrupted the unfolding 'India Growth Story'. Before the meltdown, India was booming, cruising at 8.8 per cent economic growth, from the year 2004 to year 2008.[79] It was an economic boom that positively impacted a large section of Indians, even if unequally.

Business houses launched new projects, borrowing at home and overseas. Their confidence levels rose. Big business and, later, even mid-sized firms, acquired iconic companies overseas. Demand and wages for construction labour shot up. Project books overflowed. Increments, salaries and hiring were up. If companies set up new offices, factories and businesses, then young Indians bought new houses, all funded by debt. Real estate prices soared.

The needs of cities grew. Many more house helps, watchmen, drivers and cooks were required, which rural India supplied. City demographics changed. Lifestyles changed. Consumption baskets changed. The middle class started to travel by air instead of by rail. The protein intake among poor families improved.

The way Indians lived, worked, retired, saved and consumed changed. A young population meant it would continue to be so. It had begun to seem that India's time had finally come. It was finally going to take off. With sustained high growth over an extended period, India could have approached what economists call a 'take-off', which means rapid and self-sustained GDP growth. (For instance, take-off may occur when the manufacturing sector begins to drive GDP growth, accelerating urbanization, industrialization and the pace at which technological breakthroughs happen.)

This momentum was called the 'India Growth Story'. To Indians, especially those who had missed their share in the gains from the 1991 liberalization, the new patterns represented a promise of a better future.

According to World Bank calculations, India's economy needs to grow at 8 per cent and higher per year for the next three decades to join the ranks of middle-income countries.[80] If that did happen, it would raise the income of at least 50 per cent of India's 1.3 billion people to sustain consumption expenditure of $10 a day, based on the purchasing power parity of the global middle class. India's per capita income in 2017–18 was close to Rs 86,668, or $3.7 a day.[81] The rapid pace of growth of 8.8 per cent annually from 2004 to 2008 had held out the promise of an improved economic future.

The task of the government and the RBI's economists was to make sure that the 'India Growth Story', which had been disrupted by the global financial crisis in September 2008, was not destroyed completely. It was going to have to be on pause, no doubt, given the state of the economy, and the growth pattern would have to adjust to a changed world scenario. But it was possible to minimize the impact of the crisis.

The effect on the Indian economy was not significant in the beginning.[82] The initial effect of the sub-prime crisis was, in fact, positive, as the country received accelerated FII flows during September 2007 to January 2008. As the global crisis intensified, the net portfolio flows soon turned negative as FIIs rushed to sell equity stakes in a bid to replenish their overseas cash balances. This had a knock-on effect on the stock market and the exchange rates through creating the supply–demand imbalance in the foreign exchange market. The current account was affected mainly after September 2008 through slowdown in exports, the real economy channel.

The global financial crisis had the effect in India of freezing its economy, from the monetary side, from the financial side and from the exports side.

The economy experienced extreme volatility in terms of fluctuations in stock market prices, exchange rates and inflation levels during a short duration. Despite setbacks, however, the balance of payments situation of the country continued to remain resilient despite signs of strain in the capital account that manifested in the reversal of FII investments (outflows of $15.0 billion during 2008–09) and on current account through decline in exports.[83]

In 2008–09, the merchandise exports recorded a growth of 3.4 per cent reaching 168.7 billion. While export growth was robust till August 2008, it became low in September and became negative from October 2008 to March 2009. The rupee depreciated by 21.2 per cent against the US dollar during that year. The US dollar, however, appreciated by 17 per cent against the broad index (Federal Reserve Bank, New York) between March 2008 and March 2009, suggesting that only 5 percentage points of the rupee depreciation was due to India-specific factors.[84]

The crisis slowed India for one year. GDP growth plummeted that crisis year (2008–09) to 6.7 per cent, but bounced back within a year to 8.6 per cent.[85] The RBI, under Governor Subbarao, and the government worked in tandem to make sure a quick, sharp 'V'-shaped recovery was made. But the recovery could not be sustained for too long. The following chapters show how the recovery fizzled out.

Anticipating well in time a collapse in world demand, the government and the RBI responded in coordination and consultation to the challenge of minimizing the impact on India. There were the usual turf battles, interpersonal friction and unprecedented dilemmas. And, in the midst of it all, the horrific Mumbai terror attacks. Negotiating the challenges and sidestepping precedents when needed, India avoided a full-blown economic crisis. The RBI, a conservative central bank, embraced unorthodox measures. Unlike the US Fed and the central banks of other advanced economies, the old-fashioned RBI emerged from the turbulent phase of the crisis with its reputation intact. The government too shook off pressures to restrict markets, keeping its nerve even when a clamour arose from private players for state intervention. Most significantly, no bailout situation was allowed to build up.

'The measures that were put in place in those two and a half months [the period from 15 September to 30 November after which he was moved to the home ministry] ensured that all three objectives were met: There was sufficient liquidity in the market; there was no run on any bank, which was my worst fear; and, no bank collapsed,' recalls Chidambaram.[86]

'Indian markets didn't collapse. All over the world markets collapsed.'

Shock, Not Crisis

India's success was that the shock was prevented from becoming a crisis. The benchmark equity index, the Sensex, collapsed from 13,518 on 16 September 2008 to 9647 by end December that year.[87] But even at the height of the crisis, the Indian financial markets continued to function in a fairly orderly manner. There was no drama of the sort seen on Wall Street. As the credit crisis spread, no Indian bank even came close to failing; none required the kind of emergency injections of capital seen on Wall Street. None needed huge write-downs.

India had escaped the asset bubbles and the excess liquidity created in the Western economies by design, not chance.[88] Governor Reddy had instituted a host of timely preventive measures. Two years before the global financial crisis, with private equity and hedge funds pouring foreign investments into commercial and residential real estate in India, the market had in fact begun to turn frothy, and would have entered bubble territory had it not been for the ban that Reddy placed on the use of bank loans for purchase of land. Banks had been allowed to make only construction loans, and that too only when the developer was about to commence building. Risk weightings on commercial buildings and shopping mall construction had been made conservative. As were rules regarding the capital that banks were required to hold in reserve as buffer for potential defaults. His high-interest-rate monetary policy stance for fighting inflation had dampened the housing frenzy in India. And so, nothing resembling the US sub-prime loan crisis broke out here. Mortgage loan rules required down payments of nearly at least a third of the purchase price. All lending to individuals remained based on their income. Loans could not be made without down payments. The value of a house going up could not ensure bigger loans. Exotic structures or financial instruments like securitizations and derivatives were limited. Off-balance-sheet vehicles to hide debt, in vogue among American banks, were banned.

New Delhi and Mint Street did not necessarily see eye to eye on every single detail during the management of the crisis in India after Lehman collapsed. Differences, despite all-round stress, were not allowed to turn into impasses of the sort that will be seen later in the decade discussed in this book.

The confidence with which the 2008 crisis was managed was in stark contrast to the 1991 crisis that had brought the economy to its knees. The 1991 crisis was triggered by a spike in global oil prices at a time when there were political uncertainties, and high fiscal deficits and current-account deficits (CADs) had increased India's economic vulnerability. Its short-term foreign exchange debts were high, and forex reserves low. By 2008, India had become a changed country. Between mid-2003 and 2008, its forex reserves had grown from $100 billion to $300 billion.[89] Indian finance was far more sophisticated, and tools to manage crises, as well as precautionary measures, were in place. Most importantly, fiscal headroom had been created, which could be used to advantage.

The Indian economy showed remarkable resilience in 2008–09, even as the policymakers rose to the task. But soon afterwards the seeds of future troubles were sown. The adjustment required in the follow-through was not undertaken. Political events threw policy into complete disarray. A poorly calibrated third package of fiscal giveaways was administered, which proved to be an overdose of fiscal stimulus. The fiscal-monetary coordination broke down completely, with disastrous results for inflation, investments and growth, and eventually for macroeconomic stability. Our banks' health deteriorated over time. The soured mood bred economic discontent, which in turn caused political upheaval.

During the anxious and turbulent phase of the global meltdown, governments and central banks around the world acted in concert, synchronizing policy responses. The G20 moderated this coordination. In November 2008, a G20 summit was scheduled in Washington, where world leaders assembled to assess the global response to the financial crisis. Prime Minister Singh and his 'Sherpa', Ahluwalia, made a push for a stronger voice for emerging markets on the global stage.[90] Singh cautioned the G20 that a slowdown in developing economies would push millions into poverty and called for a coordinated fiscal response for limiting the growth impact of the financial crisis, which did become one of the strategies of the economies in the grouping for a while. Singh came to be known as the 'wise economist' among the G20 leaders.[91]

There was an important difference between the advanced economies and emerging markets on how the crisis evolved. In the US and Europe, the contagion went from the financial sector to the real economy, whereas in India it was the other way round—from the real economy to the financial sector.

The standard operating procedure to mitigate a financial crisis is to douse the system with liquidity. Every country implemented this strategy and so did we in India—supplied the system with copious rupee and dollar liquidity. The main difference between advanced economies and us was of scale and the type of securities purchased.[92]

In the matter of the real economy channel, India could not have expected to remain unaffected. By 2008, India was more integrated into the global economy than was consciously recognized.[93] India's two-way trade (merchandise exports plus imports), as a proportion to the GDP, had more than doubled over the past decade: from 20 per cent in 1998–99, the year of the Asian crisis, to over 40 per cent in 2008–09, the year of the global crisis.

Looking back, the year was so fast-paced that it was more an unbroken continuum of daily challenges and struggles. Hours merged into days, and weeks into months. Most of the crisis managers confess their memories of incidents, and their experiences and reflections of that time, have faded. Only outcomes remain. Hardly anyone kept diaries or notes.

India escaped the direct impact on its banking system, in part because the financial sector had been kept insulated from the global giants, many of which fell like ninepins once the financial crisis broke out on Wall Street. Reddy writes in his memoir of the diplomatic pressures there had been in the pre-crisis years for opening up this sector.[94]

'By the time I joined as RBI governor [in 2003], the government had decided to allow foreign banks to take over our banks. I did not agree with that . . . My experience with the operations of foreign banks was that they enjoyed political and diplomatic clout that undermined effective regulation. The RBI and the government finally settled for a roadmap for the entry of foreign banks to take over our banks.'

The world economy didn't collapse, although, even ten years later, it still has not fully recovered from the impact of the crisis. The global financial system remains as vulnerable to a repeat of the lead-up to the crisis as it was then. No lessons appear to have been learnt. The shock of the global financial crisis showed that globalization comes with both benefits and costs. Globalization of finance undermines the policy space available to a nation's public authorities, making regulation difficult.[95] Of course, remaining closed cannot be the way forward either. The key would be to strengthen safeguards and regulations, and strive for effective and independent regulators. Bankers are greedy universally; it is the job of the regulator to apply the brakes when conditions turn what economists refer to as 'bubbly'. A big lesson of the global financial crisis that remains is that markets must always maintain a distance from political influence. The pre-crisis sub-prime loans market in the US was shaped, in part, by political forces that had certain social aims.

On 25–26 January 2010, on the advice of the Manmohan Singh government, President Pratibha Patel awarded the Padma Vibhushan to Y.V. Reddy. In his long career in public service, Reddy was a key player in the management of the 1991 crisis and several other important phases in contemporary Indian economic history. The steps he took 2006 onwards, as the RBI governor, to prepare India for a possible global financial shock are likely to have been among the reasons the second highest civilian honour was conferred on him. The decade following the breakout of the global financial crisis would see hardly any recognition for any of his successors for their role in managing India's financial and economic risks. Raghuram Rajan[96] would leave at the end of his three-year tenure, frustrated at a shrill campaign labelling him 'un-Indian', followed by Urjit Patel,[97] who would step down much ahead of the completion of his term after a public falling-out with New Delhi in which the government would send letters on multiple intractable disagreements to the governor under a provision that had never been used before in the eighty-three years of the RBI's history.

2

A Recovery Destroyed (2009–12)

After P. Chidambaram was drafted into home affairs, Prime Minister Manmohan Singh retained charge of the finance ministry. Singh enjoyed a rapport with many of the senior bureaucrats there, with some associations going back to his teaching days at Delhi School of Economics (1969–71)[1] or to his stint as finance minister in P.V. Narasimha Rao's cabinet (1991–96).[2]

Assisting him in overseeing the day-to-day work of the ministry were Planning Commission Deputy Chairman Montek Singh Ahluwalia, and chairman of Singh's Economic Advisory Council, C. Rangarajan—old economy hands and confidants. Chidambaram assisted Singh in answering Parliament questions related to the finance ministry.

This was essentially a reassembling of the 1991 rescue team, and it generated much hope. The burst of economic reforms of the 1990s had not been repeated, even if successive governments had stayed on course with the thrust and direction given by these reformers. True, the Lok Sabha elections were just months away, but could history repeat itself?

The expectations had to be suspended. Singh, it was announced, would go for a coronary bypass surgery on 24 January 2009 and would be away from office for the following four weeks at least.[3] The status of the prime minister's health was not widely known; even many cabinet ministers came to know about it only after he had been rushed to hospital.[4]

In December, Singh had overseen the preparation and announcement of the stimulus package, which allocated funds for infrastructure and slashed tax rates to avert a GDP growth collapse, but the economy was not yet out of crisis. In addition, a Vote on Account had to be presented on 16 February. Through this special provision, Parliament would obtain sanction for the expenses likely to be incurred in running government until the elections were completed, the new government sworn in and a full budget presented.

There was much speculation in the press about the substitute arrangements, including the chain of command in government that would be needed in Singh's absence, and as to whether a caretaker prime minister would be named. In the preceding four years, whenever the prime minister was away, for a week or even a day, a standard procedure would come into effect empowering Pranab Mukherjee to preside over cabinet meetings, although the cabinet had rarely met without Singh in attendance.[5]

Besides these standard step-in arrangements, some extraordinary provisions were put in place. For the first time since 1950, the prime minister was going to be indisposed for the Republic Day celebrations and parade. Defence Minister A.K. Antony was entrusted with all the official duties performed by the prime minister on Republic Day.[6] Mukherjee was briefed on the nuclear briefcase that fell under the prime minister's charge. He was not designated 'officiating Prime Minister', as Singh would be recuperating and therefore able to take critical decisions, if any had to be made.

The prime minister held additional charge of several portfolios: finance, coal, environment and forests, information and broadcasting, space and atomic energy, and personnel. The widely held notion in Lutyens' Delhi at the time was that sooner or later Singh would divest the additional charge of finance in favour of Chidambaram. The impression had gained currency as, although home minister now, Chidambaram had, on instructions of the

PMO, been taking meetings with the finance ministry top brass for overseeing preparations for the upcoming Vote on Account.

One such meeting of the secretaries of the finance ministry was taken by the home minister on 23 January 2009 in his chamber.[7] The home and finance ministries are housed in the heritage North Block atop Raisina Hill in Delhi. 'We had walked across,' recalls one of the secretaries. 'Everything that a finance minister could be expected to say about Interim Budget preparations Chidambaram had said in this review. (. . . so, what has happened on this, what has happened on that? . . . what are the dates?).'

As they stepped out of the meeting and made their way back to the finance-ministry wing in North Block, chit-chatting and exchanging notes, the consensus among the officials was that the charge of finance would definitely be given to Chidambaram, and he would be the one who would present the Interim Budget in Parliament and oversee the formulation of policy responses required to rebuild the economic growth momentum in the aftermath of the global crisis. It was a big deal. If the portfolios of home and finance demand tremendous responsibility and accountability, they also represent seats of disproportionate power and authority in government.

The walk back from the home to the finance ministry takes a couple of minutes. On entering his chamber, the secretary found himself staring startled at the news flashing on television—that the additional charge of the finance ministry had been allotted to Pranab Mukherjee.

'We got it so wrong,' says the secretary, reflecting on the sequence of events of that day.

Asking Chidambaram to officiate over the Interim Budget meetings, knowing that the budget would ultimately be presented in Parliament by Mukherjee, strikes one as jarring and clumsy, and an action uncharacteristic of Singh. In all likelihood, UPA Chairperson Sonia Gandhi picked Mukherjee for the job in a last-minute decision. The heavy-duty home and finance ministries, inarguably, are a handful for any individual. Gandhi and her political advisers may have calculated that nothing would be lost by letting Mukherjee, who was coming through as quite obviously disgruntled at the time, have the portfolio of his choice briefly.[8] Indeed, the press communique from the President left little scope for doubt: the reassignment of finance was only a stopgap arrangement. Mukherjee would hold the additional charge only until the prime minister's recovery.

'Originally, when Dr Singh took over, he made it clear to me that he will hold it [the ministry] until the 2009 elections. And after 2009, we will see what needs to be done. That's what he told me,' says Chidambaram. 'After election, Mr Mukherjee was already there.'

The President House communique and Singh's clear preference for retaining the ministry, as Chidambaram suggests, indicate that Mukherjee was not Singh's choice for the finance portfolio. The move to send in Mukherjee, who could obviously not have been removed after the election win, would in time prove costly—for the economy, the ministry, the UPA government and the Congress too.

Mukherjee held additional charge of finance from 24 January 2009 onwards. Except on the day of the Interim Budget, when a ceremonial signing of budget papers takes place in the finance minister's chamber, he did not visit North Block. Occasionally he called officials over for meetings at his office in the external affairs ministry at South Block, across the road from North Block. Files were carried to him and brought back.

Singh was back at work 4 March 2009 onwards.[9] Yet Mukherjee stayed in charge of finance. Upsetting the arrangement just weeks ahead of the 2009 general elections may have seemed useless to the party leadership. Elections were held and, to everyone's surprise, the UPA government returned to office. Mukherjee was sworn in as the finance minister now and began coming to North Block. The ministry was not new to him; he had held the portfolio twenty-four years ago, in Indira Gandhi's cabinet.

Finance and economics had changed since then. The economy had been liberalized; it had changed structurally and fundamentally. The work culture and mindsets in the ministry had changed too. Mukherjee, though, still seemed to swear by the socialist-era ideology that had long been retired. His approach and instinct were still defined by an abiding faith in the jaded dirigisme doctrine. The new finance minister was not as conversant with the new economic order as his post-liberalization predecessors were. Mukherjee soon earned a reputation for being old-school and out of tune with global economic affairs.[10]

'He was, in the first few months, a bit lost . . . The world had changed. He had not changed,' says the secretary who worked with him for more than two years in the ministry.[11]

V-Shaped Recovery

By mid-2009, around the time Mukherjee was settling into North Block, the economy had made a sharp V-shaped recovery (when plotting of the annual growth rate against time shows a dip and then picks up, yielding a 'V'). The shock of the global financial crisis slowed growth for a year, after which it had a rebound. Of course, this did not become known immediately, as estimates of the GDP come out after a lapse of roughly nine months at least.

The once-in-a-generation shock could have triggered, as it did in many economies, a prolonged crisis of credibility. It did not in India. A GDP growth collapse had been averted. The pullback was no mean achievement. The government and the RBI had successfully and safely steered India out of the most severe world crisis since the Great Depression of 1930. The economy showed remarkable resilience, even as the policymakers rose to the task. The RBI, under Governor D. Subbarao, had worked in tandem with the finance ministry, first under P. Chidambaram and then under Manmohan Singh.

The economy had responded well to the finely coordinated mix of fiscal and monetary measures that had been administered; the pre-shock growth momentum was set to be restored. But missteps followed with Mukherjee at the helm. This chapter will show how the fiscal and monetary policies were no longer well aligned and often worked at cross purposes. The recovery, not nurtured, proved to be short-lived.

The global financial shock of September 2008 had slowed India down for one year. But ill-advised policies and self-serving politics disrupted the nascent recoveries that followed. The result was a whole decade wasted in coping with a prolonged, policy-induced slowdown. Except for those employed or associated with the government sector, where salaries and pensions kept growing handsomely, nearly everybody else was affected. Corporate India, which had been preparing for 10 per cent GDP growth, was hit first, triggering a severe investment slowdown in the economy. Subsequently, acute rural distress followed.

The first chance at recovery was derailed when Mukherjee, misjudging grossly, announced a third fiscal stimulus package, in addition to the two that had been designed and announced under Singh's supervision. Rather than shift gears to growth-sustaining policies, he kept up the stimulus and persisted in demand-stimulation, budget after budget. And so, the fiscal policy remained in firefighting mode long after the global crisis had subsided.

Stimulus Overdose

During the first four years of UPA-1, from 2004–05 to 2007–08, P. Chidambaram had pared down the fiscal deficit, simultaneously raising the direct tax-GDP ratio.[12] The improvement in government finances led to a rise in the economy's savings and investment rates. The fiscal correction had helped greatly in creating conditions conducive for high growth, seen in the pre-global financial crisis years. After the crisis, a stimulus to stave off a growth collapse could be crafted out of the fiscal space created by Chidambaram. Manmohan Singh, before repairing for his bypass surgery, had overseen the preparation and announcement of two tranches of the stimulus.[13] Announcing the second, Ahluwalia had made it clear that it was going to be the last such injection of stimulus into the economy that financial year.

And yet, barely weeks later, Pranab Mukherjee announced a third tranche of fiscal giveaways on 25 February 2009.[14] This announcement could have been made as part of the Interim Budget he presented on 16 February, but it was not. The Interim Budget had been prepared under Chidambaram's supervision and was approved by the cabinet.

Mukherjee did not obtain cabinet approval for his stimulus package that ended up hurting rather than accelerating the economic recovery. Taken outside the regular schedule of a budget, at a time when the prime minister was indisposed, this was an unusual and clearly an unwise decision. It involved a huge sum of money, and its impact, whether negative or positive, on the economy was certainly going to be tremendous. If he did take on board the views of the prime minister, whether Singh was in a position at all at that point to give advice is difficult to say. Singh, recuperating still, held his first official engagement post-surgery ten days after Mukherjee announced the third stimulus package.[15] The future course of events would demonstrate that the finance minister rarely heeded the prime minister's advice on matters of economic policy.

As Mukherjee writes in his memoirs, *The Coalition Years*, 'I and Manmohan Singh held differing views on economic issues.'[16]

Mukherjee's package came ahead of the Election Commission's pronouncement of the dates for the general elections. The announcement, made on 2 March 2009, activated the model code of conduct, which would have disallowed fiscal giveaways.[17] Mukherjee extended the previously announced excise cuts, which would have expired on 31 March 2009. States were allowed to exceed their fiscal deficit targets. The ideal approach would have been to sit back and watch the paint dry on the previous two fiscal stimulus packages announced. But Mukherjee could not resist the temptation to cut excise duties and service tax rates to put money in people's hands—something that the industrial lobbies had been asking for, completely unmindful of how, in the medium run, the macroeconomic consequences of these sops would hurt business.

Over the next three years, Mukherjee, the dirigiste finance minister, hiked allocations for social-sector spends,[18] ignoring the revenue position, the expanding fiscal deficit and the economy's capacity for absorbing the fund releases productively. The budget for 2008–09 presented in February 2008, months ahead of Lehman's collapse, had projected a fiscal deficit of 2.5 per cent and a revenue deficit of 1 per cent. A year later, presenting the Interim Budget in February 2009, Mukherjee told a shocked Lok Sabha that the fiscal deficit had ballooned to 6 per cent of GDP and the revenue deficit had widened to 4.4 per cent. The actuals came out later in line with these projections.[19] The fiscal stimulus overdose, Chidambaram conceded in 2013, overheated the economy and stoked inflation.[20] The effects played out over time. In the next couple of years the country's macroeconomic stability diminished and the government's unpopularity with voters shot up.

The decision to administer the stimulus had been an economic one. To keep it going was a purely political one. 2009 was an election year. There may have been pressure on Mukherjee from Sonia Gandhi or the Congress party for pre-election fiscal goodies. Mukherjee, though, takes full ownership of the decisions in his memoir.[21]

Economists Sidelined

The finance minister was ideologically well disposed towards the UPA's 'pro-poor' politics. In the two and a half years he was in charge, the emergency measures announced in the three fiscal stimulus packages, which were meant to be temporary, were never revisited or reassessed.[22] Arvind Virmani, chief economic adviser till 2009-end, prepared and submitted a road map for ending the fiscal stimulus before leaving the post to assume charge as India's representative to the IMF in Washington.[23] It lay about unattended, gathering dust, ignored or forgotten.

'When a recovery is evident, reverse the stimulus,' this exit strategy proposed.[24] Virmani's second recommendation was, 'Resume reforms then for removing bottlenecks to sustain the growth recovery.' In the Economic Survey for 2009, he published a whole chapter on growth-driving reforms that ought to have guided North Block.[25]

This was a fairly comprehensive agenda for deepening reforms undertaken in the 1990s.[26] The reforms of the 1990s had created a competitive environment in which Indian entrepreneurship had flourished. The fruits of those reforms were the higher GDP growth and employment from 2003–04 onwards. Thereafter, the pace of policy reforms had slowed.

For as long as the economic growth had trended up, and before the global finance crisis disrupted that momentum, this sluggishness in policy reforms had not mattered. But in the aftermath of the crisis, industrial manufacturing growth had steadily declined for nearly eight quarters over 2007–08 and 2008–09. The durability of the recovery was still uncertain. Policy interventions were clearly necessary to rebuild the growth momentum. Especially since manufacturing had been one of the main drivers of the spurt in GDP growth recorded before the global financial crisis.

The pre-crisis acceleration in growth had given rise to a number of economic bottlenecks and constraints.[27] Conflicts over land, water and natural resources, and bottlenecks in supply of urban land, credit and employable workforce, needed to be eased. Resolution of these conflicts, including the socio-political ones, through economic policy and institutional reform was a must for sustaining high growth. Needed for that was a steady stream of reforms which removed bottlenecks as they arose, unencumbered new growth drivers when old ones were exhausted, and initiation of institutional change as old institutions became unable to cope with the demands of a more modern, higher-income economy.

Several bottlenecks and conflicts were becoming visible even as the economy was coping with the external shock of the global crisis. The evolution of institutions had not kept pace with the expanding need for urbanization, mining rights, risk capital and debt finance, and effective bankruptcy law. Conflicts were common in land acquisition and rehabilitation of displaced persons. There were complaints of rent seeking, crony deals and corruption, as laws and practices for leasing natural resources had not adjusted fast enough in response to the increased requirements of a growing economy. With faster growth in the pre-global financial crisis years, government expenditures and revenues expanded much more rapidly than what the government systems and procedures for spending and collection had the ability to cope with. Virmani's recommendations covered reforms that could have addressed some of these bottlenecks and conflicts.

Unfortunately, Pranab Mukherjee showed little interest in Virmani's blueprint for reforms. A handful of the recommended reforms were carried out by the Manmohan Singh-led government after Pranab Mukherjee's exit from the government in mid-2012. And, a few more were rolled out by the Narendra Modi government after it was voted to office in 2014. Most of the broad-based agenda, however, has remained untouched in the nearly ten years since the release of the Economic Survey in July 2009.[28]

After the elections, in July 2009, Virmani's two-year tenure as CEA had been extended by three months. In September, the Appointments Committee of the Cabinet (ACC) approved his appointment to the IMF as executive director.[29]

With his exit from the ministry, the reforms list remained unattended, and once the preliminary estimates of GDP started trickling in, the evident rebound became cause for celebration. No attention was paid by the ministry to the durability of the recovery or the steps needed to be taken to sustain it.

By February 2010, the view in the finance ministry was that the economy had responded well to the emergency measures taken in the wake of the global financial crisis as part of the stimulus packages. The Economic Survey, released on 25 February 2010, said that the recovery was well founded with pickup in merchandise exports, capital flows and credit flows. The turnaround, according to it, had come in the July–September quarter of 2009–10 when the economy grew by 7.9 per cent, year-on-year basis. The advance estimates quoted in the survey had forecast 7.2 per cent growth in GDP with industrial output growing at 8.2 per cent and the service sector at 8.7 per cent. Complacency soon set in. The policy stance remained the exact opposite of Virmani's recommendations.

Even after the rebound in the economy, the stimulus was allowed to go on. The overstimulation soon set inflation on fire.

When the crisis had struck, the government had given a free hand to its economists. Crisis over, their counsel was sidelined. The prime minister's Economic Advisory Council raised red flags in 2010.[30] The budgeted level of fiscal deficit that year, it cautioned, was beyond the comfort zone and would have been higher still but for the lower-than-expected loan waivers and pay and pension arrears. 'Such easy options will not be available in the coming years and serious policy measures to contain unproductive expenditures will have to be initiated,' it wrote in its outlook for the economy.

The marginalization of sound economics and economists, silent but still insidious during the Singh government's tenure, will grow over time. The resistance to qualified economists will assume unprecedented shrillness and toxicity in Modi's tenure, when nearly every technocrat and IAS officer holding a PhD in the subject will decamp from the finance ministry.

Why were the tax cuts and spending boosts not reversed? I asked this question of a bureaucrat who held a key position in the ministry at that time and has retired from service since.

'Who will pilot an exit from a stimulus?' the bureaucrat now says.[31] 'There was always some justification for continuing it. In government, when you have to give something, there is a decision. But when you have to withdraw, there is no decision. Because the industry will say "no".'

After a pause, he added, 'Besides, I don't think Pranab was the kind of finance minister who would take a call on withdrawing things.'

Mukherjee's policies of increased fiscal spending and lower taxes put more purchasing power in the hands of Indians, but in a way that did not make the economy more productive. When rising rural incomes improved the rural demand for protein in the form of milk, fish and pulses, the supply side of the economy could not cope with the building demand. Prices began to rise. Within two years, as happens in developing economies, this inflation was transmitted from food items to wages, and then to the rest of the economy.

As the effects of the fiscal botch-up began to play out, it sent inflation and government borrowings soaring. At one point inflation even touched the 20 per cent mark.[32]

This is not to say that the poor receiving just incomes and demanding and consuming quality food is undesirable or was in any way responsible for the economic slowdown that soon followed. To transfer purchasing power into the hands of rural India as an antidote to the global financial crisis was undeniably the appropriate policy choice. In its absence, the crisis would have depressed aggregate demand in the economy.

However, the government ought to have gone about raising demand in a planned manner. Supply-side reforms, such as reduced wastage of farm produce and steps for increasing output of proteins, should have been carried out simultaneously to avoid high inflation. Ultimately, the phase of high inflation helped no one. It added to the UPA's unpopularity with voters in the subsequent elections in 2014. High prices robbed people of their purchasing power. Cost pressures further reduced profitability as well as growth for companies that were already reeling under the effects of a global slowdown, ultimately impacting overall recovery.

The three fiscal stimulus packages came on top of an already announced expanded safety-net programme for the rural poor and the payout following the Sixth Pay Commission report, all of which added to stimulating demand.[33] The additional stimulus measures during 2008–09 worked out to about 2.9 per cent of GDP. Revenue collections were adversely impacted by the economic slowdown. Consequently, the Interim Budget for 2009–10 revised the estimates for 2008–09: the revenue deficit to 4.4 per cent and the fiscal deficit to 6.0 per cent of GDP, against the budget estimates of 1.0 per cent and 2.5 per cent, respectively. In addition, special bonds amounting to 1.8 per cent of GDP were issued to oil marketing companies and fertilizer companies during 2008–09.

The consolidated fiscal deficit of the states was expected to rise to around 3 per cent of GDP that year. The combined fiscal deficit of the central and state governments during 2008–09 was estimated at about 9 per cent of GDP.[34] Accounting for special securities issued by the central government outside the market borrowing programme, the combined fiscal deficit worked out to about 10.8 per cent of GDP.

While some of the increase in the revenue and fiscal deficits was on account of post-budget expenditure commitments, such as payment of arrears resulting from the Sixth Pay Commission award, a substantial increase was also due to the economic downturn arising from the impact of the global financial crisis. The government, in its macroeconomic framework statement, indicated that there was a compelling need to adjust the fiscal policy to take care of the exceptional circumstances through which the economy was passing. In view of this, it said, the fiscal consolidation process has to be put on hold temporarily. The fiscal stimulus packages meant deviation from the road map laid out by the FRBM Act, reversing the consolidation process of the last several years.

As the fiscal policy was looser than it should have been, to drive the macroeconomy in balance, the RBI compensated by tightening the monetary policy. But it was very slow in raising interest rates. This was a completely wrong mix of monetary and fiscal policy.[35] Adding to these two major mistakes in calibrating policies was the bad external environment, which reduced both demand for exports and sources of foreign credit and investments.

The government received a windfall from 3G spectrum auctions. But most of the revenue raised was used for expenditures, instead of for covering up the loss of revenue to tax reductions announced as part of the stimulus. In effect, the policies amounted to the opposite of what was required—despite the recommendations from Virmani, protests from Subbarao and counsel in the core group of the Congress party from Chidambaram.

India soon faltered. The economy could not stay on course to complete its recovery, and two years later slipped off the high-growth trajectory.

Virmani, who holds a doctorate in economics from Harvard, where US Federal Reserve's first female chairperson, Janet Yellen, was his classmate, could see from his vantage position in the IMF that, 'Globally, the mistake was in thinking that this was just the normal cycle. Just do the normal things and it will all go back to normal.'[36]

The G20 economies were running loose fiscal and monetary policies in coordination.

'My point was, this is once in 70 years so this is more reflective of the great depression.'[37]

Once a year Virmani would visit Delhi and try to persuade Mukherjee and other officials in the finance ministry about the off-balance monetary-fiscal policy mix and the need to tighten the fisc. But Mukherjee persisted in the reverse and set up a boom by 2010. Supply bottlenecks needed to be directly attacked through policy reform, which he ignored. With the ministry celebrating the growth bubble, the corporate sector did not realize that the underlying industrial demand conditions had changed. They did not adjust for this by reducing their exposure to debt or withdrawing from projects that were turning unviable by the changed demand and interest-rate conditions.

Virmani eventually wrote an IMF working paper on the policy errors and the required corrections. On a visit to Delhi, he gave a summary of this paper to Mukherjee.

'You have to do reforms, you have to correct the fisc.'[38]

'I am busy right now. Come back later . . . make a special trip . . . the next budget, we will do this.'[39]

When Virmani flew back from Washington later, as discussed with Mukherjee, he could not get an appointment to see the finance minister. Mukherjee did not meet him. The trip was a waste.[40]

Inflation Highs and Lows

Governor Y.V. Reddy had invoked the word 'overheating' for the economy back in October 2006.[41] He could see building demand pressures and strains on the quality of credit. The RBI was watching for signs of inflation, even as Chidambaram was sweating the fiscal correction.

The RBI had been tackling inflation since 2006, but in 2008 the global financial crisis had forced a change in its policy stance. Maintaining credibility and easing the liquidity crisis because of the shock had become the overriding priority instead. (The Wall Street firm Lehman Brothers' collapse in September 2008 set off the crisis that spread and, in days, froze money markets across the world.)

Governor Reddy had raised the policy rate as late as in July 2008 in response to rising inflation.[42] In less than three months' time, on 20 October 2008, Governor Subbarao announced the first interest-rate cut of his tenure. He reduced the policy repo rate—the rate at which commercial banks borrow overnight from the Reserve Bank—from 9 per cent to 8 per cent, reversing the anti-inflation policy stance. Monetary policy works by influencing market expectations. For extra impact, the cut was timed four days ahead of a scheduled policy review. The policy statement emphasized financial stability over growth and inflation.

By December 2008 the policy rate had been brought down from 9 per cent to 5 per cent.[43] In effect, the policy rate hikes that had taken five years on the way up were reversed by Governor Subbarao in just three months. The regular rate cuts, or a monetary policy loosening, earned him a reputation for being a trigger-happy governor.

Over 2008–09, the RBI ran an easy monetary policy—low interest rates and ample liquidity—to mitigate the impact of the crisis on the economy.

One of the immediate effects of the global crisis was a crash in international oil prices. Lower crude prices quelled inflation in India. For a few months in 2009, inflation, measured by the wholesale price index (WPI), was negative.[44] Falling global input prices were what had sent inflation into the negative zone. The deflation proved to be a transient phenomenon. Soon prices started rising rapidly. As the economy recovered from the crisis and the purchasing power injected by the fiscal stimulus started having an effect, inflation too caught up.

'Bringing inflation down by raising interest rates understandably became my foremost priority and remained so for most of my term,' Governor Subbarao wrote.[45]

The RBI began rolling back the post-crisis accommodation from the second half of 2009. The exit from crisis-driven measures started. In contrast to the policy path on its way into the crisis, when rate cuts were swift, even radical, the reversal or the way out of the crisis was slow and incremental. Interest rates had gone down to historically low levels in response to the ferocity of the crisis. Governor Subbarao avoided an abrupt reversal, fearing it would disrupt recovery. By October 2011, in a space of eighteen months, he took the policy rate up from 3.25 per cent to 8.5 per cent, raising it a total of thirteen times.[46] This slow and steady navigation of the reverse path earned him the moniker, 'Baby Step Subbarao'.[47]

Average WPI inflation during the three-year period from 2010–12 was 8.7 per cent, significantly higher than the average inflation of 5.4 per cent during the previous decade, 2001 to 2010.[48] The severity of inflation sent the UPA government's unpopularity soaring. Inflation started declining only gradually in 2012.

Writes Subbarao:[49]

Every time I met him, the Prime Minister would ask me why inflation was so unrelenting. I would tell him that our inflation was, of course, a problem, but it was a problem of success. The government's affirmative action programmes led by the Employment Guarantee under the Mahatma Gandhi National Rural Employment Guarantee Act pushed up wages without raising the underlying productivity while the expanded subsidy schemes, combined with improved delivery systems, had contributed to raising rural incomes at a record pace. A result of this rapid growth in incomes was a spurt in demand for consumption goods which, in the absence of commensurate increase in production, put upward pressure on prices. But, as they say, there are no free lunches. the government's apparent success on one side was also its failure on another front. It was spending way beyond its means by borrowing in the market . . . In telling the inflation story to the Prime Minister, I would give him both the positive and negative sides of it. As an economist, he understood my arguments, but as a politician, he felt helpless. Most of the time, all I would get by way of reply would be a wry smile.

Because the government persisted with its loose fiscal stance way beyond what was necessary, the economy went into a serious bout of high and stubborn inflation. RBI was left to do all the heavy lifting to fight this inflation.[50] In the process the RBI muffed it.[51] It took a 'softly-softly' approach to raising interest rates.

Pranab Mukherjee was locked in a 1970s mindset.[52] Whenever Governor Subbarao went to North Block for briefings, the finance minister let his team of officials do most of the talking, while he himself kept quiet, giving the impression that he was endorsing everything that was being said.[53] The main thrust of these meetings, reflecting Mukherjee's attitude, was to convey to the governor that reviving growth was an urgent priority, but the finance ministry can't do much on the fiscal side, and whatever was to be done to get the economy out of the growth deceleration would have to be done by the RBI.[54]

'I can't do anything on the fiscal side because of political compulsions. The RBI must therefore take full responsibility for reviving growth,' Mukherjee would say, recalls an official who attended these meetings. Mukherjee was not a policy wonk. He was uncomfortable with complex arguments about why RBI's efforts to revive growth would be ineffective unless the government tightened on the fiscal side.[55] He just accepted what his officers told him and used the weight of his office to put pressure on RBI to fall in line.

Mukherjee had an oversimplified view of complex economic systems. He probably assumed—as many Indian politicians do— that inflation and growth can simply be managed with monetary policy, regardless of the fiscal policy parameters.

The RBI's research showed[56] that one of the structural drivers of inflation was the changing dietary habits of low-income households, evidenced in the persistent rise in the prices of protein foods. In a $1500 per capita economy—where food is a large fraction of the expenditure basket—food inflation quickly spills into wage inflation, and therefore into core inflation.[57] This transmission was institutionalized in rural areas where the MGNREGA wages were formerly indexed to inflation. The only effective response to supply-side-driven inflation would have been reforms expanding the economy's output. But Virmani's list remained forgotten.

Governor Subbarao raised the fiscal situation with Prime Minister Singh routinely:

> The fiscal situation would, of course, figure in our conversation and my tale of woe about how the fiscal stance of the government was undermining the Reserve Bank's anti-inflation position was standard fare. To his enormous credit, he never interfered in the policy action. 'I hope you have settled this with the finance minister' was all he'd say . . . It was my standard practice to apprise the prime minister of our statement on the government's fiscal stance. He understood the economic logic but always seemed uncomfortable with the Reserve Bank pointing it out. He never intervened directly with me, but in early 2012, he told Rangarajan, the chairman of his Economic Advisory Council and my former boss when I was secretary to the council, to convey to me that he did not expect Subbarao, 'who was finance secretary in the government and understood its political compulsions' to take such a strident stand on the fiscal stance. I certainly have sympathy for this point of view but was unwilling and unable to show any accommodation.[58]

The WPI inflation finally dropped from double digits to below 5 per cent in the summer of 2013, by when Mukherjee was no longer in North Block or in the government.[59]

The supply-side constraints and governance failures sharply slowed down the economy. By 2011–12, even as inflation remained elevated, GDP growth crashed to 6.69 per cent.[60] The risk premium on investment went up as the macroeconomic situation deteriorated: the persistence of high inflation was followed by a rise in the current-account deficit (CAD), besides one in the fiscal deficit. All of this suggested that the economy was running out of control. Still, Mukherjee remained clueless about the gathering dark clouds.

Its coordination with New Delhi less smooth now, the RBI that had handled the immediate aftermath of the breakout of the global financial crisis well, misunderstood the nature of the slowdown. It kept monetary policy loose despite the surge in inflation. There was to some extent wrong management of the macro-fiscal system. The upshot was that the country was thrown into a trap of low growth and high inflation. 'With the benefit of hindsight, I must admit in all honesty that we would have been better served if our monetary tightening had started sooner and had been faster and stronger,' wrote Subbarao.[61]

Other governance problems did not help. Starting 2010, the government got tangled up in the fallout from accusations of involvement in various scams. The result was that output of critical materials, such as due to iron ore mine closures by courts, was adversely affected.

Reforms Shunned

Mukherjee offered bagfuls of promises in his budgets. However, the disinvestment proceeds, tax collections, fiscal deficit correction, borrowings reduction and growth figures consistently fell way short of his targets.[62] He failed to drive consensus for liberalization of foreign investment norms in sectors like multi-brand retail, insurance and pension with the Trinamool Congress, a crucial ally in his home state of West Bengal, offering stiff opposition to foreign investment in certain sectors. The other reforms on which he missed deadlines were formulation of guidelines for issue of new bank licences and subsidies reduction, which included transition to direct transfers of cash to the poor in lieu of subsidies for kerosene, LPG and fertilizers, and decontrol of diesel prices—Virmani's comprehensive list of reforms received no attention at all.

Besides delaying adjustments in fiscal policies, Mukherjee was not sensitive to the pressing need for institutional reform or the significance of mediating and resolving conflicts over land, water, natural resources, or bottlenecks in supply of credit, risk capital, employable workforce and absence of bankruptcy law, although as finance minister, and the main in-charge of the economic health of the country, he should have been on top of these issues. Unresolved, such conflicts diminish productivity. The urgency of putting reform back on a steady track, which was needed to address known bottlenecks and the negative effects of shocks in a timely manner, escaped him. The brief recovery induced a misplaced confidence in the resilience of the economy in him, resulting in neglect of basic economic reforms—removal of bottlenecks to growth, elimination of rents and removal of supply constraints—which were needed for sustaining the economic recovery.

The UPA government lost crucial time as the finance minister failed to drive consensus for its tax reforms agenda: introduction of the GST and the Direct Tax Code. Soon the PMO and the cabinet's energies were diverted by a political economy crisis: the policy paralysis.

Policy Paralysis

The 'policy paralysis' phase of UPA-2, called so because it was the time when files stopped moving and bureaucrats stopped acting out of fear of the 3Cs—Courts, CAG, CVC—coincided with Pranab Mukherjee's leadership of the finance ministry. The CAG's report on the 2G corruption scam that led to a washout of Parliament sessions, intense campaigning by the Opposition and the Anna Hazare movement—all decisive inflection points in the economy's mood—happened in this period.

On 9 November 2010, the month-long winter session of Parliament began. The next morning, Vinod Rai—a 1972-batch retired IAS officer of the Kerala cadre, a former student of Manmohan Singh at the Delhi School of Economics and the Comptroller and Auditor General of India—held a press briefing that marked the beginning of the end of the Manmohan Singh-led government's popularity among the people of the country.[63] From here onwards, it was a downward slide all the way for it.

Vinod Rai told reporters that he had sent an audit report on the 2G spectrum allotments by the telecom ministry to the government. He refused to share the details of the findings, in line with a loosely followed tradition: Parliament, when in session, has the first right to know. The report sparked a political storm that wouldn't subside until the Lok Sabha polls four years later.

Rai was accusing the telecom ministry of undervaluing the 2G spectrum it allotted to new telecom service providers, inflicting, in the process, a revenue loss of Rs 1,76,700 crore on the exchequer. The figure, in large font size, was published on the front pages of newspapers across the country.[64]

The CAG report named Telecom Minister A. Raja for valuing spectrum on 2001 prices while allotting it in 2008, and for changing the deadline for receiving applications to favour a select set of spectrum seekers. Its conclusion was that this was all arbitrary and that the correct value of the spectrum could only have been determined through a market-driven process.[65]

The telecom ministry's reply to the accusations, also carried in the CAG report, was that the 2G spectrum allotment and the sale of 3G spectrum, which was done through an auction, were not comparable. The 2G spectrum was not stand-alone but was bundled with licences issued for pan-India telecom operations, at Rs 1658 crore per licence. This, the ministry explained, was not arbitrary. It was based on the New Telecom Policy of 1999 and a cabinet approval of 2003, and was in line with the policies formulated by previous governments.

Most of the accusations in Rai's report were anyway getting play in courts, the Parliament and the media,[66] and the Supreme Court was hearing a public interest litigation on the matter too. Yet leaked confidential documents, copies of file notings and dispatches on the spectrum allotments from the CAG, Telecom Regulatory Authority of India (TRAI), the telecom and the other ministries, landed on editorial desks in Delhi at every stage before and after Rai's report became officially public. These were in the form of mysteriously dropped off, safely enclosed documents in blank envelopes, as if dispatched by hands unseen. The reportage and discourse ran along the precise pattern the leaked documents set, never beyond or around it. Who was behind all this was never conclusively investigated.

In the months before Rai finalized and submitted his report, the Opposition had already begun calling Raja's 2G spectrum allocation 'the biggest financial scam in Independent India'. On becoming public, Rai's audit served to energize and legitimize this campaign. By lending them documentary backing, it anchored the accusations. In the public's eye, the accusers were no longer the Opposition, corporate vested interests, activists, lawyers and journalists. It was the CAG itself.

The BJP brought Parliament to a halt, demanding a statement from the government on the floor of the House on Raja's culpability.[67]

Meanwhile, Rai's report was sent to President Pratibha Patil for her signature.

On 11 November, two days after Rai's press briefing, the telecom ministry filed an affidavit in the Supreme Court defending Raja.[68] It refuted the allegations as misconceived.

The argument was that the purported losses had been estimated by making an erroneous presumption: that since 3G spectrum had been sold through auction, the 2G spectrum should have been auctioned too. The CAG had failed to recognize that while the former was a premium service, the latter was a value-added service. How then could the proceeds from the sale of 3G spectrum be an appropriate benchmark for the market value of 2G spectrum? The ministry submitted that it was targeting higher tele-density, not revenue maximization. The low entry fee for new operators, it expected, would increase competition among telecom operators for market share, leading to lower tariffs for consumers.

In effect, the ministry was simply canvassing a free-markets policy stance.

On the allegations that the cut-off date had been advanced, the ministry's submission was that the applications received later had not been rejected; they were being considered.

Calling the affidavit a 'shameful justification of corruption', the BJP spokesperson issued a demand for Raja's dismissal from the cabinet on 12 November 2010.[69]

That day Prime Minister Manmohan Singh, who had been in Seoul for G20 Summit meetings with world leaders, was on board Air India One, en route to New Delhi. He called a press conference mid-flight. Dressed in a white shirt and his signature blue turban, he had gotten out of his *bandhgala*. The first thing that strikes someone who has not seen Singh in person before is how much taller he is than he appears in photographs. Also, he never turns just his head. His whole body turns to face a subject that draws his attention. The impression this creates is of complete engagement with the subject.

At the mid-air press conference, reporters who had accompanied the official delegation to the summit meetings asked the prime minister for a response to the call for Raja's resignation. Singh answered that as Parliament was in session, he would not comment on the matter.

Next, a question was asked about the All India Anna Dravida Munnetra Kazhagam (AIADMK) leader J. Jayalalithaa's reported offer to fill the breach in numbers that might result if the Dravida Munnetra Kazhagam (DMK), Raja's party, were to quit the government.[70]

'This is a subject I am hearing for the first time. It is for the Congress high command to take note of it. I don't know what Jayalalithaa has offered. We are in alliance with the DMK, and that alliance stands as of now.'[71]

Singh had measured his words, particularly the last three, carefully. New reports of the prime minister's press conference caught on to the message in those three words: Manmohan Singh had put the DMK and the Congress high command on notice.

Air India One touched down in New Delhi late evening that day, 12 November 2010. Raja's career in Singh's government ended in a matter of hours.

Manmohan Singh, Sonia Gandhi, Pranab Mukherjee and Ahmed Patel met to chart out a course of action.[72] The prime minister made it absolutely clear to the top leadership of the Congress that he wanted Raja out.[73] He had been opposed to the inclusion of Raja and T.R. Balu of the DMK in his cabinet from the beginning. In fact, his refusal to accept the two in his government had held up the swearing-in of the UPA-2 cabinet in May 2009. He had been persuaded to accommodate the two after the ally made the support of its eighteen MPs in the Lok Sabha to the Congress conditional on both its nominees getting the portfolios of its choice.

Things had changed since then. The Congress had moved to eject two of its own—Suresh Kalmadi as secretary of the Congress parliamentary party and Ashok Chavan as chief minister of Maharashtra—for alleged graft.

On the morning of 15 November, the Supreme Court was to hear multiple petitions alleging Raja's involvement in the 'spectrum scam'. The CAG report that had been sent to President Patil for her signature was also expected to be presented in Parliament over the next couple of days.

Singh put his foot down.

Ahmed Patel explained to the assembled Congress leadership that the DMK was no longer in a position to resist demands for Raja's resignation. Assembly polls were due in Tamil Nadu, where the DMK needed an alliance with the Congress. Its rival in the state, AIADMK, headed by Jayalalithaa, had already announced a visit to Delhi to greet Sonia Gandhi on her birthday, 9 December.

If the DMK could no longer dictate terms to the Congress, the party itself had finally come around to agreeing with Singh on Raja's position in government.

A decision was taken. Mukherjee, it was agreed, would convey it to DMK chief and Tamil Nadu Chief Minister M. Karunanidhi.

Over the next twenty-four hours, Raja met his party leader, Karunanidhi, in Chennai twice, flew back to Delhi and drove straight to the prime minister's 7, Race Course Road residence. There, on the night of 14 November, a Sunday, he handed over his resignation letter to Singh.

Before leaving for Delhi, Raja had told reporters at Chennai airport, 'There is no question of me resigning and there is no need for it.' On exiting from the prime minister's residence, he told journalists in Delhi that he had done what he had been advised to do by 'my leader'.[74]

'My conscience is clear; I have done nothing wrong,' he said.[75]

Later that night Karunanidhi issued a two-page statement in Chennai saying Raja had been advised to quit with a view to safeguarding parliamentary democracy.[76]

'Everyone had the responsibility to protect and nourish the dignity and neutrality of parliamentary democracy in India. If this principle suffered any blow, it was the duty of all to safeguard the principle.'[77]

The CAG report was tabled in Parliament on 16 November.[78] This was not the first occasion the telecom sector had evoked serious adverse remarks from the CAG. In a 2001 report, the CAG had alleged losses to the exchequer of thousands of crores of rupees consequent to the NDA government's waiver of committed licence fees on migration to a system of revenue sharing for telecom companies.[79]

The public response to the Raja report was comparable only with the response the Bofors report of the 1980s fetched.[80] Once again the course of India's political economy would change.

Quite the way the CAG's Bofors report had, the 2G spectrum report would also end up being a turning point in India's politics. It too would not be free of controversies. The procedures followed, the analytical tools employed and the motivations that drove it would be questioned eventually. If the author of the Bofors CAG report joined the BJP as a member, got elected to the Rajya Sabha and later was appointed a state governor by BJP governments, Rai too would accept sinecures from the BJP government that would replace the UPA government, the party having rode to power on sentiments his report would help whip up.[81]

The Supreme Court sent Raja and top executives of telecom companies to Tihar Jail in February 2011.[82] Raja spent fifteen months there. The court directed the central government to constitute a special court for hearing cases related to the 2G spectrum allocation. A year later, a Supreme Court Bench of Justices G.S. Singhvi and A.K. Ganguly cancelled the 122 licences Raja had issued and disallowed allocations; natural resources could only be auctioned now.[83] The cancellation at one stroke reset the telecom industry and, according to one estimate, had an impact on 5.3 crore phone connections.[84]

The judges of the Supreme Court had punished those named in the 2G spectrum case, but soon the whole economy was paying the price for the alleged wrongdoings of the accused.

Rai had not confined the CAG to scrutiny of government finance. He interpreted its mandate as a responsibility to expose the corporate-politician nexus at the root of allocations of natural resources.[85] Besides the report on 2G spectrum, reports on a number of 'scams' were produced by the CAG under Rai. One of his reports alleged a Rs 141 crore Commonwealth Games scam that landed parliamentarian and former Indian Olympic Association chief Suresh Kalmadi behind bars. A report on coal block allocation pegged irregularities at Rs 1.86 lakh crore and indicted Congress MP Vijay Darda.

Bureaucrats in key decision-making positions feared that in the prevailing atmosphere there was no guarantee that even scrupulous approvals would not invite investigations and allegations, resulting in soiled reputations. Systemic judicial and investigative delays meant that the process of being tried itself would be the punishment, even if it eventually ended in acquittal.

With the result, decision-making came to a standstill in government. Self-preservation bred a collective reluctance to clear files, creating a policy logjam.

The fallout of the chill within government reverberated across the economy. The infrastructure industry had been gearing up to build projects worth $1 trillion in anticipation of and in preparation for faster GDP growth.[86] The whole lot of infrastructure projects that had been kicked off got held up by the piling up of pending clearances, approvals and unresolved disputes in those that involved public-private partnerships (PPPs). As it is, financial constraints were weighing down infrastructure investors because they had not anticipated the global economic downturn and were finding it difficult to cope with cost escalations. The added uncertainty and bureaucratic non-cooperation completely soured the investment environment. The policy logjam triggered an investment slowdown and a related bad bank loans crisis.

A Political Maelstrom

Rai's allegations impacted national politics. The frenzy his reports generated proved damaging for the Congress politically. The India Against Corruption movement led by Anna Hazare was floated against this backdrop. The BJP inflicted a parliamentary paralysis, completely blocked pending reforms such as introduction of the GST and liberalization of FDI norms in multi-brand retail. To its corruption crusade it added a new campaign, 'policy paralysis', in preparation for the Lok Sabha elections that were then more than three years away.

The biggest victim of Rai's reports was his one-time professor. The BJP used his reports to demolish Manmohan Singh's lifelong reputation for honesty and integrity: 'People say he [Prime Minister Manmohan Singh] is personally honest . . . It is a strange honesty that he leads the most corrupt government in India since 1947.'[87] His reformist credentials were blown to smithereens.[88] The mood in the country drooped. Manmohan Singh seemed a figure of disappointment, dejection and loss of control. Debates in swish drawing rooms turned to conjectures about his resignation.

Singh had publicly upbraided Rai on one occasion at least, when he told a group of editors in 2011,

> Well, I think the CAG also leaks. It is not the function of the CAG. It has never been the case that the CAG has held a press conference as the present CAG has done. . . . it is not the CAG's business to comment on policy issues. I think they should limit themselves to the mandate given under the Constitution. We are now a permissive society, I think if the media can get away with murder, so can the CAG.[89]

Speaking in Mumbai in February 2013, months before his term was to end, and with the air of a crusader, Rai told his audience,

> 2012 will go down in the history of Indian democracy as a defining year . . . A year in which the citizen came centre stage and debunked the age-old myth of the silent majority . . . This class of people who . . . took pride in not going to vote, who looked down on caste and regional politics . . . This disparate group is now aggregating, it is uniting for a cause. It seems to feel its strength . . . What stirred them? Maybe corruption at every government office.[90]

When the estimates came, 2011–12 became the year in which the economy grew 6.69 per cent,[91] its slowest pace in nine years. The RBI acknowledged that paralysis in governance was acting as a drag on economic growth.

The growing sense of despondency in the economy peaked with the Supreme Court's cancellation of 214 coal mines that had been awarded between 1993 and 2010.[92] Investors were stunned. There was no way that a business floated in the 1990s based on an assurance of availability of coal from the government could have predicted that twenty years later coal block allocations made by government would get cancelled, jeopardizing its entire investment.

Rai appeared before the Joint Parliamentary Committee (JPC) appointed at the insistence of the Opposition to examine the 2G spectrum allotment. The auditor was asked to explain how he had arrived at the stunning figure of Rs 1.76 lakh crore. Rai made similar presentations before the Public Accounts Committee (PAC), which examines CAG reports and tables its findings to Parliament.

Congress leaders in the JPC, chaired by the Congress leader P.C. Chacko, gave Rai a tough time. Digvijaya Singh drew a parallel between Rai and T.N. Chaturvedi, the CAG during Prime Minister Rajiv Gandhi's tenure, who had raised questions in his report about the Bofors deals.[93] The defeat of Gandhi's government is ascribed to that report. On retirement from service, the former CAG enrolled to become a member of the BJP. He received two terms in the Rajya Sabha, a Padma Vibhushan and an appointment as governor of Karnataka in 2002 from the A.B. Vajpayee government.

Rai's report had presented four separate estimates of total 'presumptive loss' to the national exchequer, ranging from Rs 57,666 crore to Rs 1,76,645 crore,[94] of which the largest figure was picked and highlighted by the media. It stuck in public discourse, although the loss figure in the Central Bureau of Investigation (CBI) charge sheet was Rs 30,984 crore.

In late 2014, Rai released his book, *Not Just an Accountant: The Diary of the Nation's Conscience Keeper*,[95] explaining the models of assessment the CAG used under him for computing the loss figures. He wrote that the specific figure of Rs 1.76 lakh crore was based on rates discovered for 3G spectrum in its auction in mid-2010. 'The formula applied for computing the loss was . . . based on a logical understanding of tax laws in India and abroad. It was thus decided to use data and other indicators which were already in the public domain.'[96]

The CBI court passed its verdict in the 2G telecom spectrum case on 21 December 2017. If Rai's reports had stunned the country, Special Judge O.P. Saini's strongly worded order sent it into a state of complete shock.

> There is no evidence on the record produced before the court indicating any criminality in the acts allegedly committed by the accused persons relating to fixation of cut-off date, manipulation of first-come-first-served policy, allocation of spectrum . . .[97]

It noted that some people created a scam by

> artfully arranging a few selected facts and exaggerating things beyond recognition to astronomical levels . . . The charge sheet of the instant case is based mainly on misreading, selective reading, non reading and out of context reading of the official record. Further, it is based on some oral statements made by the witnesses during investigation, which the witnesses have not owned up in the witness box.

In effect, the trial court ruled that there had been no scam. The theory of notional loss of Rs 1.76 lakh crore stood rejected. The eighteen accused were acquitted.

The verdict brought into question Rai's estimates and the role they, and those excerpts of his reports that were leaked to the media before being tabled in Parliament, played in national politics and in the deepening of the economic slowdown by triggering a policy paralysis.

A smear campaign gained credence on the strength of Rai's reports. The public mood turned against the government of the day. The government machinery stopped functioning amidst fears of a witch-hunt. The Opposition became a clear beneficiary of a wave that was created against the government in office.

Is Rai a symbol of 'abuse of constitutional power', as Raja wrote in his book, *2G Saga Unfolds,*[98] released in early 2018?[99] In the book, Raja says, 'Rai's report in the garb of CAG is nothing but a caveman's voice not conforming to any legal pattern. His is an adventurism that makes constitutional value a mockery.'[100]

The first CAG was appointed in 1860; that makes the CAG a 158-year-old organization. Its motto is 'Dedicated to truth in public interest'. Its job is to make government more accountable. It is a watchdog of public finance, acting on behalf of Parliament, and is duty-bound to check and report any revenue not collected, or wrongly foregone, by the executive.

The framers of the Constitution did not see the CAG as merely an auditor. They expected it to hold the executive accountable for its expenditure to Parliament and the public. The oath administered to the Chief Justice of India and other judges of the Supreme Court is the same as that of the CAG. Dr Babasaheb Ambedkar had said that the CAG's 'duties . . . are far more important than the duties even of the judiciary'.[101]

It was believed that the dismantling of the 'Licence-Permit Raj' in 1991 would diminish corruption in the country. But the politician-capitalist nexus has been working on a much grander scale since. During the economic boom from 2004 to 2008, when government connections were needed to jump queues for allocation of natural resources, it acquired heightened visibility.

Politics, cutting across party lines, became a business. The spoils were no longer only for those in office. The Opposition was as much a player in the game. For, as much as policy discretion, obstructive politics too could help preserve monopolies and curb competition.

In Delhi, the hub of political capitalism, the class of busybodies expanded. Capitalists, bureaucrats, politicians, activists, lobbyists, lawyers and journalists worked symbiotically to expand their own wealth and areas of influence.

Those unsympathetic to Rai count him as one of the willy-nilly power elite in this game. For Rai went out of his way to ensure publicity for his audits. To popularize them, he had the reports crunched into lucidly written blocks of eighteen to twenty pages. These miniature versions were called the 'Noddy' booklets.[102] A media officer Rai had appointed raised the CAG's public profile. Those sympathetic to Rai say his numbers might be debatable, but he succeeded in throwing light on the murky business of natural resource allocations by governments.[103] The partial reform that followed was a clear gain. Had it not been for his reports, the sleaze would have grown unchecked. Those with a nose for conspiracies point to the downside—a deepening of the economic slowdown, a political upset and the controversies surrounding Rai's reports.

If Rai's reports accused the government of corruption, a new batch of leaks starting mid-2011, of notes written by his subordinates, put the spotlight back on him. Each one of these communiques was written well before the CAG report on the 2G spectrum allocation was tabled in Parliament.

The first of these, an internal CAG note, suggests that Murli Manohar Joshi, the PAC chairman and BJP leader, may have used his influence over the CAG. Director General (RC) R.B. Sinha wrote in a note to Deputy CAG Rekha Gupta on 13 July 2010[104] about a call he had received on his mobile at 11.30 that morning, in which Joshi demanded a briefing from the CAG office on the status of its 2G spectrum audit before the scheduled PAC meeting of 15/16 July 2010.

Sinha records Joshi telling him, 'there was tremendous pressure on him [Joshi] . . . in respect of . . . allocation of 2G and 3G spectrum and that if the probe is further delayed, the Executive would get time to cover up the issue.'[105]

After the note was released, the Congress wondered if it was appropriate for Joshi to contact the CAG before the report was tabled in Parliament, and if the CAG had an agenda.

'Was the figure [of presumptive loss in allotment of 2G spectrum] inflated? Was it made in haste? Was this at the behest of Chairman of PAC?' Congress General Secretary Digvijaya Singh tweeted.[106]

The head of the CAG team that had audited the 2G spectrum allocation made revelations suggesting that the figure in the 2G report, Rs 1.76 lakh crore, itself may have been the result of a forced signature.[107] On retiring as Director General Audit, R.P. Singh declared in November 2011 that he had never put the figure of Rs 1.76 lakh crore in his draft report. Singh disowned the final report and publicly denounced Rai for overstepping his mandate.[108] He said the CAG headquarters, through a written order, had asked him to sign on the final report, and he had complied with the instructions even though he did not agree with its findings.[109]

Singh's own loss estimate had been much smaller, Rs 2645 crore.[110] An internal note dated 8 July 2010 circulated in his department said, 'We are not on strong grounds in the argument made . . . however, since the headquarters wants a draft, we may forward it.'[111] A letter Singh sent on 31 May 2010 to the CAG headquarters expressed his difficulty over quantifying the losses. It said that the price used for 3G spectrum couldn't be used to calculate the losses in 2G spectrum allocation because, 'charging for 2G spectrum was never recommended by TRAI or the government has never contemplated any charges for the spectrum other than entry fee.'[112]

Raja appears to have leaned on TRAI's consistent stated policy. The TRAI Secretary R.K. Arnold's communication on 20 August 2010 to CBI confirmed Singh's notings.[113] The regulator's consistent view, the TRAI secretary wrote, was 'that telecom services and spectrum should not be treated as a source of revenue for the government. It is against this background that TRAI did not recommend any increase in the entry fee for new players, by way of indexation or otherwise.'

Rakesh Mohan, whom Prime Minister A.B. Vajpayee had appointed as member of TRAI, had dissented in the early 2000s with the majority recommendation of the telecom regulator for auctions as the appropriate mechanism for allotting licences for new private-sector landline companies. His dissent note argued for a fixed licence fee and allotment of many licences so that the new tariffs would not be burdened by the obligation of these new companies to pay off high licence fees. Prime Minister Vajpayee's office had accepted the dissent note, and the policy Mohan favoured was adopted.[114]

Mohan wrote in 2018 in a tribute to Vajpayee on his death:

> This was perhaps the root of the later first-come-first-served policy with which UPA government ran into great trouble in the 2G spectrum allotment process. The subsequent adoption of auction processes for spectrum allocation, once again, has resulted in excessively high bids which are now resulting in significant difficulties for the spectrum winners in the form of high debts, which are also inhibiting new infrastructure investment in the sector.[115]

Singh's revelations—in particular his disclosure that CAG officials had been called to Joshi's residence on a holiday to help him prepare the PAC's 2G spectrum allocation report—could have been embarrassing for the BJP and Joshi had the noisy discourse of those times not drowned them out.[116]

Singh had, incidentally, also been the director, audit, for the Bofors report. His battle with lung cancer ended in December 2014.[117]

In February 2016 Rai accepted the job of chairman, Banks Board Bureau, the body which advises the government on top-level appointments at PSBs and the clean-up of bad loans—areas crying for reform, but where government's record is the weakest. The Supreme Court in 2017 conferred on him responsibilities for transparently running the administration and reforming the Board of Control for Cricket in India.

Journalist Akshay Deshmane wrote of Rai,

> In the ongoing tenure of the National Democratic Alliance (NDA) government, however, the former CAG's engagements in the public sphere have not been as frequent and vocal. This is significant because he has now taken over two new responsibilities which are in sync with his self-described role in his book as the 'nation's conscience keeper' . . . Clearly, reticence has taken over a once media-savvy public official.[118]

Constitutional authorities have failed to hold the Modi government accountable for decisions that have inflicted economic distress on the nation—demonetization, defence purchases, the introduction of electoral bonds, an opaque source of political funding that lends itself to use for channelling corruption receipts, and the handling of NPAs, where profits are privatized but losses socialized. Episodes such as the collapse of IL&FS may be putting the financial system at risk. Rai has spoken against none of these threats.

There is no doubt that Rai tried to sensationalize his 2G report, a populist report that sought to build the reputation of one institution, the CAG, undermining public faith in another, the telecom ministry. What made the hawkish Rai the UPA government's bête noire?

Rai, Manmohan Singh's student, was serving in the finance ministry before his retirement from the IAS in 2008.

'In the CAG report on the 2G spectrum, the calculation of the losses was certainly exaggerated, especially the implication that there was a loss to the government of Rs 1.76 lakh crore or that there was corruption of the order of Rs.30,000 crore,' says a former bureaucrat.[119]

Subbarao, who was finance secretary when the 2G case played out, was called in as a prosecution witness in the court case. He took the view in his deposition that the 2G case presented the government with a choice between revenue maximization and welfare maximization.[120] The government could have extracted market price for the spectrum, but that would have raised the costs to consumers. On the other hand, the government could sell spectrum below the market price so as to keep the costs low and affordable even to low-income segments. 'It is perfectly open', he said, 'for a democratically elected government to forego revenue in order to deepen phone penetration.'[121]

The CBI judge, in his judgment on the 2G spectrum case, called Subbarao a stellar witness.[122]

Of all the CAGs in the institution's 158-year-old history, Rai's post-retirement acceptance of positions offered by the Narendra Modi-led NDA government, is reminiscent of T.N. Chaturvedi.

GST Stalled

In the budget for 1986–87, Finance Minister Vishwanath Pratap Singh had proposed a major overhaul of the excise taxation structure.[123] A decade and a half later, in 2000, Prime Minister Atal Bihari Vajpayee, introducing the concept of GST, set up a committee under then West Bengal Finance Minister Asim Dasgupta to design a GST model. In 2003, a task force under the economist Vijay Kelkar, then adviser to the finance ministry, recommended a number of tax reforms. A year later it recommended GST as a replacement for the tax regime in place.

On 28 February 2006, the GST debuted in the budget speech, with Finance Minister P. Chidambaram setting an ambitious 1 April 2010 as deadline for its roll-out and requesting the empowered committee of finance ministers to prepare a road map for it. Two years later, this committee was constituted. The preparatory work, such as computerization of commercial tax systems for rolling out the proposed GST, was under way. However, political consensus on the constitutional amendments needed to provide the legislative framework for rolling out the GST regime was proving difficult.

A GST regime could not have been created within the federal arrangement laid out in the Constitution. Amending it required a political process, in which all the states and union territories would agree to give up their right to impose sales tax on goods (VAT), and the centre would agree to give up its right to impose excise and services taxes. Next, they would have to agree to a new amended federal arrangement, in which each state and the centre would receive a share of the GST collected nationally. This meant that instead of every state imposing a tax, all the states would sit together and decide what that tax rate should be. Individually, states saw this as an erosion of their financial autonomy.

Mukherjee met, one by one, almost all the state chief ministers. He held a number of meetings with members of the empowered committee, but a consensus continued to be elusive.[124] Two states in particular, Gujarat and Madhya Pradesh, stood out in active disagreement. Despite Mukherjee's efforts, Madhya Pradesh Finance Minister Raghavji remained ferociously opposed to the very idea of a redistribution of taxation powers between the centre and state. Along with Saurabh Patel, Gujarat's finance minister, he vetoed the bill, holding the introduction of GST to ransom.

Mukherjee ascribes the BJP's blocking of the GST to the arrest of former Gujarat Home Minister Amit Shah in the Sohrabuddin Sheikh murder case in July 2010.[125] On 4 August 2010, the Gujarat government made detailed written submissions before the empowered committee:

> The proposed constitutional amendment . . . fundamentally alters powers of the States to levy and collect indirect taxes. The power to determine rate of taxes is a basic function of legislative body like Parliament or, as the case may be, State Legislature. Article 265 very clearly states that no tax shall be levied or collected except by authority of law. Thus, provisions of proposed Article 279A

run counter to the existing provisions of Constitution. I find it difficult to agree to wide ranging powers given to GST council. These powers shall remain within legislative and administrative purview of State and cannot be ceded to the council as it will take away entire financial autonomy of the State.[126]

On 11 February 2011, the Gujarat government raised the pitch:

The new constitutional amendment draft proposed by the Government of India is retrograde in nature and completely against the tenets of fiscal federalism . . . Gujarat does not support the proposed constitutional amendment in its present form.[127]

Amit Shah's arrest may have hardened the BJP's position, but the party had been cold to the bill even before. On the eve of the Lok Sabha session in 2009, to resolve the stalemate over the bill, Manmohan Singh had invited L.K. Advani, Sushma Swaraj, Arun Jaitley and Pranab Mukherjee for discussions over lunch.[128] That morning, L.K. Advani, followed by Swaraj and Jaitley, turned down the overture. They informed Mukherjee of their inability to engage with the government, refusing to show the prime minister the courtesy of directly informing him of their decision. The BJP was so disinclined to accept GST that even Mukherjee's legendary powers of persuasion could not make its leaders in Parliament see reason over the GST. Nor was Mukherjee, the government's chief troubleshooter, able to make two states, Gujarat, under Narendra Modi, and Madhya Pradesh, under Shivraj Singh Chouhan, support the GST.

With the BJP's support not forthcoming, the bill could not be moved in Parliament. The centre's consultations with chief ministers and empowered committee members continued.

Finally, a thaw became possible in 2011. The government tabled the 115th Constitution Amendment Bill in the Lok Sabha on 22 March.[129] A week later it was sent to the parliamentary standing committee on finance headed by BJP's Yashwant Sinha. Here the bill languished, and the UPA government missed the deadline it had given to itself for rolling out the GST.

In his budget speech of 2013, Chidambaram—back in the finance ministry with Mukherjee's election as President—said that the groundwork and IT-enabled infrastructure for GST had been put in place during the period 2009 to 2012.[130] The only thing holding back the roll-out was the passage of the Constitutional Amendment Bill that was pending with the parliamentary standing committee.

Sinha, who took two years and four months to submit his report on the bill, finally sent it in August 2013.

Even after Sinha returned the report on the bill, as late as October 2013, Gujarat Chief Minister Narendra Modi opposed it saying the state would incur losses worth Rs 14,000 crore every year as a result of GST.[131] On 23 October, the Modi-led Gujarat government opposed the UPA government's attempt to pass the bill. Its finance minister, Saurabh Patel, told the national empowered committee meeting, 'If the union government through an ordinance enacts the GST regime, Gujarat will have to bear Rs 14,000 crore loss per annum due to the destination-based taxation principle . . . Gujarat is facing a severe problem of realization of revenue due to economic slowdown.'[132]

Unable to make Modi see the value of GST as a tax reform, the UPA government gave up, and instead decided to devote itself to building support for the Land Acquisition Bill and the National Food Security Act (which was passed on 5 September 2013). The BJP found it difficult to stall the two legislations and voted in favour of both in Parliament. The inevitable result was that the Constitutional Amendment Bill lapsed without getting passed in 2014, as the Lok Sabha was dissolved ahead of the general elections.

Why could the UPA government not pass the GST Bill? Multiple forces seem to have been at play.

The first was that the BJP had come to be dominated by GST atheists. At every meeting of the empowered committee of state finance ministers, the BJP states would offer systematic opposition, rallying behind the vocal finance minister from MP, Raghavji.[133] The issues they raised were all centred on the premise that the GST's introduction would erode the state legislatures' fiscal sovereignty. In a genuine GST regime, the state finance ministers' options to change tax rates are circumscribed and, therefore their clout is drastically reduced. These politicians—genuinely or mistakenly— confused individual discretion with state autonomy. For, a GST system typically has fixed rules and rates of taxation, and shrinks the leeway for making changes, and therefore the clout of finance ministers too.

In an interview to *India Today* in October 2010, Mukherjee explained the stalemate:

> I don't think politics should be mixed with major economic decisions. If you look at the BJP manifesto, they have . . . accepted GST. There is a broad political consensus about the necessity of GST, about the need to remove multiple points of taxation. There are reservations from some states who feel that a uniform rate of taxation will deny them the autonomy of imposing taxes which they believe is their sovereign right. It may take some time, but it will be possible.[134]

Second, the resistance to the GST in Parliament was a purely political strategy. The GST had for all practical purposes become a UPA initiative, although the idea had originated as part of a process put in place by the Vajpayee government. Manmohan Singh had become the first prime minister since Pandit Nehru to return to office, having delivered quality economic growth never seen before in independent India. The BJP, keen to make him and the UPA government seem ineffective, was in no mood to facilitate passage of the bill and let them walk away with further credit.

Sinha says,

> I was perhaps the only voice in the BJP, when we were in the opposition, which was supporting the GST. Was Modi [as Gujarat Chief Minister at the time] bothered about GST? His Finance Minister [Saurabh Patel] came before the Standing Committee which I was chairing and opposed GST. [The] Madhya Pradesh government opposed GST. Arun Jaitley, Sushma Swaraj, L.K. Advani, Rajnath Singh all these leaders they were completely unconcerned. I recommended that it should be passed, but who in the BJP was bothered about GST?[135]

Sinha is certainly a reformist, and the empowered committee, which used to always be headed by the finance minister of an opposition party, was his innovation back in 2000 for monitoring the harmonization and reform of indirect taxes, including the Central Sales Tax (CST) system, and the switch over to VAT. It became the basis of the institution of the GST Council, for which he should get extraordinary credit. He was the one who had introduced the three-tax-rates model in the extant CST, which was meant to be the template on which the GST ought to have been built, and probably would have been had any other government piloted the GST.

Yet, while the BJP was stalling the GST through parliamentary and empowered committee tactics, Sinha showed little efficiency or urgency in readying the report. The delay at his end only helped his party's unconstructive politics.

If Sinha was doing his party's politics, the Congress should have found political solutions to break the impasse. But it failed to. Mukherjee, the master numbers stringer and problem-solver, either proved ineffective, or worse, did precious little to drive consensus and overcome the BJP's tactical resistance.

That he couldn't make the GST's opponents see it as a tax reform and that they kept looking at it as a power struggle also suggests that there may have been another force at play, something other than obstructive politics: the issue of ownership. The GST was identified with Chidambaram. Mukherjee was perhaps not that interested in pushing it. The Congress party could not prevail upon Mukherjee to get the reform through.

Says Jairam Ramesh,

> Mr Mukherjee did nothing from 2011 to till he became President in July 2012 to push the bill. I used to meet Sumitra Mahajan every third day to get my Land Acquisition Bill report out. And she produced the Land Acquisition report in nine months. That was as complicated as the GST Bill. It went to her in September. In May, she gave the report. That's because I kept talking to her, explaining to her. Mr Mukherjee did not do anything.[136]

The fact is, none of the politicians rose above petty politics.

The objections from the BJP-governed states never vanished even after the government led by the BJP, with Modi himself at the head, was sworn in at the centre in 2014. Rather, they were simply papered over. The party never engaged adequately with the concerns its own members raised. As a consequence the BJP lacked the conceptual clarity required to evolve a smoothly functional GST.

When the GST eventually landed in the hands of a political leadership that was not convinced about the indirect tax in the first place, it led to a malfunctioning design and flaws. The tardy rate structure and implementation scheme dealt a debilitating impact on the economy. Did one state's—Gujarat's—insecurities and philosophy cast a dark shadow on India's GST? More on this a little later in the book.

Tax Terrorism

In his Finance Bill for budget 2012, Pranab Mukherjee had inserted provisions to undo a Supreme Court verdict that had gone in Vodafone's favour. The court had held that the Income Tax department had no right to tax capital gains in the $11.08 billion Vodafone-Hutchison transaction that had paved the way for the UK-based company's entry into India in 2007.[137]

The finance minister now proposed to amend the Income Tax Act with retrospective effect to empower the tax department to tax indirect transfers of shares where the underlying assets are located in India.[138] The motivation was to gain around Rs 40,000 crore from various similar cases pending before various courts.[139]

Before Mukherjee moved the provision in Parliament, Chidambaram, in a meeting of the core group, which included Manmohan Singh and Sonia Gandhi, had advised him against proceeding with retrospective taxation.

Mukherjee discloses in his memoir, *The Coalition Years: 1996 to 2012,* that he had pressed on with the retrospective amendment defying the counsel from Manmohan Singh, Sonia Gandhi, Kapil Sibal and P. Chidambaram, all of whom were convinced it would create a negative sentiment for FDI in the country.[140]

He pressed on, unmindful of their advice. The move ended up souring the investment sentiment, and it was criticized severely as 'tax terrorism' on the part of the UPA government. The recourse to retrospective amendments for undoing a Supreme Court judgment was seen as a return to the old socialist ways. Vodafone counsel Harish Salve severely criticized it:

> We should show that we have institutions in this country that work. I think the country will pay a dear price for this. I think we are on course for elections this year. It's a government which is politically rattled. They don't want to take tough decisions and introduce reformist measures. This is waging war on foreign investment. If a client asked me 'should I invest in India today?' I would say 'no'.[141]

In his book, Mukherjee defends the retrospective amendment, arguing that taxation cannot discriminate between domestic and foreign companies.[142] He maintains that the apex court had not said that capital gains are not taxable. All it had said was that the language used in the IT Act did not adequately reflect the intention to tax capital gains. The retrospective amendment was a way to bridge that gulf between language and intention.

Leaping across briefly to 2014, in the very first address Mukherjee made in the Central Hall of Parliament to the congregation of the newly elected members of the sixteenth Lok Sabha and those from the Rajya Sabha, just after the Modi government had been sworn in, he read out the new government's promises. One of them was a tax regime that would be predictable and non-adversarial.[143] The irony was lost on no one. Then, two years later, in 2016, adding injury to insult, Chidambaram criticized the Modi government for not repealing the retrospective taxation on Vodafone.[144]

Chidambaram too had squandered the opportunity to repeal it when he was brought back as finance minister following Mukherjee's election as President.

The fact is, no one would repeal the troubling provision because everyone had cast their vote for it in Parliament.

Why was Mukherjee not overruled? I asked Chidambaram.

'I don't know. I think he should have been advised not to introduce the retrospective provision. It could have been made prospective.'[145]

Mukherjee's handling of the other crucial tax reform, the Direct Taxes Code (DTC), too came in for criticism. For instance, parts of the version of the DTC that Mukherjee released in June 2010 disregarded previous judgments of courts in cases involving the Income Tax Act 1961, which has evolved over several decades, and which was now being sought to be replaced. 'Some of the proposals [in the DTC] are highly debatable and may defeat the objective of simplification and reduced litigation,' the Institute of Chartered Accountants of India said in an editorial in its in-house magazine.[146] Among the risks pertaining to the DTC, it listed 'the limited horizons of those tasked with implementation'.

Seeds of the NPA Crisis

The second G20 Summit was held in London in April 2009. As the Indian delegation waited for the proceedings to begin, the prime minister spoke of his own days in North Block to Ashok Chawla, 'In my time, there used to be a single post of Secretary, Financial Services, and Secretary, Economic Affairs, and, although even in those days there was a proposal to have a separate secretary, I had opposed it, as Secretary, Economic Affairs.'[147]

'For better coordination, it should be one post,' the prime minister had added.

The Government of India has for long persisted with separate departments for banking services and economic affairs, just to avoid reducing a secretary-level position. Banks transfer and store people's money and allocate people's savings, in the form of loans, to business. But often banks trip and begin to malfunction. That is when they start absorbing losses from businesses and transmit those back to savers and taxpayers. In the aftermath of the global financial crisis, it was clear that the American taxpayers would be made to bail out global financial giants. The global crisis was spilling over from financial markets to the real economy in the United States.

Singh thought it prudent that the arms of the policy scissors—banking and economic affairs—should work together to minimize the spread of the contagion from banks to the real economy. Within days of returning to Delhi after the G20 summit, Chawla was given additional charge of financial services, and G.C. Chaturvedi was appointed additional secretary (he was later appointed, post-retirement, as chairman of ICICI Bank in 2018).

The two officials set about the task at hand. The global financial crisis had demonstrated the destructive potential of the greed and incompetence of bankers. India's mostly outdated public banking system was already in dire need of reform. Singh, as the RBI governor in the post-nationalization period, and then in the 1990s as finance minister, had seen the rot up close. A round of capital infusion into PSBs had already been made part of the second stimulus package.

It was felt that more than twenty PSBs were too many. Experts had on occasion recommended consolidating them into six or seven large banks, each a diversified powerhouse offering the whole range of financial and banking services.

Chawla, with the intention of setting that process in motion, called a meeting with four or five of the bigger PSBs and discussed their appetite and strategy to take on weaker ones. He then wrote the minutes of this discussion. A formal examination of proposals was to follow. Mukherjee was not impressed. He called Chawla.[148]

'This is an exploratory meeting . . . I thought, this is maybe something which you may like to look at,' Chawla told Mukherjee.

'But from the policy point of view this is not an area which one is going to take a look at all.'

That was the end of it. Mukherjee had taken a stand. Streamlining the public banking system was now ruled out.

In the preceding four years, 2004 to 2008, the banking system had got rid of almost all the PSBs that were a regulatory discomfort. Reddy records in his book how Chidambaram gave him 'unstinted support' for the mess to be tidied up through mergers, obliging him even outside office hours.[149] The state-run banks escaped the regimen because of Mukherjee's gruff resistance.

One day, a little before the end of 2009, Chawla was at the cabinet secretary's office for a meeting when the cabinet secretary, K.M. Chandrasekhar, asked him, 'What happened? What's the problem? FM not happy with you in banking?'[150]

'No, why?'

'He's been asking for a separate secretary, giving the reason there is too much work for one secretary.'

Chawla was a bit taken aback, and visibly somewhat hurt, probably as the minister had not informed him directly. The cabinet secretary also shared the name of the replacement the minister had in mind.

Later, Chawla told Mukherjee about what he had come to hear. 'Sir, that's your prerogative and the government's.'[151]

'No, Ashok, I think, you need to concentrate here more.'

A new secretary, financial services, of Mukherjee's choice was appointed on 4 January 2010.[152] Just about four months later, in April, Chaturvedi was also packed off from the ministry.

Mukherjee thus dismantled within months the administrative arrangement the prime minister had put in place to make sure that the public banking system and economic priorities remained closely aligned. He had edged out Singh's first choice, Chidambaram, from the all-important ministry. Now he was replacing at will officials Singh had hand-picked.

Candidates he preferred filled up senior positions in most banks. They were not always the top-rated in the shortlists sent to the ACC.[153] Singh, who chaired this committee, let the finance minister have his say most of the time.

Mukherjee soon had a grip over the men and women who ran the financial services department in the finance ministry, the banks and the banking system.

Loans extended in the years 2006 to 2008 had begun to run into trouble by 2010.[154] In those boom years, companies had overcommitted themselves to projects.[155] Bankers had sanctioned loans when economic growth was strong, expecting the growth momentum to continue; they also went by the record of previous projects that had been completed on time and within budget.[156] An unforeseen shock—the global financial crisis—had changed everything. The demand projections on the basis of which projects were being built and had been financed no longer held. Global demand had collapsed. A global economic downturn, the worst since the Great Depression of the 1930s, was looming. But the lending banks remained blind to what lay ahead.

Political developments in Delhi and the related disruptions compounded the challenges. The CAG's reports led the Supreme Court to cancel 2G spectrum licences, mining leases and coal block allocations. Bureaucrats feared politically motivated investigations. Government approvals came to a grinding halt. Parliament remained deadlocked. Political uncertainty peaked. Business confidence dipped.

As projects stalled and cost overruns escalated, debts became unserviceable. When the global crisis struck in 2008, many companies tried to pause and rethink the viability of their projects, but then continued borrowing and investing in 2009–10 to try and finish the projects, becoming progressively more weighed down by debt.[157] Eventually, the need to deleverage became urgent in the face of stagnant demand and necessitated the abandonment of ongoing projects as well as cancellation or postponement of new investments. The debt burden became so high that it continues to inhibit investment recovery even now, nearly a decade later.

Lenders should have reassessed the economic prospects and course-corrected to scale back projects and write down the loans that had turned uncollectable. Promoters should have been forced to bring in more equity or lose their projects. Nothing of the sort was undertaken.[158]

Promoters, hopeful of riding out the difficulties, took on even more debt to keep projects afloat. Bankers went out on a limb, throwing more good money to avoid the blot of bad loans on their books. Loans were restructured, but the projects remained stuck. Bureaucratic inaction, political mud-slinging and the clampdown by courts on supplies of natural resources only worsened the situation.

Stress piled on bank and company balance sheets. Plummeting GDP growth precipitated the crisis. But banks still could not see the looming threats to their financial health and went on approving loans with more and more leverage and less promoter equity. In some cases, due diligence was omitted, and loans were made based solely on project reports prepared by promoters' investment banks. Bankers were either not trained to—or failed to—detect inflated costs of capital equipment through over-invoicing.

It was in this way, in the years Mukherjee was at the helm, that the seeds of the NPA crisis were sown. PSBs went on financing promoters long after private banks had begun exiting loans.

Prime Minister Modi would later call this a 'phone-a-loan' scam.[159]

The continuing push for infrastructure creation, an asset stimulus, was not an inappropriate goal. But it should have been clear that there were no obvious sources for financing these long-gestation capital-intensive projects. Funding strategies ought to have been given more attention. The private sector was already hobbled by low-demand conditions, shrinking profits and growing debt problems. Budget allocations were ruled out because the fiscal stimulus had already blown the deficit to the sky. It is for these reasons that the task of funding infrastructure had fallen upon PSBs—under instructions from Delhi, as suggested later by Modi.

Who might have made these calls? I asked a top government source who had handled the matter first-hand. 'The popular perception is that NPAs were caused by crony capitalism. There certainly was some of that, but there were many other causes as well. Pranab was a crafty politician with a lot of political IOUs . . .'[160]

Banker exuberance bordering on irrationality, incompetence and lack of training, and possibly susceptibility to malfeasance (yet to be established in a court of law so far), pushed the economy into an investment slowdown from 2011–12 onwards. This was a reversible slowdown but indecision and policy failures, both before and post-2014, would prolong and deepen it.

The Vijay Mallya Case

Some of the most reckless lending by banks happened in this period, a lot of it to promoters who were later declared wilful defaulters or fraudsters (as against defaulters who failed to pay loans due to the eroded profitability of their companies). The most controversial of the wilful default cases, IDBI Bank's Rs 900 crore loan to Kingfisher Airlines, was sanctioned within a mere twenty days of the bank being approached for a loan, although the (now-defunct) carrier did not even have an account in the bank till the day of disbursement of the loan.[161] The loan was made during Mukherjee's term in the finance ministry. The consequences of the NPA crisis became most visible in the case of IDBI Bank; 25 per cent of its outstanding loans having gone bad, the bank was on the brink of failure when, pressed by the Modi government, Life Insurance Corporation (LIC) bailed it out in 2018.[162]

On 9 March 2016, attorney general of India, Mukul Rohatgi, told a Bench of Supreme Court Justices Kurian Joseph and Rohinton Nariman that Vijay Mallya had left the country on 2 March 2016—the very day the banks to whom he owed over Rs 9000 crore moved the Debt Recovery Tribunal.[163]

Appearing for thirteen banks from this consortium, which was led by State Bank of India, Rohatgi said he had been told about Mallya's departure by the CBI.

Barely twenty-four hours earlier, on 8 March, the banks had moved the apex court to restrain Mallya from leaving the country. The banks had wanted the court to seize Mallya's passport. Chief Justice of India T.S. Thakur had posted the case for 9 March.

Mallya, still a Rajya Sabha member, had pre-empted the banks' petition to bar his departure. Did Mallya leave because the banks had moved the tribunal? Or, had the banks moved the tribunal because they had an inkling that Mallya had left? Will we ever find out? Why didn't the CBI restrain him? He had visited the Rajya Sabha, with his bags, ahead of his departure, and even had a brief exchange with Arun Jaitley, the finance minister at the time.[164]

In a Facebook post, Jaitley later confirmed that Mallya had told him in person, as he was walking to his room in Parliament: 'I am making an offer of settlement.' To which Jaitley said he had replied, 'no point talking to me and he must make offers to his bankers.'[165]

Rohatgi asked the court to pass orders directing Mallya to appear before the Bench, passport in hand.[166] Most of Mallya's assets are abroad, the attorney general informed the apex court.

'Only a fraction is in India . . . maybe one-fifth.'[167]

'Then how did you give these loans? Were there no secured assets on these loans?' asked Justice Kurian Joseph, who was on the Bench with Justice Rohinton Nariman.

Rohatgi replied that the loans had been granted at a time when Kingfisher Airlines was still a brand at its peak, with assets worth some thousand crores.

'It crashed.'[168]

'We had some assets [as security] for the loans advanced.'[169]

The banks had moved the Supreme Court, telling it that the threat to their financial interests was immediate and grave, after the Karnataka High Court refused to pass an ex parte order against Mallya.[170]

Before moving the high court, the banks had filed four pleas before the Debt Recovery Tribunal in Bengaluru on 2 March, for immediate freezing of Mallya's passport and issuance of an arrest warrant.[171]

The Supreme Court ordered Mallya to appear before it in person with his passport on 30 March. He never did.

That same day, 9 March, in a separate hearing, a Delhi court fixed 27 April as the date for hearing final arguments in a two-decades-old case against the liquor baron.[172]

Later that week, newspapers reported that Mallya had flown to London on 2 March, by first class on a commercial flight, and not in one of his private jets, taking seven heavy bags along with him.[173] There was no travel bar on him the day he flew out. The CBI had lowered the lookout notice on him from 'detain' to merely 'inform'.[174]

The CBI had registered a case against Mallya, Kingfisher Airlines, and some IDBI Bank officials in July 2015, taking suo motu notice of alleged fraud.[175] Mallya was questioned at least twice and the agency conducted searches.

Days after Rohatgi stunned the nation with the disclosure that Mallya had left the country, in Mumbai the Enforcement Directorate's questioning of former IDBI chairman Yogesh Agarwal focused on the substantive issue in the case: Why did IDBI Bank disburse a hefty loan of more than Rs 900 crore to Vijay Mallya's negatively credit-rated Kingfisher Airlines in what appears to be extraordinary efficiency?[176]

'Profit and loss are part of the business,' Agarwal said, defending the bank's decision.[177]

Agarwal had been on the executive committee that screened Mallya's loan application, giving it a favourable report. He was the chairman of IDBI Bank at the time.

The investigators then asked what had made the bank sanction the loan despite the evident uncertainty about Mallya's repayment capacity, given the status at the time of a loan made earlier by a consortium of banks.[178]

The team that had sanctioned the loan told the investigating officers that they 'were asked to consider the brand value of Kingfisher Airlines'.[179]

The Enforcement Directorate officials who questioned Agarwal were quoted as saying they had reasons to believe Mallya had secured the loan with the speed and efficiency that he did due to political intervention.[180] The charge sheets and FIRs related to the IDBI Bank loan to the airline contain the details about the transaction.

On 1 October 2009, Mallya directed the chief financial officer of his company, A. Raghunathan, to 'immediately' file an application for a loan from IDBI.[181] Kingfisher Airlines moved an application for a corporate loan of Rs 50 crore on the same day.[182] Both went to the IDBI headquarters on 5 October and met Yogesh Agarwal and B.K. Batra, deputy managing director of the bank.[183]

They met again on 6 October.[184] The day after, Raghunathan submitted a letter to IDBI Bank seeking an urgent sanction of Rs 150 crore as loan for a period of six months. The letter stated that the money was for meeting certain critical obligations to overseas vendors; however, no documents were attached to substantiate that claim.[185]

According to the CBI, Mallya had already convinced Agarwal to sanction the loan before he wrote the letter, as a 'hastily drawn memorandum to the credit committee recommending sanction' had been submitted on the same day by Buddhadev Dasgupta, a senior official of IDBI Bank.[186]

The loan was sanctioned the same day.[187]

Dasgupta recommended the sanctioning of a loan of Rs 150 crore to Kingfisher despite its weak finances and without referring with the risk department of credit ratings.[188] No reason for not getting the ratings, nor any explanation for the emergency, was provided.[189] The loans were disbursed to Mallya on 9 October.[190] The CBI discovered that Kingfisher Airlines did not even have an account with the Nariman Point, Mumbai, branch of IDBI Bank till 8 October.[191] It was only on the day of disbursement of the loan that it opened a current account in the bank.[192]

After the entire amount had been disbursed, the proposal was referred to the risk department for post facto ratings on 20 October.[193]

Kingfisher did not pay the processing fees of Rs 41 lakh from its own reserve.[194] The airline rerouted the loan amount through another bank and then, five days after the loan was sanctioned, paid this fee on 12 October.[195]

In November, Raghunathan wrote to the bank, referring to a meeting between Agarwal and Mallya, and requesting an ad hoc release of Rs 200 crore.[196] Once again, the amount was released.[197] Later, it was subsumed into the corporate loan of Rs 750 crore that IDBI Bank released to the airline on 27 November.[198]

Part of the problem in India is that the wheels of justice move slowly. It was only as late as on 4 January 2018 that Mallya was declared a proclaimed offender by a Delhi court in a FERA (Foreign

Exchange Regulation Act) violation case of 1995, unrelated to Kingfisher Airlines.[199]

A few months later, in mid-2018, the Modi government pressed LIC to bail out the beleaguered IDBI Bank by acquiring equity in it.

The Legacy of Pranab Mukherjee

Mukherjee's sharp differences with Singh, and their impact on decision-making in government, became apparent when the former blocked an extension to RBI Deputy Governor Usha Thorat in October 2010, despite Governor Subbarao's strong recommendation of a two-year extension for her, as per convention. Subbarao met the minister in person to requisition the reappointment, but, he writes in his memoirs, Mukherjee would not budge.[200]

The refusal was the price, writes Subbarao, that they were made to pay for asserting the RBI's independence. A regulatory issue on Thorat's watch had not gone down well with Mukherjee. Thorat's expertise lay in determining the 'fit and proper' criteria for bank owners. Subbarao has not disclosed the details of this controversial case, but they are known well in banking circles.

A student of Singh's when he taught at the Delhi School of Economics, Thorat had been appointed to the RBI by Singh and Chidambaram, on request from Reddy.

'Later, when the time for a call on Subbarao's reappointment came, Mukherjee again had other ideas.

He did not speak on the subject to Subbarao even once.[201] Seven weeks short of completion of his term, Singh, after a regular pre-policy briefing at 7, Race Course Road on 21 July 2011, asked the governor if the finance minister had spoken to him about his extension. The governor said 'no'. On 28 July, principal secretary to the prime minister, T.K.A. Nair, called Subbarao to check if the finance minister had spoken to him about his extension. The governor informed him that Mukherjee hadn't. The ritual was repeated on 4 August.

By this time, as far as possible Mukherjee was avoiding Singh, communicating rarely and indirectly through the messengers the prime minister would send on pressing matters. C. Rangarajan and Nair were among the go-betweens.[202]

Even after repeated reminders from the PMO seeking the finance minister's recommendation for extension to Subbarao, the file was not moved.[203] This time Singh put his foot down.[204] Days before Subbarao's three-year term was to end, the PMO sent a missive to the finance minister's office.[205] The prime minister would have no hesitation in issuing the orders for a second term for RBI Governor Subbarao, pending a formal recommendation.[206]

On the morning of 9 August, Subbarao found out about his two-year extension from a television news flash.[207] It was followed by a call from Nair fifteen minutes later, informing him about the extension and congratulating him on behalf of Singh.[208]

The formal announcement came from the PMO, on its website, rather than from the ministry of finance.[209]

It was only after several calls that Subbarao managed to reach Mukherjee on the phone, and only at 10 p.m.[210] 'Oh, that was just a formality. You've earned the extension by your performance. There was never any question of replacing you at this stage. Best of luck.'[211]

Mukherjee held the finance portfolio until 26 June 2012, after which he ceased to lord over the government's purse strings and 70 per cent of the country's banking system. He was elected the country's President. For more than three of UPA-2's five years, Mukherjee had been the finance minister.

This phase marks the start of a protracted investment slowdown in the country. The banks' bad loans (NPAs) crisis, responsible for the investment slowdown, can be traced to the years when Mukherjee was at the helm. Some of the most reckless lending by banks overlaps his tenure, a lot of it to promoters who were later declared wilful defaulters. Enforcement Directorate investigations are probing for political influence in the dubious cases.

Decisively anti-reform, Mukherjee felt no hesitation in defying the prime minister's authority. His decision to impose capital gains tax on Vodafone brought disrepute to the country's image as an investment destination. Investors from around the world said India practised 'tax terrorism'.

Supposedly the government's troubleshooter, Mukherjee was unable to persuade two states, Gujarat, under Narendra Modi and Madhya Pradesh under Shivraj Singh Chouhan, that the GST was not a compromise of the fiscal autonomy of states. The UPA government missed deadlines it had given to itself for rolling out the GST, as the bill for amending the Constitution languished owing to opposition from Modi and Chouhan.

Within twenty-four months of Mukherjee's entry into the finance ministry, the GDP growth rate crashed from 8.9 per cent in 2010–11 to 5.5 per cent in 2012–13,[212] as he, instead of withdrawing the fiscal stimulus, took decisions that weakened the investment sentiment, stoked inflation and hurt the macroeconomic parameters of the country. India went from being a miracle economy to one of the 'Fragile Five' economies.

As finance minister last in the pre-liberalization era, Mukherjee's style of functioning was a throwback to the socialist 1970s and 1980s, when the concept of economic policy was limited mostly to increasing government spending.

'He was quite sort of, at that stage, in the first few months, a bit lost,' recalled an official in the ministry who had worked closely with Mukherjee.[213] 'His world of finance was one in which you collect what you can. Rob the rich, spend it on programmes which are politically important. The finance minister's job essentially was that of a tax collector and then expenditure, according to the political economy priorities that had been chosen. All the levers basically be controlled by the government, which is what nationalization was, and he talks very warmly about nationalization.'

At least two bureaucrats who worked in the ministry with Mukherjee attest to his outdatedness, his deep differences with Singh and his general opposition to reforms.

Mukherjee articulated his economic philosophy in his own words as soon as he became President on 25 July 2012, when he spoke at the historic Central Hall of Parliament[214] shortly after he was sworn in as the thirteenth President of India. For real development to be achieved, he said, to a burst of applause, 'The poorest of our land must feel that they are part of the narrative of rising India.' In his brief acceptance speech, he placed 'economic equity' above all the basic 'fundamentals' of a modern nation—democracy, secularism, equality of every region and language and gender equality.[215] As he expanded on the theme of eliminating poverty, it did not go unnoticed among the gaggle of ministers, governors, chief ministers and MPs who packed Central Hall that Mukherjee, dressed in a black achkan and white churidar, was taking a gentle swipe at the economic reformers whom he had left behind in the government that he was part of until recently.[216] 'Trickle-down theories do not address the legitimate aspirations of the poor,' he stressed in his home-grown English, which the smart set of his party has named 'Pranabese'.[217] Nice-sounding words, except that he took not a single step to broad base the economic growth model and relied only on redistribution policies.

Unapologetic about being old-school, some would say. Misfit, others would retort. But even when he left for Rashtrapati Bhawan, it was not without inflicting one last embarrassment on the government.

'He was no believer in the Fiscal Responsibility and Budget Management targets [FRBM]', says one of the secretaries, a retired IAS officer who had worked under Mukherjee.[218] Says a second secretary, also now retired, who worked under Mukherjee, 'This was a whole new world where capital was flowing from all over the world, where you have to protect yourself from overflows.

And if flows are less, then you try to attract them to meet whatever internal deficit you have . . . These are all which he didn't even really want to understand. Or, it wasn't really his cup of tea.'[219]

Here was a minister locked in a pre-liberalization mindset, negotiating a post-liberalization economy. Mukherjee represented everything Singh had in 1991 proved wrong-headed and had dismantled. Even two decades after Singh had rid the ministry of the Licence Raj mindset, Mukherjee still swore by it and stubbornly refused to give it up.

'He shot down reform proposals. He thought all these things don't give any power. Because his thing was, how does one get authority in the political system? How does he control big business? How does he control his own colleagues? Because *unko paisa dega toh* they will come and say *hum ko paisa do*. Mamta will come Railways *ke liye paisa do*. [The finance ministry's role of allocation of funds to ministries and states will bring his colleagues to him asking for funds. Mamta will come and seek funds for Railways.] Lalu will come . . . Because that is the power of the finance ministry,' says the retired official who worked with him.[220]

The draw of the finance ministry for an individual of a certain persuasion is that it is indeed a powerful one. Therein lie the country's purse strings, and its arms are also vested with surveillance apparatus.

'He was a 60s–70s classical finance minister and he may have been rated as one of the good finance ministers of those days, but for this period nobody will give him any marks. The world had changed, he had not changed. I don't think he had mentally any desire to change. He still believed in the old system of giving some concessions here giving some excise exemption there. The whole impression I always used to get was here is a finance minister who is more political than interested in finance. Who really had no desire to get to the bottom of the nitty-gritty. Who had a very good overall shrewd political sense. He was more interested in pleasing segments of lobbies. Public interest was not paramount. This has been his style all along. It was honed to perfection in finance,' the retired official says.[221]

Paradoxically, corporate lobbies had a free run of the finance ministry headquarters in North Block during Mukherjee's tenure. For instance, ahead of a budget presentation one year, a strange file came into circulation at the highest level.[222]

The protocol was that no file, including budget proposals, could go to the minister without the approval of the finance secretary. Budget meetings went on first at the secretary level and after that at the finance minister level. Ahead of one of the budgets, all files had been discussed and the required decisions were in place for being taken up further with the finance minister. Then the revenue department people sent some additional files to the finance secretary. Most of them were okayed to be put up to the finance minister. Then, at last, came out a file in which a major concession to petroleum refineries was proposed.[223]

The officials, the retired official told me, were asked by the finance secretary what this new matter was, and they said, 'We were called and told to put this up.'[224]

'*Isme kya aur kisko faida hoga aur kitna hoga* [Who will benefit from this, in what way, and by how much]?'[225]

'Sab, only one company,'[226] was the jittery reply.

'*Kitne hazar crore* [How many thousand crore]?'[227]

'4,000 crore.'[228]

'I am not signing it. *Discuss karenge, uske baad fir dekhenge* [Will discuss and take a call].'[229]

The whole file noting was based on an unsigned note given quite obviously by a corporate fellow who used to float around at the time.[230]

'*Yeh dikhao toh sahee, kahan se aaya hai . . .* Where is the letter?'[231]

'Sir, there is no letter, there is an unsigned note.'[232]

'Have you consulted the petroleum ministry? *Aise kaise approve ho sakta hai?*'[233]

The file was sought to be cooked up in such a manner that it would fetch approvals from a couple of higher-ups in the ministry.[234] Decisions that no officer wanted to approve were at times escalated further to the level of the Group of Ministers.[235]

'It was not populism. It was politics by a personality—favours, ambition, rivalries—Lutyens' Delhi stuff. Throwback to the old style, reversal [of the 1991 market orientation of the economy and dismantling of government controls and Permit Raj]. Intrigue,' says one of the ex-secretaries quoted above.[236]

The character of North Block changed. Bank appointments became the talk of the town. There were attempts to smuggle ideas, proposals and even officials into the system.[237]

'Appointments is how he exercised control. Having the right man in the right position was crucial for an interventionist philosophy, best way to control the levers . . . There were stories of some agent sitting in a [top Delhi five-star] hotel who was taking orders . . . The bank fellows, they say, used to go and strike deals . . . And of course because of not letting the economies slip and all that . . . it became a very convenient thing for them to keep giving oral instructions to banks through [an officer in charge of banks in the ministry].' *[References to names blanked out in this quote]*[238]

Pranab Mukherjee was certainly out of his depth in finance. Singh's Economic Advisory Council tried to caution Mukherjee on his unchecked profligacy, perhaps a signal from Singh to Mukherjee that the latter completely ignored. In core-group meetings Mukherjee paid no heed to advice from Singh.

Says Chidambaram, 'The second and third [fiscal] packages were between the FM and presumably the PM, if he was in a position to give advice. My view then was, and remains, that while the second package was perhaps understandable, the third package was unnecessary. We were not facing that kind of a dip in growth. There was enough domestic demand to keep the economy clicking at about 6-7 per cent. So, we should have accepted the fact that thanks to the international crisis, the rate of growth will decline from say 8+ per cent or 8.5 per cent to, say, about 7 per cent. We should have accepted it. Why did we have to aim at 8+ per cent growth when the external environment certainly did not support such a rate of growth? Unless exports dramatically went up and foreign capital poured into the country, you couldn't expect 8 per cent growth.'[239]

'This was just before elections, so you think electoral calculations influenced the decision?' I asked Chidambaram.

'Maybe,' he said. 'Perhaps they wanted to keep the growth number high. But what they gained in the growth number they lost in the inflation. Inflation was far too high. We just managed to scrape through [in the elections] because inflation had not started biting the people. There's a lag. Inflation started to bite the people after the election, therefore we paid a price that way.'

In 2010, Mukherjee forced an ordinance just five weeks before the monsoon session of Parliament to create a super-regulatory structure that came in for criticism.[240] The senior-most bureaucrat in the ministry, Finance Secretary Ashok Chawla, opposed the plan on the grounds that it was not for the ministry to discipline regulators.[241] At a cabinet meeting, Chidambaram, home minister since December 2008, and deputy chairman of the Planning Commission Montek Singh Ahluwalia likened the ordinance to trying to swat a fly with a sledgehammer.[242] Mukherjee dug in his heels.[243] The troubleshooter had become the troublemaker, it seemed. For the UPA, bringing him into North Block began to seem to be a mistake.

Mukherjee's many failures in the crucial role raise interesting questions. There is the matter of what explains his non-performance. Was he nursing a consuming ambition to replace the prime minister, or at least become President, which distracted him from his finance ministry responsibilities? Second, when he was clearly out of depth, too dated for the finance ministry, why was he given the responsibility? Why could the party and the government not remind him of his duties?

Without question there was a failure of oversight in the banking department and a complete stalling of reforms. That Mukherjee didn't pull back the stimulus was an avoidable error, but is understandable. Exactly the same mistake was being made around the world at that time. The pushback from Singh was not strong enough. Governor Subbarao's account in his memoir details delicately how helpless Singh was in the face of his finance minister's outdated fiscal stance. The prime minister intervened only when it was absolutely crucial to do so. Singh and Mukherjee had a complicated manner of negotiating their deep ideological differences.

The relationship never reached a point where Singh would say something to the effect, 'You might differ, but do as I say'. The prime minister rarely overruled Mukherjee, barring the odd instance, such as Subbarao's extension. That episode too, in particular, shows that there were not only deep differences between them but a struggle for control too. The reliance on emissaries also suggests that communication between the finance minister's office and the PMO was certainly uneasy. This clash—which has not been written about enough—was less about personality differences and more a conflict of pre- and post-liberalization ideas. It symbolized the loss of power of an old-timer of a finance minister and his quest to regain it. Pranab stood for everything Singh had taken apart in the 1990s.

Mukherjee had accepted the new way, but had not adjusted to it. So he strived to recreate the old way—because that's what he knew best.

'It is easy to understand Pranab Mukherjee's frustration. It was he who appointed Manmohan Singh as RBI governor during an earlier stint as finance minister. And now, Manmohan Singh has become prime minister and Mukherjee is having to serve under him. This frustration defined the core relationship between the two of them during UPAII,' says a top official who regularly interfaced with the two on economic matters.[244]

This was in sharp contrast to the practice before Mukherjee's appointment.

'P. Chidambaram was meticulous about keeping the prime minister in the loop. He informed the prime minister always about what he was doing. The prime minister had a lot of respect for his intelligence and competence. Whereas Pranab Mukherjee treated the ministry as a fiefdom that had been carved out for his own agenda,' says the official.

There was clearly a mismatch between Mukherjee's troubleshooting reputation and his record in the finance ministry. He was busy, but not as the country's finance minister. 'The FM's heart is in everything but the MoF [ministry of finance],' an official told me at the time.[245]

For officials, the wait for an audience with Mukherjee could sometimes last a couple of days.[246] 'There are no discussions on his [Mukherjee's] views on the plan for the MoF for the next few years,' this top bureaucrat in the ministry said back then. 'At a senior level, what do officials need from FM other than direction?'[247]

What was the FM's heart in, then? Mukherjee, an astute politician of immoderate ambition, wanted to be prime minister. Or at least President. P. Chidambaram confirms that not just Mukherjee, but the Congressmen too had the settled view that Mukherjee should be prime minister or President.

When he entered North Block, Mukherjee had the decor of the finance minister's chamber redone, leaving no one in doubt that this was a man who took the contours and image of his office space seriously. The chamber that he had inherited was too bare and drab for his taste, comfort and ambition. The high-ceilinged room overlooking South Block, which had barely been touched since 1991, now underwent a dramatic makeover, acquiring a luxurious look and feel. The floor and walls were panelled with wood. Leather-bound seats and lighting effects usually seen in five-star hotels were installed. The look and feel matched his personality—the watch on a chain he wore with his bandhgalas, the pipe always close, even decades after he had given up smoking. A man of habit and ritual, he had refused to change. Journalists were invited to his yearly Durga Puja at his ancestral home in West Bengal. Hilsa was served at the annual winter lunch. The joke in the corridors of North Block was that the chamber had ceased to reflect the low-income-economy status of India and was finally in step with its newly earned middle-income standing.

The PMO could be seen across the road towards the right from the windows in the chamber, and farther down, the forecourt of Rashtrapati Bhawan.

To be in public office is to have ambition. Rare is the person who occupies one and does not aspire to higher positions.

I asked Chidambaram if Mukherjee's resentment at being subordinate to Singh was apparent.

'No, he was always very respectful to Dr Singh. Throughout. From day one he was extremely respectful to Dr Singh.'[248]

But it was Mukherjee's legitimate ambition to want to be prime minister.

'Yes, but it was a choice [of Singh as PM] made by Mrs Gandhi.'

Did this choice complicate in any way decision-making in government?

'I wouldn't know . . . he was extremely supportive of the prime minister in the Cabinet. And the prime minister always deferred to Mr Mukherjee.'

Pranab Mukherjee gave the first indication that his chosen path led inexorably to Rashtrapati Bhawan in an interview he gave to *India Today* in 2011.[249] He presented a picture of perfect harmony and good cheer, concealing his ambition and embracing humility. Instead of showcasing a sense of hurt or injustice, he threw down a challenge. 'Personally, I believe that the office of the President is not to be sought after, but is to be offered. It is the highest office. And it is always offered to a deserving person.' He made it known that he had been pushed thus far, he would be pushed no further. He refused to serve in any more Congress governments under any other prime minister. He also tried to dislodge the impression that he was having trouble with Singh in the matter of day-to-day decision-making in the finance ministry by profusely praising the prime minister. He was respectful, not deferential, to Singh, though. 'India is fortunate to have a prime minister like Dr Manmohan Singh. I have great respect for him,' he said.

But the interview did pose an open challenge. He had subtly suggested that the choice before Sonia Gandhi was either to reward a humble servant or appear thankless for his yeoman service to the country and party. It was a coming-out moment, a well-calculated riposte.

Pranab Mukherjee probably settled for the position of President when he realized that the last chance to be prime minister was gone and that time was running out. Being deputy prime minister may no longer have been acceptable to him. He had indicated he wouldn't serve another government, signalling that he had given up the quest for 7, Race Course Road. But it must have been clear to him that there would not be another Congress government in the immediate future. Staying relevant for five more years would be difficult for him with the Congress in the Opposition.

Within the Congress, Mukherjee was held in regard for his razor-sharp mind, his command of a panoramic sweep of issues and his dispassionate eagle eye for forging alliances. He became the Congress candidate and won the election despite not being Sonia Gandhi's first preference. One could say he outwitted her in garnering widespread support in favour of his claim to the position.

The government was, by then, under attack for 'policy paralysis'; its policy reforms relating to foreign investment in organized retail and insurance were in a limbo, and it had failed to make headway in implementing taxation reform. Rating agencies Standard & Poor's (S&P) and Fitch downgraded their outlook on India's sovereign rating from 'stable' to 'negative', citing slowing economic growth, high deficits and policy inaction.[250]

Foreign investors and the markets were spooked by Mukherjee's provision for taxing transactions retrospectively and the planned introduction of general anti-avoidance rules targeting deals structured in such a way as to avoid payment of tax.

Mukherjee's election as President ensured Singh a greater degree of freedom in handling the economy. But what if Singh had not needed the bypass surgery and had carried on holding the additional charge of finance?

'This event [Singh's bypass surgery] was a Black Swan event,' says Chidambaram. 'A completely unexpected event. Otherwise it was going smoothly. Dr Singh will be the Finance Minister and I will handle the Parliamentary work. It was going for whole of December and practically the whole of January. It was work, lot of work. This was a completely unexpected event. In fact, some of us came to know about it only after Dr Singh had been rushed to hospital.'

As it turns out, destiny had a hand too in the grave mistake the UPA made by bringing Mukherjee into the finance ministry ahead of Singh's bypass. With Singh indisposed, perhaps the decision makers had no choice. But it has become increasingly clear that the Congress and the economy have paid a heavy price for it. Before Mukherjee's appointment as finance minister, India was on the verge of being christened a miracle economy. By the time Mukherjee exited, large fiscal deficits and a high net international debt position had made the country vulnerable to global financial shocks and terms-of-trade shocks. Within a year, India would earn the ignoble distinction of being one of the 'Fragile Five' economies.

P. Chidambaram, unlike Mukherjee, is held in high opinion by regulators, bureaucrats and technocrats, despite his reputation of being arrogant (and now allegedly corrupt).[251] The Mukherjee phase coincided with the recovery's destruction, and Chidambaram's return with the reversal of that. The difference in approach of the two ministers does seem to at least partially explain the trends during their respective tenures.

His extremely poor track record, though, did not sully Mukherjee's public image. Be they leaders of the left parties, the RSS or the Congress, and even Modi and his ministers, everyone only seems to have positive things to say of him.

His great quality seems to have been that he had made very few enemies. If a parliamentarian posed searching questions, instead of going on the back foot, Mukherjee would compliment the questioner profusely for raising issues of importance and give a generic response about greed being the enemy of progress, blunting the pointedness of the question—evocative of an old-world charm, in the grip of ambition, but never losing grace.

3

A Slow Recovery Again (2012–15)

Damage Control

With Mukherjee ascending up Raisina Hill, from North Block to Rashtrapati Bhawan, Manmohan Singh took charge of the finance ministry once again, as was his plan before the bypass. He threw himself into damage control mode and set about changing the narrative. As P.V. Narasimha Rao's finance minister in the early 1990s, when he freed the economy of stifling government controls known as the 'Licence Raj', he had relied frequently on press interactions to explain to the people the changes being driven by the government.

Early July, in an email interview to *Hindustan Times*,[1] Singh identified his focus areas for the short term; the list read more like a compendium of positions Mukherjee had taken on policy matters that were going to be reversed: controlling the fiscal deficit, achieving clarity on tax matters, reviving the mutual funds and insurance industries, clearing a backlog of foreign investment proposals, and boosting infrastructure.

Singh cited investment plans lined up by Coca-Cola Co. and furniture group IKEA as proof that things had not deteriorated greatly. 'The chairman of GE captured the picture correctly when he said, "The mood in the market is worse than the mood on the ground." I agree with that.'

He said he wanted to show that his government would be fair and was keen to cut red tape—an allusion clearly to the ill repute

Mukherjee had brought upon India through his retrospective Vodafone provision.

'We will . . . work towards improving the response time of government to business proposals, cut down infructuous procedures, and make India a more business-friendly place . . . We want the world to know that India treats everyone fairly and reasonably, and there will be no arbitrariness in tax matters.'

Consumer durables and automobile inventories had grown, sales were down, production had been halted or shifts reduced. Mukherjee's only response had been to pressure the RBI for rate cuts. Lowering interest rates without doing anything else only lowers the savings rate. When inflation is soaring at the same time, savings are converted into gold. A better policy response would have been to reduce government consumption and to vacate borrowing space for private consumption and investments, along with interest rates reduction. That required coordinating fiscal policy with monetary policy: a fiscal tightening with monetary loosening.

Singh sought to address some of these structural imbalances that were posing risks to the macroeconomy.

> The absence of investment avenues has pushed Indian savings into gold. We need to open new doors so that savings can be recycled into productive investments that create jobs and growth, not into gold. A lot of investment avenues are opening up in railways, roads, ports and civil aviation. The doors are open for the world to strengthen our hands and contribute to these vital sectors, which will give a further push to the economy.

Singh signalled his desire to push back against the ideological drift within the Congress party in general, and, in particular, correct the course of economic policy. Mukherjee's own philosophical persuasion had brought reforms to a grinding halt and nearly wrecked government finances. The economic reforms agenda and public finances were in need of rejuvenation.

It is necessary that we change the discourse from a critique of an open economy to a critique of what is needed to make an open economy work better for the welfare of the people . . . there is the issue of distribution. We have lifted millions out of poverty. But I worry that the fruits of an open economy will be increasingly captured by fewer people. I worry that a large segment of our population will be left out of the benefits of economic growth. We need to correct that fast . . . important is that we need political consensus in the government on some policies. These are genuine differences in opinion. So, in a democracy, consensus building is the key to long-term economic success, and we are steadily moving ahead in doing that.

Lastly, he said he had

> . . . tried sincerely throughout my life to make India a better place to live, work and lead a fulfilling life . . . We have tried to build a peaceful, harmonious, secure, friendly, prosperous India where every citizen can aspire for the best in life. We have an unfinished agenda. I will leave it to history to judge whether I was successful.

Time magazine had run a cover portrait of Singh, dubbing him an 'under-achiever'.[2] Three weeks later, Singh brought P. Chidambaram back to the finance ministry, in the hope that the 'Dream Budget' finance minister would succeed in reviving the animal spirits of India's economy.

Power Minister Sushil Kumar Shinde succeeded Chidambaram in the home ministry.

In the cabinet, Chidambaram was the one, besides Ahluwalia, most closely aligned with Singh's personal economic ideology.

Singh reconstituted the empowered group of ministers (EGoMs), group of ministers (GoMs) and cabinet committees to rebalance the government's ideological bent. Already a member of the core group since his appointment to the home ministry,

Chidambaram now also headed more panels than any other minister, virtually stepping into Mukherjee's 'troubleshooter' role.[3] He was on more cabinet committees, eight out of ten, than any of his colleagues in the council of ministers. While Defence Minister A.K. Antony remained the virtual number two and sat on the right of the prime minister in cabinet meetings, Antony was on five committees, while Sharad Pawar sat on seven.

Immediately upon taking charge as finance minister, Chidambaram overhauled portfolios in the ministry, sending out a clear message that tidying up the mess on the tax side was a priority.[4] The impression that had gained ground, of India being a hostile tax jurisdiction, needed to be addressed. He was particular to take out of the revenue department Finance Secretary R.S. Gujral, who had presided over some of the controversial tax decisions of the government—such as the general anti-avoidance rules (GAAR) and the retrospective amendments to tax the Vodafone-Hutchison transaction.

Singh had signalled a relook of GAAR shortly after taking over the reins of the ministry, by appointing a panel under Parthasarathi Shome, a former adviser to the finance minister, to draft the rules taking into consideration industry's feedback. A series of moves aimed at image correction included postponement of GAAR and an assurance that retrospective tax cases wouldn't be as virulent as was feared, followed by appointment of another committee under N. Rangachary, a former Central Board of Direct Taxes (CBDT) chairman, to look into some of the taxation-related aspects for the information technology sector.

The revenue department's two tax boards, the CBDT and the Central Board of Excise and Customs, saw a change of guard. Chidambaram hit the ground running, visiting Mumbai, Hyderabad, Bengaluru, Chennai and Kolkata, pushing tax officials to meet revenue targets so that the fiscal deficit could be contained.

Sumit Bose was brought in as revenue secretary. A letter on the virtues of integrity went out from the new revenue secretary to the tax officials in the field.

The redrawn strategy included finalization of the Direct Taxes Code Bill after incorporating the recommendations of the standing committee on finance (neither the UPA government nor the Modi government would implement it). Time was too short to see through the passage of legislations, including a constitutional amendment, required for the roll-out of GST.

The government set about changing the country's image to make it appear friendlier to business. State minister for commerce, Jyotiraditya Scindia, launched a website, a single platform on which entrepreneurs could apply for all fifty-seven clearances needed to start a business. The twelfth Five Year Plan document rooted for 8.2 per cent GDP growth over the five-year period of 2012–17.[5] In September, the UPA government cleared the way for global retail giants such as Walmart to set up shop through a notification allowing 51 per cent foreign ownership in multi-brand retail stores.[6] Foreign players able to invest a minimum of $100 million were allowed to set up multi-brand retail outlets in cities with populations of more than 10 lakh. The proposal to liberalize the sector had been hanging fire for months, with the Opposition creating a big brouhaha over its feared impact on neighbourhood *kirana* shops and mom-and-pop stores. Some sections within the Congress had offered stiff resistance too. States and union territories were given the choice to decide if they wanted to open their doors to foreign players in multi-brand retail. Around ten had conveyed their willingness. FDI norms in single-brand retail were tweaked to relax the condition requiring 30 per cent sourcing from the micro, small and medium enterprises (MSME) sector, as long as those purchases were from India, paving the way for the entry of Swedish retail giant IKEA.

FDI in civil aviation was liberalized up to 49 per cent.[7] Plans were announced for increasing the foreign ownership limit in insurance companies to 49 per cent.[8] The cabinet approved foreign investors owning up to 26 per cent (or 49 per cent, depending on the successful enactment of the amended insurance laws) in pension-related businesses.[9] The foreign ownership liberalization for insurance and pension businesses was likely to become more challenging as they needed parliamentary approval. 'After a long wait, the government seems to have reignited reform efforts,' global rating agency S&P said in October.[10]

But the 'policy paralysis' was about administrative collapse of governance, not only about policy. Stumbling blocks to growth and investment remained—land acquisition, forest and environment clearances, delays in decision-making. In mid-August 2013, the UPA government introduced the Prevention of Corruption (Amendment) Bill, 2013, for amending the Prevention of Corruption Act, 1988.[11] The bill was moved in the Rajya Sabha rather than in the Lok Sabha, where pending bills would lapse at the conclusion of its five-year term.

Section 13(1)(d)(iii) of the Act sought to penalize a public servant for enriching a private entity 'without any public interest'.[12]

This particular provision was bereft of the basic requirement that a criminal act should emanate from a criminal intention, or 'mens rea'. It afforded staggering discretion to investigative agencies and courts in deciding whether a commercial decision taken by a public servant benefiting a private entity was devoid of public interest, the notion of public interest itself being subjective.[13] There could well be cases in which the investigators and the courts were unwilling or unable to appreciate genuine and well-intended motives behind decisions.

The provision dated back to the pre-reforms era, when the private sector was viewed with distrust. The private sector's role in infrastructure creation and economic development had increased since then. The heightened activism in the CAG, the CVC and the Courts—the 3Cs—had the effect of a heightened fear among bureaucrats of misuse of the provision, ultimately leading to 'policy paralysis', characterized by a reluctance among officials to take decisions. This stalled projects. The government does not penalize inaction or delays in decision-making. Nor does it reward decision-making. Consequently, the entire incentive structure for bureaucrats had tilted towards avoidance of decisions, with adverse consequences for the economy. The amendment would finally be passed in 2018.[14]

During Chidambaram's previous stint as finance minister, India had received a credit-rating upgrade after a gap of nearly seventeen years to investment grade from global rating agency S&P in January 2007.[15] S&P had downgraded India to sub-investment grade in March 1991, when the country had faced a foreign exchange crisis. During this stint in running the ministry, he sweated to stop India's descent to 'junk' status. The country had come perilously close to losing its barely investment-grade rating during Mukherjee's term. Both S&P and Fitch warned they might lower India's score, given its slow growth, stalled reforms and high borrowings. In October 2012, S&P reiterated there was at least a one-in-three chance of a downgrade.[16] If carried out, such a downgrade could create further problems for the current-account deficit (CAD). Losing the 'investment grade' could have made the country even more unattractive to foreign investors.

'When I came back, after doing some firefighting in the home ministry, we had to do some firefighting in the finance ministry,' recalls Chidambaram. 'I knew we had lost the plot when inflation crossed double-digits. I didn't want a collapse. I just wanted to retrieve as much as possible.'[17]

He told the prime minister: 'You have given us exactly eighteen months to pull it [inflation and other macroeconomic indicators] back. We will pull it back as much as we can, but what is it we can do in eighteen months and one Budget?'

Unrelenting Food Inflation

Manmohan Singh had long held that despite substantial investment in agriculture and rural development, a decent quality of life remained outside the reach of large sections of the Indian population, chiefly because of structural distortions introduced by policies.[18]

Speaking in the Lok Sabha on 14 September 1991, he had said:[19]

> How has India become poor? There is a conspiracy of silence when we talk about the root causes of poverty in this country. Now, all these years, in the name of planned development we have provided indiscriminate protection to Indian industry. And when you give protection to somebody, this protection is at the cost of somebody else. The rural sector, the farmers of this country, have been the worse sufferers of this excessive protection that has been given to the Indian industry. Today complex fertilisers are available from abroad at the rate of Rs 6,500 per tonne. Our domestic industry, because of various factors into which I do not wish to go, produces the same thing at Rs 8,500 per tonne. Now why should our farmers be made to buy this high-cost fertiliser? . . . Therefore, we must create an environment where the Indian industry . . . does not flourish at the cost of our farmers, and the development of industry does not become a tax on agriculture.

As prime minister, he ensured that from 2004–05 onwards, but especially from 2007 to 2013, the UPA government pursued a policy of sustained hikes in foodgrain Minimum Support Prices (MSPs).[20] The idea was to bridge the difference between low domestic and high global agricultural prices. The proposition had the backing of sound economic logic. But its implementation was botched up, which made 2009 to 2013 a period of high food price inflation.

The launch of the national food security mission and a global food prices crisis necessitated hikes that were more aggressive than was originally planned. With the MSPs rising year after year, farmers kept increasing production. Foodgrain production surged by 42 million metric tonnes in the four-year period. This was more than double of what had been targeted, all of which the government was forced to procure because the high MSPs had edged out private traders from the market.

The guaranteed large-scale procurements at higher and higher MSPs were raising market prices, benefiting farmers. The result was a severe inflation in food prices in the country. The UPA government's MSP policy was blamed for the sticky double-digit inflation in food prices from 2009 to 2013. The procurement side of the policy cannot be faulted for the food inflation. In truth, the problem lay with the food stock management policy.[21] The procurement policy was not complemented with a stock management policy. The procured stocks of rice and wheat were not offloaded in the open markets to dampen the market prices. There were no transparent rules about how and when to release foodgrain from the stocks. In the absence of a standard operating procedure, decisions were (and continue to be) taken on an ad hoc basis by the Cabinet Committee on Economic Affairs. Whereas what is needed are automatic releases when prices rise.

Kaushik Basu, chief economic adviser then, documented the mindset behind the reluctance to release stocks to cool rising prices. The argument was pushed that selling at a price lower than the purchase price (MSP plus carrying costs) would inflict losses on the exchequer and add to fiscal deficit. But since procurement spending is a sunk cost, not selling implied even higher losses to the government. Basu writes:

> It is often argued in official documents that unless the government sells food at a price above the purchase power (plus other sundry costs like that of storage and transport), this will add to the fiscal deficit. What this does not take into account is that if by trying to sell the food at such a price the government does not manage to sell the food at all and the fiscal burden is even greater. This is because the cost of procurement is a sunk cost. Therefore, from a fiscal accounting point of view, not selling procured grain is equivalent to selling it at zero price.[22]

Starting from 2009, India had nearly five unbroken years of inflation, ranging between 7 per cent and 11 per cent per annum.[23] Average WPI inflation during Pranab Mukherjee's three-year stint was close to 8.7 per cent, significantly higher than the average inflation of 5.4 per cent during the previous decade 2001–10.[24] At one point, the rate of inflation breached 10 per cent in early 2010.[25] From October 2009 to March 2010, the year-on-year food price inflation announced every week hovered at around 20 per cent.[26] Around May–June 2010, international wheat prices were 30 per cent lower than in India, yet consumers were forced to pay more.[27] The UPA had sought to address a structural issue on the producer side but managed to botch up the consumer prices. It also skewed incentives in favour of carbohydrate-rich foodgrain production, and against protein-rich food production, and thus against balanced diets.

Inflation is the most important economic variable that influences the mood of the electorate, with virtually no time lag. In the 2014 general elections, higher inflation and sluggish growth helped Narendra Modi build a campaign on economic management and trounce the Congress, which had long counted the rural poor as its core constituency. Small farmers had been hit by rising living costs but benefited little from rising food prices because of the web of middlemen in India's agricultural markets.

If government's food stocks are never going to be used, they may as well not be there, wrote Basu.[28] Continuously building the stock will, over time, have an effect on the economy. Either some other subsidy will have to be reduced, or it will blow the fiscal deficit out of the sky. Or, some other, more important expenditure will get crowded out. These choices were swept under the carpet and the fiscal deficit kept growing, as did inflation.

Governments seek to influence prices to smoothen them out—both for consumers and farmers.[29] In the absence of state intervention, prices would soar in bad-weather years and plunge in good-weather years. High prices would hurt consumers, and low prices would hurt farmers.

If the government wants to have in place a mechanism where it will intervene to cushion prices for consumers during inflationary periods and procure from farmers during deflationary phases, then fiscal costs cannot be eliminated. They can, however, be economized. There's a misconception that this subsidy is only for the farmers and for the poor through the Public Distribution System (PDS). But the operation benefits open market prices too, and therefore all consumers. The better-off people may not receive direct subsidy, as those with Below-Poverty-Line (BPL) cards do, but they gain from the market price being lowered.

The governance failures sharply slowed down the economy. In 2011–12, even as inflation remained elevated, GDP growth crashed. The only effective response to supply-side-driven general inflation would have been reforms expanding the economy's output, something Mukherjee had failed to demonstrate an inclination for. Instead, he kept pressing for the RBI to tackle high inflation through use of monetary policy instruments.

His cabinet colleague, Agriculture and Food Minister Sharad Pawar failed at stocks management, a consequence of the overall decision-making paralysis the government was suffering from.

'Mr Sharad Pawar is a very fine minister,' recalls Chidambaram.[30] 'No question. Very capable minister. But I think there was a reluctance to or a fear of taking bold decisions. We should have unloaded those huge stocks of foodgrain and made sure it reached every part of India. But they were very fearful, "what will happen if there is a drought . . . what will happen if the monsoon fails. I mean what if . . . what if . . ."

'The real problem was inflation, and we should have squelched inflation. And we did it with monetary tools and whatever fiscal tools were available, but unless those who were managing the supply side pulled their weight, how much can you bring down inflation?'

A cocktail of politics, structural issues and policy failures had brewed a full-blown macroeconomic crisis. For the RBI, the battle against the decade-high inflation segued into a defence of the rupee.

Taper Tantrums

On 27 April 2011, Ben S. Bernanke became the first US Federal Reserve Chairman in the central bank's ninety-eight-year history to hold a scheduled news conference.[31] The bespectacled, bearded former college professor, speaking from the top floor of an annex behind the Federal Reserve's headquarters in Washington DC, explained his management of the economy, in the hope that increasing transparency would improve the central bank's image and clarify its actions.[32] The size of the Fed's investment portfolio, called QE (quantitative easing), had grown by then to more than $2 trillion, in the central bank's efforts to stimulate the US economy, but without great success, which challenged public faith in it.[33] The Fed had decided that morning to conclude QE2, as planned in June.[34] Flanked by an American flag and the Federal Reserve flag, Bernanke gave the first indication that if the US economy faltered, then it could become difficult for the central bank to provide fresh support thereafter because of growing inflationary pressures in the US economy.[35] Investors saw that as a signal for the countdown to a withdrawal of the QE.

It proved an optimistic view. Just four months later, in September 2012, which was four years after the Lehman collapse, the Fed opened a new chapter in its so-far fruitless efforts to help the US recovery, with a third round of QE.[36]

The Fed finally gained confidence in the durability of economic growth in June 2013 and announced an expected gradual retreat later that year from its monthly purchases of US Treasury securities and mortgage-backed bonds.[37] Bernanke announced intentions to scale down and finally end the QE once the US unemployment rate reached 7 per cent.[38] The Fed expected this rate to be hit by the middle of 2014.[39] Unwinding the rest of its extraordinary stimulus campaign would then take several more years, as the Fed expected to raise short-term interest rates slowly from essentially zero to more normal levels.

The prospective taper of the asset purchase programme reverberated across the world through the summer of 2013. Capital flew out of emerging markets such as India back to the US on expectations of the economy there staging a recovery. The panic selling by dollar investors plunged emerging market currencies to new lows, and this dramatic reversal came to be called the 'taper tantrum'. The turmoil across emerging markets continued all through May and June.

As the tide turned, the dollar stampede out of India sent the rupee plummeting sharply, from 55.52 to a dollar on 22 May, the day after Bernanke's statement, to 67.03 on 4 September 2013, the day Governor Subbarao stepped down from office and Raghuram G. Rajan was appointed governor of RBI. This amounted to a depreciation of 17 per cent in just a little over three months.[40] In the hope of arresting the slide, a number of measures had been put in place by the government and the RBI, such as a reduction in the maximum amounts individuals and corporates could take out of the country and restraints on gold imports. But the exchange rate had kept on weakening.

On 28 August 2013, Chidambaram told the Rajya Sabha that besides the 'taper tantrum', domestic problems—that had originated, at least in part, during the tenure of his predecessor—were also contributing to the economy's travails.[41]

'There are not just external factors, there are also domestic factors. One of the domestic factors is that we allowed fiscal deficit to be breached and we allowed current account deficit to swell because of certain decisions that we took during the period 2009 to 2011.'

He was speaking on a day the rupee had posted its steepest fall in eighteen years, ending at 66.24 to the dollar.[42]

'It [fiscal stimulus] brought us growth, it stabilized the economy. We swayed off the very serious consequences of the 2008 collapse of the US economy. But it cost us in terms of fiscal deficit and current account deficit,' said Chidambaram.

Days before he briefed the Rajya Sabha, he had told the press, 'We did allow the FRBM [Fiscal Responsibility and Budget Management Act] targets to be breached. We allowed WPI [Wholesale Price Index] and retail inflation to cross 10 per cent. And now much of it is trying to retrieve ground.'[43]

The rise of the fiscal deficit to 5.8 per cent of GDP in 2011–12 against the budgeted 4.6 per cent, chiefly because Mukherjee had failed to rein in spending and subsidies, had resulted in the rating agencies putting India's sovereign rating on watch.[44] Now Chidambaram wielded the axe on spending, ensuring a lower deficit of 4.9 per cent of GDP in 2012–13.[45] Very high still, it nevertheless satisfied the rating agencies, and a downgrade was averted, but a price was paid in terms of growth, which fell to a decade-low of 5.5 per cent[46] during the year.

Alongside a widening fiscal deficit, the economy had also run a huge CAD for two years in a row. Which meant the economy's total import bill had far exceeded the total export earnings, increasing the dependence on external financing for filling the gap. The CAD was 4.2 per cent of GDP in 2011–12, 4.8 per cent in 2012–13; and most forecasts put it at over 4 per cent for 2013–14 (when the final figure came out at the end of the year, the forecasters were proven wrong. The CAD had been contained at 1.7 per cent of GDP).[47] This was well above the RBI's sustainable limit of 3 per cent of GDP.[48]

As global liquidity conditions tightened as a consequence of the 'taper tantrums', portfolio debt outflows intensified, bringing the currency, equity and bond markets under significant pressure. The CAD rose because of the flight of dollars. Investor concerns were amplified by the persistently high inflation, weakening growth prospects, large current account and fiscal deficits, and increased domestic political uncertainty.

The increased imports bill was also expanding the CAD. With inflation running high, people were shifting their savings to gold. Imports of gold surged, more than doubling, from 1.3 per cent of

GDP in 2007–08 to 3 per cent in 2012–13.[49] The spike in the global price of gold did not deter buyers of the precious metal. Savers turned to it as protection against the persistently high inflation that was eroding the purchasing power of money.

Judicial orders unwittingly became a source of heightened stress on the CAD.[50] The Supreme Court's cancellation of coal block allocations made by the government to private parties resulted in a sharp decline in domestic production and forced power producers to meet the shortage through imports. The Supreme Court also banned iron ore mining, on environmental grounds, which affected ore exports. Global crude prices had spiked too, which was adding to the imports bill, and thereby to the CAD. The fast-depreciating rupee was inflating the cost of crude imports.

The CAD has expanded so much because, while there had been focus on individual items of the CAD, such as gold, the fiscal tools available to the government had been used inadequately. Macroeconomic stability calls for balance of external and internal elements. India would have had a smoother adjustment to the taper with a reduction and eventual elimination of the revenue deficit. Government dis-saving could not be stopped. Had it been done, it would have helped investments and brought down the CAD.

A strategy controlling government expenditure was needed, but with the Opposition breathing down the government's neck over fuel prices a political decision was taken to limit the pass-through of the increasing burden of global crude prices. This had further strained the fisc, in addition to Mukherjee's loose fiscal stance.

Balance of payments came under stress in the summer of 2013 as external shocks interacted with domestic macroeconomic vulnerabilities. In these circumstances, going forward, restoration of fiscal and current-account balances to the trends prevalent before 2008–09 was now crucial.

The building macroeconomic crisis seemed a redux of the balance of payments crisis of 1991, which had also been an outcome of the fiscal profligacy of the 1980s, financed by borrowings that were way beyond the country's means. The potent mix of the twin deficits destabilized the macroeconomy in 2012, but could not bankrupt the country as it had in 1991. The shock of the 1990 Gulf war had pushed the deteriorating balance of payments into a full-blown crisis, leaving the country's reserves with just enough foreign exchange to cover the import bill for barely three weeks, and the country itself on the verge of a default on its external loan repayment obligations. The trigger for a crash came this time from the US Fed. Pressures on the rupee mounted as foreign investors pulled out to cut losses, setting the exchange rate into a free fall. The floor seemed to cave in after May 2013. The rupee, in a free fall, seemed headed to 70 to the dollar, a historic low.

India, One of the Fragile Five

Soon after taking over as the twenty-third governor of the RBI on 4 September 2013, Raghuram Rajan went live on national television. India had been named one of the 'Fragile Five' emerging market economies. The epithet referred to the emerging market economies of India, Brazil, South Africa, Indonesia and Turkey that were hit the most by the 'taper tantrum'. Rajan was keen to send out the message to foreign investors that India had institutions like the RBI that could push reforms forward even when Parliament was stalled.

'These are not easy times, and the economy faces challenges . . . Our task today is to build a bridge to the future over the stormy waves produced by global financial markets. I have every confidence we will succeed in doing that . . . At a time when financial markets are volatile, and there is some domestic political uncertainty because of impending elections, the Reserve Bank of India should be a beacon of stability as to its objectives.'[51]

Rajan ended his speech quoting Kipling's 'If'.

'If you can trust yourself when all men doubt you,

But make allowance for their doubting too.'

Lionized internationally as the oracle of the financial meltdown of 2007, he became the comfort factor for foreign investors in India and for the domestic markets. He wrote later that he had strategized to send out four messages through that speech: a facade of confidence to the public and investors that the RBI knew what had to be done; a commitment to reducing inflation, an ability to be bold, that standards were being set for transparency and predictability.[52]

Rajan had spent a year familiarizing himself with government, as the chief economic adviser. During this period he wrote two reports. The first was on evolving a composite development index for states, in a move that was attributed to the UPA government's attempt to woo Bihar Chief Minister Nitish Kumar.[53] The Bihar government had been asking that it be classified as a backward state so that more central funds could be allocated to it. The committee proposed a backwardness criterion, along with a general methodology for determining devolution of funds from the centre to the states, based on both a state's development needs and its development performance. The performance index captured the progress that states had made over time in terms of the Composite Development Index. BJP prime-ministerial candidate Narendra Modi's showpiece Gujarat figured among the 'less developed' states in the country.[54] Some proponents of the Gujarat model had been arguing that more than the level of Gujarat's development indicators, how these indicators were changing over time was of significance.[55] The performance index focused on performance in the decade of the 2000s, Gujarat's putative best, but the state was found to slip from ninth to twelfth position in the ranking of twenty major states.

Rajan's second report was on financial-sector reforms, and also examined the case for an inflation-targeting monetary policy.[56] Rajan held that to be effective, such a redefining of the RBI's mandate would have to be preconditioned on the government's commitment to, first, maintaining fiscal discipline, and, second, not holding the central bank accountable for the level or volatility in the nominal exchange rate—a policy position influenced by Montek Singh Ahluwalia and presumably Manmohan Singh himself, on the unrelenting inflation problem.

The reports would leave a heavy mark on Rajan's career in the RBI. His detractors in the BJP and its affiliates would leverage them, in addition to his policies in other matters, to sour relations between him and Prime Minister Narendra Modi, negating his chances for a second term as governor in 2016.

Even so, in 2013 he played a key role in restoring macroeconomic stability. His opening statement had the desired effect. Slowly, the market and investors regained confidence in the RBI's ability to ride the rupee and the macroeconomy out of the storm. The stress was not allowed to become a crisis, but for the first time since 1998 recourse had to be taken to special financing arrangements for balance of payments support.[57]

Special financing refers to public policy initiatives for instituting extraordinary mechanisms to make up for shortfall in normal capital flows. NRI bonds, called Resurgent India Bonds, were raised through State Bank of India (SBI) in 1998 for managing the impact of the US sanctions against India on the balance of payments. These bonds did not come with exchange rate guarantees from the RBI. A unique mechanism devised by the RBI allowed SBI to take upon itself a bearable modest extent of gains as well as losses. Anything beyond on either side was to be absorbed by the government. Since the rupee never depreciated after that float, no foreign exchange impact had accrued at all.

To tide over the 1991 crisis, similar bonds had been issued by SBI to NRIs, the foreign exchange risk on which was borne entirely by the RBI. But soon after, the idea of a central bank bearing the foreign exchange risk had been discarded as part of the reforms undertaken. In 2001, a follow-up issue to the Resurgent India Bonds, called India Millennium Bonds, was raised, but to add to forex reserves rather than as a response to a crisis or any special circumstances.

In 2013, the special financing arrangements were for mobilizing foreign exchange, in a bid to ease the pressure on the rupee, through three-year NRI deposits, called foreign currency non-resident (FCNR) deposits.[58] The proposal had been received from bankers who were confident of raising dollars, converting them into rupees and investing in India. In return, they wanted a cheap rate at which they could convert rupees back to dollars three years later, at the time of maturity of the deposits.

If the RBI could assure the forward dollars, this was a great deal for the bankers. They would get rupee interest income and a guaranteed cheap price at which they could swap the maturing rupees back to dollars. The cost of such a subsidy to the issuing banks would of course have to be borne by the RBI and the economy as a whole. But, on the other hand, if the rupee were to continue depreciating as fast as it had been and did not move to a more fundamental value, the import costs to the economy would approximately inflate by Rs 40,000 crore for every Re 1 rise in the rupee-dollar exchange rate. If the rupee remained undervalued for three years, lakhs of rupees could be lost to such a blow-up in import costs. But if the scheme the bankers were proposing succeeded even mildly, the payout by way of the subsidy would be a lot less. There could have been cheaper ways of restoring confidence in the rupee, but time was of the essence. On balance, the scheme seemed a viable solution. And if the rupee appreciated after the inflow of dollars raised through the deposits, the forward subsidy required to be provided to bankers would be even less. On the flip side, if the rupee continued to depreciate unabated even after dollars had flowed in through the scheme, the costs would mount.

Governor Rajan decide to go ahead with the FCNR deposits proposal. Since the rupee's troubles were because of the US Fed's 'taper tantrum', the RBI agreed to guarantee the exchange rate on these deposits. For the first time since 1991, the RBI was taking on exchange rate risk. The FCNR scheme brought in $26 billion more than anticipated. More importantly, the mood changed. Confidence picked up. The rupee strengthened. Averting a crisis of confidence is usually half the battle won. The political projections of a likely pro-business government getting elected in 2014 played a role in changing the discourse. The forward swaps could be covered cheaply. The rupee became one of the most stable emerging market currencies for a while.

The corrective measures the government and the RBI had instituted were: liquidity conditions were tightened, limits on FDI and external borrowing were eased, capital flow measures were introduced, and gold import duties were increased sharply, which succeeded in curtailing imports.

In the pre-Lehman Brothers era, FDI flows had more-than-financed the CAD. FDI covered only about a quarter of the deficit in 2012–13, even as there was a corresponding increase in reliance on debt flows. And so, in its final eighteen months, the UPA government undertook multiple steps to bolster capital inflows, including liberalizing some of the caps on FDI inflows. The RBI moved towards improved communication of its views, further reducing the risk of volatility.

Inflows respond with a lag typically, but these policy initiatives reduced vulnerabilities by changing the outlook. The measures taken—to narrow external and fiscal imbalances, raise policy interest rates, accelerate project approvals, manage market volatility and strengthen capital flows—were positive corrective signals of a pullback.

After years of fiscal profligacy, measures were announced for shrinking energy subsidies, allow the exchange rate to adjust, bolster capital inflows, and alleviate supply-side constraints.[59] There was some movement forward on reforms: Parliament passed the pension and companies bills, and the Cabinet Committee on Investment, set up as a response to the 'policy paralysis', approved previously stalled projects worth around 5 per cent of GDP.[60] It succeeded in unlocking infrastructure projects worth more than $95 billion, which translated into a pickup in activity in the final months of 2013–14.[61] On the fiscal front, corrective steps included higher pass-through of higher global crude prices to retail diesel prices, a paring down of the financial losses of state electricity boards through tariff hikes, and sharp central government spending cuts. Expectations of a favourable monsoon helped. Exports improved, remittance inflows remained solid, and higher import duties and quantitative restrictions discouraged gold imports.

As external pressures eased, the government was able to unwind the earlier steps taken to tighten liquidity and partly reverse restrictions on capital outflows. In addition, non-oil, non-gold imports declined in line with weak domestic demand, and capital inflows resumed.

Out of the Fragile Five

In February 2014, the IMF team that conducted the annual Article IV consultations observed that India had demonstrated its ability to respond to shocks and market concerns, although the more chronic problems, such as persistent inflation, lingered.[62] A clear agenda for preserving this hard-earned macroeconomic stability and consequent nascent economic recovery emerged from the Article IV consultations. (Article IV of the IMF's Articles of Agreement provides for bilateral discussions between the fund and each of its members every year. Most international investors and global rating agencies place high value on these Article IV consultation reports in making investment or rating decisions.)

State Electricity Boards (SEBs) had raised tariffs, but much more needed to be done for eliminating their losses. The pricing and allocation of a wide range of natural resources (including coal, natural gas, electricity and fertilizers) were still subject to complex and cumbersome mechanisms and regulations. The pricing and allocation of natural resources needed to be moved towards a market-determined basis for making them more transparent and for raising investment. Power linkages were a significant bottleneck. The strict labour regulations needed to be relaxed for raising productivity, increasing formal-sector employment and improving potential growth. For easing the skill mismatch in industry, educational and vocational training was required. The agriculture sector needed to be reformed. In particular, the administrative inefficiencies in food distribution, pricing and storage needed to be reduced. Farm-sector productivity needed to be improved.

Finally, for building human capital, health and education outcomes needed to be enhanced, which could only be done by sustainably increasing spending, improving the quality of health and educational services, raising the efficiency of social programmes and focusing on inclusiveness. More effective health and education spending was key to ensuring that the so-called 'demographic dividend' would pay off for India.

In other words, a rebound in growth was conditional on the resumption of structural reforms—something Arvind Virmani had flagged back in 2009. There was very little space for a counter-cyclical policy stimulus to kick-start the economy. Rather, a tightening of fiscal and monetary policies was needed to narrow macroeconomic imbalances, supported by actions to relieve supply-side bottlenecks. The only feasible option to boost both actual and potential growth was to create jobs to absorb the rapidly growing labour force and reduce poverty. That needed structural reforms. Nothing else would work.

Singh's government had barely weeks left in office. But even the new government that would join office in May 2014 would ignore this counsel and strive for designing a fiscal stimulus. Just as the UPA, it too would fail to pursue structural reforms.

What Chidambaram did in eighteen months was to ensure that the deficit numbers began to look more respectable, although the quality of the deficit numbers he reported was hardly enviable. The current and fiscal account deficits for 2013–14 came down sharply.

Among emerging markets and BRICS countries, India stood out for accomplishing the sharpest turnaround in its macroeconomy since the US Federal Reserve started reversing its zero-interest-rates monetary policy. India was no longer among the 'Fragile Five'. In October 2014, the IMF India Mission chief declared the country best prepared among emerging economies to deal with the Fed's anticipated winding down of its QE. 'India is the odd man out from the emerging markets and BRICS economies that were being called the Fragile Five last year . . . But the story for India changed quickly . . . India is better prepared for shocks today than when the US Fed's tapering started and more prepared than other emerging markets,' IMF India Mission Chief Paul A. Cashin told me at the time.[63]

'Three percentage points down [of the CAD] is a lot . . . in the IMF's history there are very few cases of that . . . Retail food inflation in India has been growing at a 10 per cent plus rate . . . Few countries have had such problems for such long periods of time.'

When, post-elections, Chidambaram's successor, Union Finance Minister Arun Jaitley, tabled the Economic Survey 2013–14 in Parliament, this first assessment of the health of the economy by the new government opened with a reassurance that in 2014–15 the economy was poised to stage a gradual recovery.[64]

The survey said that the macroeconomy had stabilized, that there had been a dramatic improvement in the external situation and that the fiscal deficit had declined for the second year in a row. The surging financial markets were reflecting this, besides the expectations of a change for the better under the new regime.

Chidambaram now says, 'Fiscal deficit was sharply reduced. The Current Account Deficit in fact had been contained substantially by squeezing. Some very harsh decisions were taken, which of course affected growth and it did not give us the kind of advantage that we should have got if inflation had been lower. Ultimately, we lost [the 2014 Lok Sabha elections] partly on, apart from the corruption charges, we lost on inflation'.[65]

By April 2014, Singh, Chidambaram and Rajan would ready for rolling out an underrated and unglamorous—but potentially effective—institutional reform for inflation management. Directed at placing a check on the Pranab Mukherjee-style fiscal populism that hobbles monetary policy, it would be implemented by the next government. The reform, although not the ideal solution for the kind of inflation that strikes India episodically, was a second-best compromise, necessitated by the stubborn reluctance of Indian politicians and bureaucrats to treat moderate inflation and fiscal rectitude as sacrosanct for macroeconomic stability, even twenty-five years after liberalization. The reform would be based on the report Rajan had written on inflation-targeting monetary policy and submitted to the Planning Commission.

Populism Strikes

Prime Minister Manmohan Singh's efforts at course correction and perception management did not go far, though. Wherever his ministers who were in sync with his economic persuasion were the boss, decisions moved on unimpeded. This happened in the narrowing of the current account and fiscal deficits, which was overseen by Chidambaram, in exports promotion and in foreign investments liberalization, both of which fell under Commerce and Industry Minister Anand Sharma. But wherever the governance agenda required the concurrence of varying interests in the Congress party and the cabinet, Singh and his like-minded colleagues could not push through reforms. Even after Mukherjee's departure from government, economic policies did not shed their slant to the left. Nor was support for populist legislations hamstrung by his absence. The UPA government restored order inside Parliament and made sure the National Food Security Act (FSA), 2013 and the Right to Fair Compensation and Transparency in Land Acquisition, Rehabilitation and Resettlement Act, 2013 (also called Land Acquisition Act, 2013) were passed.

The legislations, though, had been finalized by glossing over the assessments made by the economy heavyweights in the cabinet.

'Ahluwalia, including me, expressed reservations about our ability to fund the Food Security Act when it is fully rolled out,' says Chidambaram.[66] 'In 2013, we certainly were not flush with funds to fully roll out the FSA . . . Our reservation was about our ability to fund the full roll out of the FSA in the year 2013–14. Look at what's happening today . . . First three–three and a half years of this government, they were flush with funds. Yet they have not rolled out the FSA.'

The FSA, on full implementation, was expected to benefit 720 million people through availability of 5 kg per capita per month of subsidized foodgrains (rice, wheat and coarse cereals) at a much lower rate than that in the open market. The supporters of the legislation believed it would make food available to all and enhance nutritional status. Nutrition security, as well-meaning critics point out, is a much wider concept than food security. It includes adequate and safe intake of protein, energy, vitamins and minerals.

On the Land Acquisition Act (LA Act), the differences in Singh's cabinet and the Congress party were even sharper.

'The Land Acquisition Amendment was pushed by the rural development ministry [headed by Cabinet Minister Jairam Ramesh] and, I think . . . the NAC [National Advisory Council headed by Sonia Gandhi],' says Chidambaram. 'I think it was the right decision to get rid of the old LA Act. Because the old LA Act was a colonial, anti-farmer law that gave a pittance to the farmer while conferring a bounty upon the industrialist for whom the land was acquired. The procedure was totally undemocratic. What made the Act appear to be an obstruction to industrial development was not the compensation part. But the procedural part which became too difficult for any district collector or any land acquisition officer to negotiate. How do you get the consent of 75 per cent or 80 per cent of the landowners? No district collector, no land acquisition officer had the capacity or the wherewithal to negotiate those provisions which were written into the law, although on paper they appeared very democratic and very liberal.'

I asked if he agreed with the amendment.

'No, no, I had expressed my reservations. I'd said, nobody can acquire land in this . . .'

If there were reservations, how could the legislation go through?

'But it's not a dissenting vote. It was consensus finally. A lot of ministers went along with the LA Act. The National Advisory Council was behind it. I still believe the intent of the Act was good, but the provisions were such that no one could have negotiated that Act to acquire land required for industrialization. Unless states have land banks. Some states do and many states do not have land banks.'

The laws passed cast legal obligations on states. Even years later, states are writing memoranda to the centre complaining about the laws.

Although, years later, the Modi government would be criticized widely for its poorly designed, inadequately thought-out and populist policies, the Singh government's food security and land acquisition legislations too suffered from a similar disconnect between policy objectives and policy tools. The difference between Singh's and Modi's governments was that of the powers enjoyed by the ministers. Singh's cabinet colleagues could obstruct reforms and force populist decisions. The reformers were outnumbered and overruled. Modi's cabinet colleagues would be mute spectators, a mere rubber stamp on decisions taken in the PMO.

In Singh's cabinet, conflicting views jostled to block structural reforms and push incrementalism and populism. Modi's government would suffer from confusion and obfuscation. The result will be the same: incrementalism and populism.

In the cabinet meeting called by Singh's government to approve the important reform of urea pricing decontrols, the minister in charge himself blocked the decision, on the laughable pretext that he could not read the note prepared by the ministry for the cabinet's consideration because of language problems.

On another occasion, even as the cabinet was deliberating on a low-key scheme, certainly less earth-shattering than, say, urea pricing, a secretary-level bureaucrat passed chits to Pawar, approached him and whispered something into the minister's ear, and the whole proposal was cancelled.[67]

In yet another, similar instance, the sports ministry had proposed a law for instituting a code of conduct for the various sports federations in the country. The note for the cabinet's consideration was circulated. None of the concerned departments sent in any objections, but in the meeting of the cabinet no less than eight ministers—including Agriculture Minister Sharad Pawar, Aviation Minister Praful Patel and MSME Minister Virbhadra Singh—spoke against the draft.[68]

Many of those who vetoed it held portfolios that had nothing to do with sports. 'Each one of them spoke against it. It got torpedoed. You were left completely nonplussed. They won't say anything at a previous stage . . . at the meeting, they would start off,' says a bureaucrat, now retired, who was involved in the drafting of the law.[69]

'This was in sharp contrast to what used to happen even under the most indecisive prime minister, P.V. Narasimha Rao, who, people have told me, would hear everybody out and then just say, "ok, this is the decision".'

Besides dissonant voices in the cabinet, there was actual evidence of corruption against at least one minister, who was dropped belatedly. 'But why did they not stop her in her tracks?' says the retired IAS officer, who held important positions in government at the time. 'That phase of 2011–14. I don't ever want to see again . . . Most frustrating and disappointing. This is the time when economy was doing well.'[70]

UPA Minister Salman Khurshid explained in an interview to *The Hindu* the reason for the lack of direction in government. In his assessment, it was the duality of authority between Sonia Gandhi and Manmohan Singh.[71]

> Our set up (Congress) was divided between a Prime Minister and a President. In the past, the years that I have been in public life, the Prime Minister and the Congress president were the same people. Now that [one individual holding dual responsibilities of being both party president and prime minister] in this country is a huge pressure. Even Mr. Modi can't do it despite having incredible energy. He has got Amit Shah [as party president] whom he can trust. But in our [Congress's] structure, it is required that one person be party president and Prime Minister. You can imagine what pressure it may have been on a single person to carry that burden. So when Mrs Gandhi decided not to accept the Prime Ministership and chose Dr Manmohan Singh . . . he was focussed on governance without bothering about things like a local body election and the [coordination with other] political parties [that were part of the coalition] was done by Mrs Sonia Gandhi. There couldn't have been a better model for the efficient governance of the country. But we as a party were accustomed to one single window. So when you went, you went to the Prime Minister and the Party president who's the same person. Having two separate things meant we had to visit two people.
>
> But my experience is that whenever I went to Mrs Gandhi, she would tell me why are you telling all this to me, tell the Prime Minister! She was very particular that the PM take the call . . . there was no platform, no place where all this was discussed. All we could do was to go privately and talk to them. Now that was exacerbated by the fact that there were people from another party. We didn't have much equation with Mr Raja [Telecom Minister] . . . I got involved when I became Law Minister to get bail or to get a good lawyer. That's the first time I got involved [in resolving the political crisis that followed the release of the

CAG's 2G report]. Otherwise, it wasn't the kind of camaraderie where we would immediately go and say we will handhold you. Don't worry, this is a collective problem. Nobody treated it as a collective problem but the problem of the telecom minister.

That the cabinet was not functioning like a well-oiled machine was evident even in the case of Congress ministers, not just the coalition partners. Said Khurshid:

Look at what happened to Kapil (Sibal). He made that statement about zero loss [in the sale of 2G spectrum]. It was not an off-the-cuff remark. He sat and explained to me a week before he said it . . . the Planning Commission and the entire government had consciously said we are not looking for money [in the sale of 2G spectrum]. Our concern is not revenue but tele-density, network, mobile penetration etc. On that basis he was saying zero loss. So I knew why he was saying zero loss but, perhaps, nobody else in the government knew why he was saying it. And everybody said I am not going to get involved. We were just being pushed to the wall.

Chidambaram agrees and ascribes the controversy that erupted over the 2G sale and the CAG report over it to 'administrative mishandling. There was nothing wrong in the first-come first-serve policy. Successive telecom ministers had followed that policy. Maybe the manner in which it was implemented, there were some errors or mistakes. But I don't think there was anything wrong fundamentally with the first-come first-serve policy. If government only asks for a huge bid amount, at a premium, it's a rent you are collecting at a time when the man starts the business, you are inflating the costs. That has consequences for the industry.'[72]

Since it was a political crisis more than an economic policy, in his view, the responsibility of finding solutions lay principally with Gandhi and the prime minister.

Singh's personality certainly seems to have been a key factor in the internal collapse—it recurs in conversations even with his staunchest fans.[73]

'He abdicated responsibility. His attitude always was, "do not let anything bad happen in my time", "solve problems on your own",' says a former bureaucrat who worked closely with Singh both when he was finance minister in the 1990s, and later when he became the prime minister.[74]

'He was uninvolved and not passionate, but well-intentioned and good-natured . . . He was concerned about the crisis but did not want to get actively involved in the nitty-gritty of actions to resolve the crisis,' he says.

Khurshid described the crisis,

> The courts were giving us orders, saying that by next date of hearing this should happen, that should happen . . . They [the Court] were actually monitoring the investigation and asking the CBI to report, they were selecting prosecutors. . . . can you imagine the Attorney General of the country being cross-examined in Patiala House? As Law Minister I used to go and sit with him just to make him comfortable. And I have mentioned here that I told Justice Singhvi [Supreme Court judge then] that he is the law officer. And poor Justice Singhvi said, what can I do? If I walk across to his house, there would be a scandal here! But the comments that were being made in court every day and they were being reported in papers, and they were hurting us more than the judgement finally did.

The Congress, Khurshid disclosed, never had a strategy to deal with the political challenge mounted by the India Against Corruption movement:

> Mr Kejriwal and his group destroyed us completely . . . We had no way of knowing how to handle him. The best of us, Pranab

Mukherjee, who can't be outwitted by anybody was outwitted by him because he [Kejriwal] would speak to Mr Mukherjee in a very submissive voice and go out and say something completely different.

The Opposition's onslaught complemented the public shaming. Says Chidambaram:

These guys [BJP] . . . talk about policy paralysis. They would not let Parliament work. We used to go there. Shouting would begin and we would come back. Anything we wanted to do would be completely stalled. So, we were just going through the motions. We were not really able to do anything.

The mishandled political crisis had grave economic consequences. Says Chidambaram, 'The CAG report was a clear attempt to sensationalize. Look at the consequences of the 2G and the coal report. The economic consequences. Forget the legal, political ones. The economic consequences of the 2G report and the judgement. The coal report and the judgement. We are bearing the brunt of the economic consequences. There is no international telecom company barring Vodafone which is in India today. Everyone packed their bags and left or did not enter at all.'[75]

And yet there is little accountability for the 2G scam report's author, then CAG Vinod Rai. This points to the crying need for administrative and institutional reforms that both Singh's and Modi's governments neglected.

'Unfortunately, it is the PAC which has oversight over the CAG. But here, because of the peculiar situation where the PAC Chair is occupied by an Opposition leader, far from providing oversight, he was providing encouragement from what you tell me . . . [responding to author's question about M.M. Joshi calling the CAG officials about the 2G report; see sub-section on Vinod Rai] These things have to be re-thought. The arrangements that were apparently good arrangements in the 1950s and 1960s have to be re-thought today,' says Chidambaram, on the sheer absence of institutional accountability.

Said Khurshid:

> Even as the government was creaking under a whole multitude of pressures, a new challenge came up. 'While we are doing all this, Nirbhaya happens. In that situation we couldn't even go across to Hyderabad House for President Putin's dinner. We had to squeeze ourselves into the Prime Minister's residence, because we couldn't cross the road. There were crowds of these beautiful kids who were just angry and were facing all kinds of adversity there—weather, water—and none of us had the courage to step across and talk to them. I think it was [Former MP] Sandeep Dikshit who tried to talk to them but his car was overturned. None of us had the courage to go talk to them. Can you imagine what a pathetic situation it was? We were ministers who didn't matter anymore.

The UPA then, Khurshid said, went to the 2014 polls 'accepting defeat . . . [even as] Dr Manmohan Singh's government gave the impression of being a lame-duck government since 2012'.

The Modi Wave

When the economy fails, anxieties find political expression. Just as material progress relieves political anxieties, economic anxieties convert quickly into political upheavals. The poor handling of the economy from 2009 to 2012 did exactly that in India. That is also when radical politicians who challenge the prevailing order trounce moderate leaders. This was exactly how Modi pitched himself to voters. His campaign for the 2014 elections was premised on projecting him as an anti-establishment challenger subverting the prevailing order for a better future, 'achhe din'. Indians voted for an economy in which more and more people would get quality jobs, health and education. Corruption would be less, banks safer, quality of life better and economic justice more equitable. In the promised land, the rich and the powerful would be held to account.

The political battleground was made fertile by the political economy of rising inflation and corruption. An impression was created among non-rural Indians that their economic prospects had dimmed for two reasons: the UPA was frittering away resources, sending them to the poor through anti-poverty programmes from which they were all leaking away, or being given to the rich and powerful through corruption. The people were now left with the bills for the appeasement in the shape of inflation, taxes and lost opportunities. The narrative of corruption may not have succeeded had the economy been growing as fast then as it was in 2009.

Rural Indians bought into the aspirational tonality of Modi's campaign: the promise of an improved, all-new future. Tools of new technology were used to create confusion, controversy and crises among voters craving, ironically, for a cleaner, more decent, more transparent political process. A big success of Modi's campaign, and his '*Vikas Purush*' avatar, was that he was able to convert the tremendous pessimism in the country into a near-irrational exuberance. From Uttar Pradesh to Rajasthan, voters were thrilled that they were voting to make the whole country a la Gujarat, which they had been persuaded to believe was a model state in governance, development and social justice. They remained woefully unaware of the growing literature questioning the state's record on social indicators.

The UPA government, despite having the knowledge, analysis and skill sets in place for addressing the prevalent problems, failed to act. The slow erosion of institutions, especially the cabinet and the PMO would, in a continuum of a slide, give way over time to a complete breakdown in the next government's tenure. At the economic policy level, the dialogue of the deaf and the tower of Babel would be replaced by a complete absence of discussion. If earlier dissenters were not heard, in the coming years scandalously wrong-headed decisions would be taken against zero protest. If power was too diffused under Singh, it would be centralized and centrifugal under the new prime minister. But before that there would be a brief phase of extraordinary hope—both in government and among the people—for far-reaching change.

Modi Arrives in Delhi

On 4 June 2014, a week after he was sworn in as the fifteenth prime minister of India, Modi met close to ninety secretaries led by Cabinet Secretary Ajit Seth. Panchavati, the five-bungalow complex in Lutyens' Delhi that serves as the official prime-ministerial residence, throbbed with a sense of hope as Modi went around familiarizing himself with the officials, most of whom he was meeting for the first time. He invited comments from the assembled bureaucracy.

IAS officers love to talk. This was their chance to be noticed. Among the significant comments made was then secretary, Petroleum and Natural Gas, Saurabh Chandra's exegesis on a legal provision. 'Please amend the Prevention of Corruption Act, 1988 Section 13 (1)(d)(3) if you want us to function,' he said.[76] This pre-liberalization clause was, as explained earlier in the book, at the root of the 'policy paralysis'. The Manmohan Singh government had moved amendments to it that were finally cleared by Parliament in 2018.

The interaction was interspersed with the prime minister's interjections.

In an obvious reference to the 'policy paralysis', he said, '*Peeda hee prerna ban sakti ha . . . kaam na karne ki thakkan nahee, kaam karne ka utsah* [At the end of the day, be tired because you worked hard, not because work was paralysed].'[77]

The bureaucracy, eager to charm Modi, was bewitched. It felt reassured and encouraged. 'It was one of those rah-rah moments . . .

a lot would get done,' recalls a participant, one of the IAS officers who attended the meeting.[78] 'My colleagues believed every word of it.'

By 8.10 p.m., after listening to everyone, Modi spoke again. He summed up the proceedings and reassured everyone present categorically, 'I don't believe in transferring officers; transferring an officer who is no good or inefficient to another department amounts to transferring inefficiency essentially.'[79] He invited the officers to have faith in government, meet often and work as teams to reduce administrative fragmentation and strive for departmental convergence. '*Sarkar mein bikhrav hai, jodna hai*' (the administration is fragmented, we have to rectify this).[80]

Another point he sought to impress upon his audience was, 'My government is not media-driven.'[81]

He asked the IAS officers to study the BJP's election manifesto issued weeks earlier, as well as the one released ahead of the 2009 Lok Sabha polls. He wanted to be apprised of the status in 2014 of the goals set for their respective departments in the BJP's 2009 manifesto.

'It was unprecedented for a prime minister to bring up a political party manifesto at an official meeting with the bureaucracy,' recalls the retired secretary.[82]

The lines between the political and the administrative fields would blur often under Modi. More than a year later, in February 2016, a presentation would be made to a group of secretaries set up by the prime minister. This proposal had been submitted in the run-up to the 2014 elections to the BJP's former president, Nitin Gadkari, as an input for the party's vision document on matters such as taxation.[83] The idea, which originated from a right-wing Pune-based research outfit, Arthakranti, advocated the abolishment of income tax along with over thirty other state and central tax levies. In place of these taxes, Arthakranti recommended the imposition of a single 2 per cent levy on receipts deposited in bank accounts. The presentation to the secretaries envisaged a system that would not impose any taxes on the consumption of goods and services or on income. Instead, it proposed to tax the 'velocity of money'. Quirky proposals are routinely received at the central government. But rarely do zany ideas receive a hearing on an official platform. Needless to say that the group of secretaries made to sit through the presentation did not pursue the idea.

The minutes of the 4 June 2014 meeting with secretaries circulated by the cabinet secretary sought presentations on follow-ups to the prime minister's directions. These presentations went on through the next couple of months. The bureaucracy was impressed with how much patience the prime minister had to sit through hundreds of slides (the cabinet secretary had told them to restrict themselves to twenty slides per presentation, but many secretaries used smaller font size to pack information from ten slides into one). Modi listened carefully and asked searching questions that were punctuated by observant comments. Occasionally, when his interest flagged, he would appear to switch off. If something or someone ever annoyed him, it never showed.

So much face time with the prime minister was a new thing for the bureaucrats. A man of few words, Singh had held far fewer in-person interactions. One-on-ones with the civil service were rare during his tenure. The two prime ministers seemed a study in contrasts.

Singh was evidently brainy, intelligent, scholarly, with a great understanding of economics, and always fully aware of all that was going on. At G20 meetings, as has been described earlier, world leaders turned to him for advice, calling him the 'wise economist'.

Modi, on the other hand, had a flair for on-ground solutions. The new prime minister's mantra was, 'Policy translated on ground'. 'I don't want any more reports or more theorizing . . . Please show me results . . . What works on ground,' was the message from him to the bureaucracy, recalls the retired secretary.[84] 'He had no patience with intellectual inputs, or with a strategic, forward-looking approach. But down on the ground, he seemed very practical. I was impressed and hopeful.'

Bureaucrats, regardless of the individual holding the office, are always in a contest to impress a prime minister. The difference with Modi was that bureaucrats got into trying to second-guess him, since it was quite clear that he was a prime minister with strong and obvious likes and dislikes. They would try to present to him what they thought he wanted to hear. When you get to only hear what you want to hear, or what people think you want to hear, the truth starts getting filtered out. This is a problem leaders often encounter.

Second-guessing Modi soon became the game in Lutyens' Delhi. Every secretary vied for new programme launches and results on the ground to impress him. Make In India, Mudra, Deen Dayal Upadhayaya Grameen Kaushalya Yojana, Pradhan Mantri Jan Dhan Yojana, HRIDAY—Heritage City Development and Augmentation Yojana, Sukanya Samriddhi Yojana, Smart Cities Mission, AMRUT, Pradhan Mantri Awas Yojana, Pradhan Mantri Kaushal Vikas Yojana, Stand Up India, Start Up India, Skill India, Pradhan Mantri Bhartiya Jan Aushadhi Kendra were some of the programmes that were launched. Many of them merely involved repackaging or renaming schemes that had been running for years.

Designing programmes is not the bureaucracy's job at the centre. Programme implementation is carried out by state governments. The bureaucracy lost its way, forgetting its core function, which is policy advice and policy formulation. Many of the ministries urgently needed policy work, but officials stopped short of even stating what needed to be done. A whole lot got confused between policy advice and programmes, and started pandering to the prime minister, pitching programmes to him. The prime minister visibly enjoyed being in the limelight, something launches of programmes ensured. On the other hand, the regime, it was pretty clear to senior officials in government, did not like bureaucrats or ministers to set the agenda, which championing policy invariably requires. 'Agenda-setting is not to be done by domain experts. Domain experts who are also assertive personalities just do not fit in . . . [In ministries of] petroleum, home, finance political sensitivity is ten times magnified, [so, the PMO] will set the agenda,' said a senior IAS officer who, in Modi's four years, had already served in three different ministries.[85]

Of course, there were notable exceptions.

Coal Secretary S.K. Srivastava put it in no uncertain terms that something simply had to be done about the acute shortage of coal in the country.[86] The shortage had the power-generating industry in a panic. As a result, auctions were conducted, and coal imports dropped sharply over the next two years, although the coal sector became stressed again thereafter despite the policy changes.

Secretary, financial services, Hasmukh Adhia made an exhaustive presentation on the deepening problem among PSBs, their growing NPAs, their loss of market to private banks, their eroding profitability, their impaired assets, the large number of top-level vacancies, the stress from power discoms, and the crying need for capitalizing banks.[87]

Modi had brought Adhia, a 1981 batch IAS officer, to the centre from Gujarat in early November. Adhia had last worked at the centre from 1994 to 1999, as director in the industry ministry. One of the prime minister's most-trusted officers, Adhia spelt out in thirty-five slides the potential solutions and strategies, and short of privatization, the way forward.[88] Over the long term, he said in precise terms, all PSBs must be consolidated into four or five large banks. The presentation left nothing to the imagination and pulled no punches.

Resolving the government-owned PSBs' problems was essential to revive investments by the private sector. These had been slowing since 2011–12. Without reversing this investment slowdown, the steady but weak GDP growth recovery Modi had inherited from Singh was difficult to sustain. Alongside reforms, a sharp pickup in investments had contributed to India's economic growth since the 1980s.[89]

Modi's failure to act on this advice would disrupt the economic recovery that was gradually gathering pace year after year. The economy that was on a smooth recovery path for four years, from 2012–13 to 2015–16, would slow for the first time in five years in 2016–17, as the banking sector's growing problems would begin to dampen the growth impulses. This loss of growth momentum April–June 2016 onwards would show in the quarterly GDP estimates. Eventually, demonetization, announced in November 2016, and later the incompetently designed GST rate structure and collection systems would further hurt growth. More about the delays in addressing the banking sector's problems later in the book.

By the end of 2014, signs of the economic upswing had begun to become discernible in the data being presented in the prime minister's reviews on infrastructure. Planning Secretary Sindhushree Khullar projected that there would be small recoveries in the major IIP (Index of Industrial Production) sectors by May 2016 and that each of these sectors needed one or two key triggers to kick-start recovery.[90] The action that needed to be taken was also laid out.

The macroeconomy, inflation in particular, was an immediate priority. Fortunately, global crude prices, which had been testing the $120-a-barrel mark in June 2014, dropped to $50 a barrel by January 2015, and seemed headed for $25 a barrel by January 2016.[91]

Institutional Framework for Managing Inflation

Governor Y.V. Reddy had announced a self-imposed flexible target for inflation in April 2007.[92] This medium-term ceiling for inflation was 5 per cent, and the RBI's resolve, going forward, was to condition policy and perceptions for inflation consistent with the range considered conducive for maintaining self-accelerating growth over the medium term. Reddy's self-imposed target sought to influence perceptions about the socially tolerable rate of inflation. 'The level of inflation tolerance in India, that is, the level at which political leadership reacted with special measures, was close to 10 per cent till then,' he writes in his memoir.[93]

Growth trickles down to the disadvantaged with lags, but the pinch of price instability is felt instantly. By the time prices cool, the poor, who typically have limited risk-bearing capacity, may have suffered permanent setbacks.

Despite Reddy's self-imposed target, the inflation record during much of UPA-2's tenure was poor. Reddy's successor, Subbarao, was forced by the global financial crisis to shift focus from an anti-inflation stance to preserving financial stability as the principal goal of monetary policy. Pranab Mukherjee's liberal allocations for the social sector thereafter, in the absence of reforms to ease the supply rigidities in the economy, fanned inflation expectations. As had the spike in oil and food prices, which account for a dominant part in the price indices. Food prices are influenced by the minimum support price, public procurement and food stock management, all of which derive from government policy. UPA-2's handling of each of these policies stoked food inflation, as discussed earlier in the book.

Large elements of subsidies and taxes in oil and food prices make them, and consequently the demand for these consumables, unresponsive to monetary policy. The sustained food inflation set off inflationary expectations, which became virtually impossible to fight with monetary policy. An easing of supply-side bottlenecks would have been the appropriate response to control runaway inflation, but the policy paralysis that set in had completely jammed the chances of that happening. And so, during the UPA-2 years, the burden of managing inflation had to be borne by the RBI. The RBI's ability to deliver on the inflation objective when the spending authority, the government, ran high fiscal deficits, was seriously constrained. Subbarao's meetings with the team of officials led by Mukherjee had shown that the fiscal-monetary policy reforms undertaken in the 1990s were at risk of getting reversed.

Negotiating the distribution of responsibilities and authority between the government and the RBI on a day-to-day basis became increasingly tense. The UPA-2 obstructed transmission of the monetary policy by guiding state-controlled banks to maintain lending rates at levels different from what the RBI's policy was driving at. Borrowers prefer lower rates so that the cost of borrowings is minimized. Borrowers tend to be organized as industry chambers and are able to lobby the government. All governments are susceptible to pressures from industry lobbies on lending rates. No finance minister, from Mukherjee to Chidambaram, and eventually Jaitley, has been able to resist them. In any monetary policy action, political economy considerations are inevitable, since there will be losers and gainers.[94] Savers favour higher returns on deposits, and so are better served by higher interest rates, but they are dispersed and have no voice, unlike large borrowers. The interest rate should ideally balance the needs of both savers and borrowers or investors.

Considerations of the political economy and the structural characteristics of inflation meant that there was a growing need for ensuring the independence of RBI's role as a monetary authority from the fiscal authority.

Against this backdrop, Chidambaram and Manmohan Singh thought of inflation targeting as a way to increase the RBI's monetary independence. The idea had first emerged just before the disruption of the global financial crisis.

On 26 August 2008, Finance Secretary D. Subbarao was to fly out of the country to attend the G20 deputies meeting in Brazil.[95] In the morning he went up to Chidambaram in his chamber to say he was going to be away, as a courtesy, since the finance minister had of course approved the trip on file. Chidambaram inquired as to when he would be back, and then, after a pause on hearing the date, asked if Subbarao would be interested in being considered for the RBI governor's job—Governor Reddy's term was ending in September. Subbarao thanked Chidambaram for putting his name on the shortlist and requested him to take his candidature forward.

Chidambaram said the prime minister had wanted him to explicitly check with Subbarao since he was in line to be the next cabinet secretary.

Since Subbarao's flight out of India was in the middle of the night, Chidambaram asked, 'Could you then come to my house at 8 p.m. for a chat with Dr Rangarajan and myself? Rakesh [Mohan] is coming in at 7 p.m.'[96] Reddy had recommended Rakesh Mohan, RBI deputy governor, as his successor.

At the interview that evening, Chidambaram asked Subbarao if he would back the proposal of a monetary policy committee (MPC) for deciding RBI's monetary policy.[97] A discussion among the three ensued on the experiences in this context in advanced countries, the Federal Open Market Committee in the US, the MPCs of the Bank of England and the Bank of Japan, and even the rather opaque system of the People's Bank of China.

Subbarao's substantive stance at this discussion was that an MPC was the direction in which India must proceed.[98] But, he said, the governor must have a veto, at least during the transition period until the institutional structure stabilized.

Chidambaram did not agree.[99] His point was that the governor should try to persuade the MPC members to his point of view. Subbarao agreed with this but countered that a governor would succeed only if the members of the MPC felt no pressure to push the government's point of view in the committee.[100] Subbarao was suggesting that the members should not owe any allegiance to the government only because it had appointed them. The interview ended well past 9 p.m. Chidambaram walked Subbarao to the car parked in the driveway of his house and wished him a safe flight.

Subbarao's appointment as the twenty-second governor of the RBI was announced in early September.

On 12 September, a committee on financial-sector reforms headed by Raghuram Rajan presented its report to Prime Minister Singh.[101] Another high-profile committee report by former World Bank economist Percy Mistry had come out earlier.[102] The debate about inflation targeting started to pick up. Mistry made a strong case for reorientation of the RBI towards a transparently independent inflation-targeting central bank. Rajan held that to be effective, such a redefining of the RBI's mandate will have to be preconditioned on the government's commitment to, first, maintaining fiscal discipline, and second, not holding the central bank accountable for the level of or volatility in the nominal exchange rate.

A growing number of central banks, starting with New Zealand's in late 1989, had been making the shift to targeting monetary policy almost exclusively towards stabilizing inflation.[103] This approach had seemed successful in the years leading up to the global financial crisis, an extended period of price stability accompanied by stable growth and low unemployment, also called the Great Moderation. But the global financial crisis showed that the premise of inflation targeting—that if policymakers took care of price stability, financial stability would be automatically assured—was flawed. Single-minded pursuit of an inflation target had blindsided central bankers to threats of financial instability. The originator of inflation targeting, New Zealand, had abandoned it.[104]

The shift towards inflation targeting did not come through in Governor Subbarao's tenure. His principal reservations were that in an economy where short-term inflation is driven more by supply shocks, be they of food or energy, than by demand-side pressures, could the RBI really deliver on an inflation target?[105] Would the government support the RBI by remaining committed to fiscal responsibility? Or, would inflation targeting become hostage to fiscal dominance? And, how effective could inflation targeting be in a situation where monetary policy transmission is impeded not just by fiscal deficits but also by administered interest rates on small savings and in ill-liquid bond markets? Would the RBI's policy so far, of managing large and volatile capital flows to subdue their impact on the exchange rate, compromise inflation targeting?

In the face of compulsions peculiar to the Indian situation, inflation targeting, Subbarao worried, could lock the RBI into a no-win situation. If people lost confidence in an inflation target, it would become hard for the central bank to persuade them to trust a target again.

On taking over, in the midst of the rupee's free fall and high CAD and inflation, as the governor of the RBI in September 2013, Rajan said the reforms strategy he intended to pursue included strengthening the country's monetary policy framework.

Among the steps he announced he had already taken was to ask Deputy Governor Urjit Patel, along with a panel of outside experts and RBI staff, to come up with suggestions in three months on what needed to be done to revise and strengthen the country's monetary policy framework.[106]

The RBI takes its mandate from the Reserve Bank of India Act of 1934, which says the RBI was constituted, 'to regulate the issue of banknotes and the keeping of reserves with a view to securing monetary stability in India and generally to operate the currency and credit system of the country to its advantage'.[107]

The goals of monetary policy in India have been set through interpretation of this preamble and the Act, as price stability and growth. The relative emphasis between the two was determined by the specific circumstances at any given point in time. Safeguarding financial stability, for instance, had emerged as a consideration in monetary policy upon the collapse of Lehman Brothers.

The primary role of the central bank, Rajan reminded the nation, was monetary stability—in other words, to sustain confidence in the value of the country's money.[108] Ultimately, this meant low and stable expectations of inflation, whether that inflation stems from domestic sources or from the changes in the value of the currency, from supply constraints or demand pressures.[109]

Rajan refused to be pulled into the debate as to whether in India the chief sources of inflation are on the demand side, which monetary policy can influence, or on the supply side, against which monetary policy is blunt. Consumer price inflation in India at the time was the highest among the large countries of the world. It was concentrated in food and services. Indian households were turning to gold because inflation was making financial savings unattractive. How would the economy finance investments without recourse to household savings?

'We can spend a long time debating the sources of this inflation. But ultimately inflation comes from demand exceeding supply and it can be curtailed only by bringing both in balance. We need to reduce demand somewhat without having serious adverse effects on investment and supply. This is a balancing act which requires the Reserve Bank to act firmly so that the economy is disinflating even while allowing the weak economy more time than one would normally allow for it to reach a comfortable level of inflation.'[110]

Urjit Patel's game-changing report came in by mid-January 2014.[111] It recommended a complete overhaul, a reshaping and retooling of monetary policy. One of the recommendations was that the central bank abandon its focus on the WPI for its inflation management and adopt in its place the Consumer Price Index (CPI) which tracked more closely the prices suffered by the basket of goods people bought in their daily lives.[112] Consumer price inflation had exceeded wholesale price inflation for some time. Bringing it under control meant interest rates, and therefore lending rates, would have to go higher in an election year when GDP growth had slowed sharply.

By April, before the polls were through, the RBI set out on a glide path with clear milestones for bringing down CPI inflation into the target range of 4 per cent, with a band of plus or minus 2 percentage points, as the Urjit Patel report had suggested.[113]

WPI inflation had, as per the latest available reading (for February 2014) at the time, fallen significantly to 4.7 per cent from 7.5 per cent in November 2013.[114]

'I think we would see WPI as also closely linked to international prices, and international prices have been flirting with zero, especially when you add energy prices. It would be good news for inflation if over time it seeps into our CPI inflation,' Rajan had explained at the time in an interview to me.[115]

The Urjit Patel Committee had also recommended that the central government ensure that its fiscal deficit as a proportion of GDP is pared down to 3 per cent by 2016–17, and further, that the 'significant impediments to monetary policy transmission and achievement of the price stability objective', such as administered prices, wages and interest rates, are eliminated.[116]

Chidambaram cut fiscal deficit to 4.5 per cent of GDP by 31 March 2014, even as the RBI embarked on the glide path to bring CPI inflation down to 8 per cent by January 2015 and to 6 per cent by January 2016.[117] (Although the less-than-ideal quality of this fiscal consolidation was commented upon by Rajan).[118]

Chidambaram also directed North Block's mandarins to draft a proposal on an inflation-targeting mandate for the RBI from the government. He asked for the new framework to specify in clear terms that the main objective of monetary policy would be to maintain price stability, 'while keeping in mind the objectives of growth'.[119] The rationale was that this condition would discourage the RBI from adopting a rigid approach to achieving the inflation target with no consideration at all for growth objectives.

Chidambaram's insistence on a flexible approach stemmed from the fact that GDP growth and inflation are not independent variables. Targets for growth and inflation cannot be set simultaneously.[120] If one is fixed, the other gets automatically determined. Of course, monetary policy can only provide a conducive environment for growth to reach its potential; it cannot raise the potential itself.

The flexible inflation-targeting approach is closer to the mandates of the US Federal Reserve and the Bank of England. The Fed cannot focus exclusively on inflation as it has, by law, a twin mandate, requiring it to balance price stability with maximum employment.[121] In the UK, the objective of monetary policy is to deliver price stability—implying an inflation target of 2 per cent—and, subject to that, the objectives of growth and employment.[122]

Conventional inflation targeting, as was practised before the global financial crisis, focused on meeting a predefined target for inflation, ignoring other objectives of growth, employment or financial stability. The logic was that by setting a clear target of low and stable inflation, and thus gaining credibility, the central bank could keep interest rates low and generate high, sustainable economic growth.[123] Growth and financial stability were thus consequences of low inflation rather than separate objectives. The post-crisis received wisdom is that when inflation is low, central banks may have to resort to unconventional policies to jump-start growth. At the same time, unconventional ultra-low interest rate policies can spur risk-taking and produce asset bubbles.

Neo-conventional or flexible inflation targeting incorporates the lessons learnt after the crisis. It essentially extends the time period for hitting an inflation target.

By the time the flexibility condition was written into the proposal for the new monetary policy framework, worded to Chidambaram's satisfaction, and Prime Minister Singh's approval had been recorded on file, the 2014 polls were close.[124] Chidambaram then added a remark that the approved file should also be placed before the incoming government, for the proposed mandate for the RBI was a major policy change with far-reaching implications.[125]

After the new government was sworn in, the file was put up to the Modi government's finance minister, Arun Jaitley, who signed it without posing a single question, and in a matter of minutes.[126] The officer who put up the file stiffened a little seeing the lack of fuss with which Jaitley had conferred his approval. It was suggested politely that the minister could take some time to study the proposed new policy if he wanted.

'There is no hurry, Sir.'[127]

'Two of the finest minds in the country [in the context of inflation targeting and central bank policies] have applied themselves and come up with this solution. I don't need greater endorsement,' Jaitley responded.[128]

If Singh is scholarly and Chidambaram analytical, Jaitley's approach to policymaking is pragmatic. Many times over the next couple of years, he sought to take credit for improved inflation management. On each occasion he criticized the previous regime for its record of runaway inflation, never once disclosing publicly that inflation was finally reined in through a mechanism designed and approved by the Manmohan Singh government.

Nevertheless, he could have ordered a re-examination of the policy. So the credit for not delaying further or obstructing the reform goes to Jaitley and Modi. The RBI, it was decided, cannot set for itself an inflation target level of 4 per cent with its chosen band for all time to come. It is best that inflation targets are set by governments elected by the people rather than by bureaucrats and economists in the RBI.

The RBI signed an agreement in February 2015 with the government, in which it committed to bringing consumer price inflation below 6 per cent by January 2016.[129] This was in line with the glide path it had set for itself earlier. The consumer inflation target for the financial year 2016–17 was set at 4 per cent, with a band of plus or minus 2 percentage points.

The main mandate of the central bank was thus defined formally as targeting consumer price inflation. Under the new regime, the centre specifies inflation targets for the RBI to achieve within a time frame; the RBI sets these as the top priority in its policy statements. Inflation has become the primary factor deciding interest rates.

In the event of the target being missed, the framework agreement enjoins the governor to report to the government the reasons for the failure, as also the remedial action being taken to return inflation to the target range. This safeguard minimizes the probability of the RBI pursuing the inflation target at any cost.

Institutionalizing the fight against inflation made it more credible. Inflation has remained within target. On the downside, the mandate has, as was expected, limited the considerations of GDP growth or exchange rate management in monetary policy setting.

Next, broadly as recommended by the Urjit Patel Committee, with just a slight departure from the report, an independent six-member MPC took over the setting of interest rates from the governor. The RBI Act had empowered the governor 'singularly' and 'solely' to set interest rates. In the new regime, the MPC, three of whose members are appointed by the government, votes to decide monetary policy action and stance. Decisions are by majority vote.

Patel was elevated as the twenty-fourth governor of the RBI in September 2015. Unlike his predecessors, Patel was not the deciding authority on the RBI's monetary policy. He was one of the six members of the MPC.

Since the 1960s, monetary policy had been subordinated to fiscal compulsions. More recently, there has been shrill clamour on behalf of industrial lobbies and big business borrowers for low lending rates, regardless of the consequences for inflation and the savings rate. The new monetary policy architecture redefined for ever the government-RBI relationship, and especially the government-governor relationship. The idea behind the MPC is that a committee is subject to less political pressure than a governor.

It was expected that the RBI's agreement with the government would reduce political influence (and the influence of the business interests close to politicians) on the setting of monetary policy; and it may even place checks on expectations and the pursuit of fiscal profligacy. These would turn out to be false hopes. By 2018, however, RBI-government differences would have led to Patel resigning his position nine months before the completion of his three-year term. Rajan's departure from the RBI would be nearly as controversial, although he would serve out his three-year term. Monetary policy would be one of the sources of the growing tensions.

So, has India resolved the problem of inflation?

Theoretically, a rules-based framework can, by signalling commitment, increase the credibility, and therefore effectiveness, of the monetary authority. Second, it is less vulnerable to political pressures from Delhi.

The new monetary policy framework yielded satisfactory results in the initial years. Runaway inflation, the kind that was seen in the UPA-2 years, did not make a comeback during the tenure of the Modi government, but this was also a period of benign global crude prices and often depressed farm-sector prices.

The RBI committee's precondition for making the shift to inflation targeting was a reduction in fiscal deficit to 3 per cent of GDP by 2016–17. The agreement between the RBI and the government for targeting a given level of inflation was signed, but the government never managed to reach the fiscal deficit target, which, at the end of March 2018, was 3.5 per cent. The message to the government was loud and clear: since it was running a larger fiscal deficit than the target, the monetary side was having to sweat to contain inflation, and that meant borrowing costs were not as low as the government would have liked.

The other question is whether the effectiveness of influence of inflation-targeting monetary policy would be limited in India, since inflation is driven mainly by food or oil prices, both of which are determined more by fiscal policies than monetary action; or, when food inflation quickens because of dietary changes, would using the interest-rate tool to cool prices be successful? These are valid apprehensions. The transmission channels of monetary policy changes into the economy are very different from those in developed countries, where unbanked populations are not as large as in India and the drivers of inflation very different.

Rajan responded to such worries in an interview to me:[130]

If there is something horrendous that knocks out, let's say for the sake of discussion, a significant part of agricultural production, food prices go through the sky. A central bank tasked with getting inflation under control will not try and restore the price level that existed before the food shock. That's a misconception a lot of people have. Instead, you will say I am not going to try and contain inflation this year to 0 or 5 or whatever my target is because given that food prices are 50 per cent higher; there is no way I can do it. Instead I am going to try and bring inflation back within the 5 per cent range over the span of the next two years. In other words, what you are doing is accommodating the supply shock and saying you can't reverse that, that's supply demand, but what you can do is prevent that supply shock from feeding into second and third round effects. That is, people shouldn't now start saying okay, food is now so much costlier, my wages are going to be so much higher then, because wages are higher and other output goods get higher and you get into a spiral. That's what we can try and curtail.

Advent of 'Modinomics'

The Bharatiya Janata Party released its election manifesto on 7 April 2014, the first of the nine 'poll days' of the sixteenth general elections, in the face of the Election Commission of India's displeasure.[131] It was not that the BJP had not done its homework on its manifesto ahead of the 2014 Lok Sabha elections. In fact, its preparations began earlier than the other major parties', with the October 2013 launch of a website inviting suggestions from voters for its manifesto. While most other parties, national and regional, came out with their largely elaborate exercises before the 'poll days' began, the BJP failed to unveil its manifesto sooner. (Even the preface signed by the manifesto committee chairman, Murli M. Joshi, bears the date 26 March 2014.)

When it was released, the manifesto made a definitive stride leftwards.[132] It devoted space and significance to welfarism and committed the party to give the country a government of the poor, the marginalized and those that had been left behind.

'The only prayer of a Government should be the welfare of its people.'[133]

'Our Government will be a government of the poor, the marginalized and left behind.'[134]

A full-fledged programme for 'Rural Rejuvenation'[135] was proposed; this included 'Institutes of Technology for Rural Development',[136] a 'Pradhan Mantri Gram Sinchayee Yojana' for irrigation, with the motto, '*har khet ko paani* [Irrigation for every field]'[137] and a massive low-cost housing programme to ensure that by the time the nation completes seventy-five years of Independence, every family will have a pucca house of its own.[138] Despite all its criticism of the Congress's rights-based approach, the BJP was clearly saying that it wouldn't abandon any of the Congress's entitlement laws. Instead, it promised to build on them. The party committed to spend 6 per cent of GDP on education.[139]

The most striking promises were around the concept of the 'Industry Family'[140] for organized industry owners and labour and the setting up of a 'Workers' Bank'[141] to strengthen pension and health insurance safety nets for all kinds of labourers. A review of labour laws was proposed, which 'will ensure that the interests of labour in the unorganised sector are protected'.[142] The manifesto, while silent on disinvestment, proposed a new public-sector unit: the Organic Farming and Fertilizer Corporation of India.[143] There were none of the expected promises of shiny new infrastructure or a big push to the economic growth rate. The manifesto contained no specifics at all on economic proposals. The growth plan proposed was to harness the '5 Ts'—Tradition, Talent, Tourism, Trade and Technology[144]—for capturing the advantages of the '3 Ds'—Democracy, Demography and Demand.[145] On fiscal consolidation, there was a single sentence: 'We will strictly implement fiscal discipline without compromising on funds availability for development work and asset creation.'[146] The only tax benefit promised was for setting up old-age homes.[147]

Overall, it read like a randomly compiled menu of promises with no clear economic agenda, strategy or vision backing it. That may have been the result of a deliberate strategy for a party that was still haunted by the ghost of its 'India Shinning' debacle in the 2004 Lok Sabha elections. Or a reflection of unresolved tensions between the old guard in the BJP manifesto committee and the aggressive Modi team. Whether the manifesto leaned leftwards in a tactful shrugging off of the 'Shining India' image or out of muddle-headed thinking, one would not know. However, well after the new government was sworn in, conflicting doublespeak on its direction and agenda continued.

Subsidies had found no mention in the BJP manifesto. Former Union minister, BJP leader and Harvard-trained economist, Subramanian Swamy, made a case for rationalizing them on the strength of the experience of the 'Gujarat Model' that had proved that distortionary subsidies, such as in the power sector, could be eliminated.

'I am not in favour of subsidies at all; the PDS [public distribution system] should move to coupons encashable by shopkeepers only through a bank account to eliminate leakages,' Swamy told me in an interview on 10 May 2014.[148]

Rationalization of subsidies had emerged as a pressing issue. The 2014–15 Interim Budget presented by Chidambaram in February had provided Rs 2,55,708 crore for subsidies, which was more than a quarter of the proposed total net tax revenue for the year for the centre.[149]

Asked why the BJP manifesto had not specifically addressed the issue of subsidies, Swamy said, 'Revolutionary ideas have to be introduced in small doses and cannot be outlined in the manifesto.'

It's not as if the party did not have ideas. Some thought-out positions on stressed sectors crying for attention could be heard alongside oversimplified public posturing.

On new jobs creation, for instance, Swamy said, 'Agriculture will be the most important industry for a government led by the

BJP's prime ministerial candidate, Narendra Modi. Modi will focus on building agriculture as an industry and will free up exports of dairy products and foodgrains, etc., with full back-end support for cold storage as there is no other real way of creating jobs in rural India.'

Modi's government would look to 'globalize' India's agriculture through development of back-end support for the agriculture sector, cold storage, and packaging and processing, he said. 'Given that the prices of rice and milk and other farm sector produce in the global market is several times that in India, Mr Modi would like to give a big push to agricultural exports, for which output of the sector will have to expand fast.'

The thinking was that developing the farm sector was important for creating jobs in rural India and arresting migration from villages. The bulk of India's population resides in the countryside and would likely find non-farm jobs, such as those in the industrial sector, somewhat alien. The Modi government would abandon this line of thinking and take a completely different direction with 'Make In India' and the Land Acquisition Amendments, which envisaged taking mega-industry to the villages.

The potentially constructive and doable ideas were mostly drowned out by a proposal to abolish income tax over five years that found many takers in the party, including Swamy, and other statements emerging from 11, Ashoka Road, the BJP headquarters, which were completely lacking in vision and limited to attacks on the previous government or on RBI Governor Raghuram Rajan.

'Only the richest 40,000-50,000 . . . the billionaires . . . must pay income tax but they must be allowed to deduct savings parked in certain productive instruments from their taxable income,' said Swamy.

This was an odd proposal, given rampant tax evasion. Barely 4 per cent of India's voters were paying tax, and only 15.5 per cent of the net national income was being reported to the tax authorities.[150]

This proposal, said Swamy, was not discussed by the BJP during the election campaign to avoid being seen as pro-rich.[151] Its campaign was perhaps aimed at reaching out to the disaffected middle class that was bristling with discontent. The prevalent feeling was that UPA-2 had taxed this growing segment of Indians merely to dish out 'doles' to build its constituency of disadvantaged voters. The sense of estrangement was heightened by the Congress party's image of being steeped in corruption. The message sent out by the BJP was that robbery through taxes was for transfers to vote banks via corruption-ridden and leaky so-called poverty-alleviation programmes. In other words, it was a way for the Congress to enrich itself. The Congress's rout in the 2014 polls was interpreted as an angry backlash to policymaking seen by voters as corrupt and divorced from the real concerns of the people.

The charges of corruption scams and scandals seemed to confirm that public wealth was being stolen for illegitimate private gains. With infrastructure acutely deficient, and public healthcare and education in shambles, the private-sector suppliers priced these basic services exorbitantly. Overall, the aspirational middle class felt it was getting little from the state in return for the taxes it was paying.

Once in office, Modi strived to outdo the UPA government on launch of schemes and programmes—without rolling out any comprehensive reforms for revitalizing failing institutions, administration systems and delivery mechanisms. Modi's schemes offered simple, quick solutions. But the outcomes may well be as unflattering as the UPA's flagships. Can the numbers of toilets built be the sole determinant of sanitation and health outcomes any more than passing a legislation guaranteeing food security to reduce malnutrition?

The scapegoating of Rajan was perhaps intended to reassure the advantaged. Rajan was already by the time speaking up against the impunity with which the rich were passing off their losses to PSBs.

Swamy told me:[152]

> If Rajan gets one more term you can safely say bye to all
> investment and therefore high growth in this country. He is not
> fit for this country. We need to immediately drop interest rates,
> doesn't mean that we do it in one go. There can be a road map,
> but businesses must know that cost of capital will come down.
> Deposit rates, on the other hand, need to rise. Bank account
> holders must get assured 12 per cent interest on deposits of
> three-year duration.

What this implied then was that banks' profitability needed to
improve so that they could lend funds at lower rates despite paying
more for raising deposits.

BJP's manifesto and the utterances of its leaders presented a
picture of a complete ideological mishmash. The questions that
remained unanswered included: What would the 'Gujarat Model'
translate into at the centre? What were the tenets of 'Modinomics'?

With the rise of 'Sonianomics', 'Pranabnomics' and
'Rahulnomics', 'Manmohanomics' had receded into disuse.
The people's disillusionment with the cocktail of 'Sonianomics',
'Pranabnomics' and 'Rahulnomics' had driven UPA-2 out of
power.

What development philosophy, policy guidance and strategy
of governance was going to replace it?

Modi had outlined a slew of slogans and promises in his
campaign speeches, in the BJP manifesto, in the President's address
to both the houses of Parliament for the inaugural session of the
sixteenth Lok Sabha, and in subsequent speeches thereafter. What
route was his government going to take to deliver on the promises
it had made?

Every economic model is constrained by political reality. But
what were the basic foundations of the new model, the Modi
model?

The answers would continue to elude everyone.

In November 2013, on the exit of Dipak Dasgupta, the post of principal economic adviser in the finance ministry had fallen vacant, following which Economic Affairs Secretary Arvind Mayaram asked Ila Patnaik, columnist and RBI Chair Professor at the National Institute of Public Finance and Policy (NIPFP), to apply for the vacancy.[153] Ila Patnaik had applied once before for the position. Now Patnaik applied for the position for the second time. The process kicked off. The routine security checks done before such appointments were carried out, but the recruitment process went cold after that. The background checks had marked her as being a 'communist' since, at age twenty-one, she had contested the student union elections at Jawaharlal Nehru University and she had been a joint secretary of the AISF (All India Students' Federation), affiliated to the CPI. It should have been evident from the body of her writings, from both her columns and her research papers, that she had been arguing consistently against leftist ideology and that her economic philosophy over the years had been decisively pro-effectively regulated market. The record was eventually updated to reflect this change in her profile.

The outgoing government had taken the call to keep the chief economic adviser's position vacant for the incoming government to fill up. It had been vacant since August, upon Rajan's transition to the RBI. Chidambaram presented the Interim Budget in February without a chief economic adviser or a principal economic adviser.

But it was clear in the department of economic affairs of the ministry of finance that an Economic Survey would have to be brought out as part of the incoming government's maiden budget expected to be presented in July 2014; and that there may not be enough time for the new government to appoint a principal economic adviser or a chief economic adviser who could write the survey. The department did not feel confident about bringing out a survey without a professionally trained economist. With this in view, Patnaik was asked to join on deputation from the NIPFP as principal economic adviser by 1 April. She joined on 1 May 2014.

The outgoing UPA government approved the appointment even as the BJP approached the Election Commission to stop the government from appointing a new navy chief and Lokpal midway into elections.[154] At the time, it was assumed that Patnaik was a political appointee. Although Mayaram's mother had been a minister in a Congress government in the state of Rajasthan, the IAS officer may have approved the appointment in view of the ongoing preparation for bringing out the survey.

In the run-up to the polls, a number of world-renowned economists of Indian origin had begun positioning themselves for plum positions and key advisory roles in the Modi government, should he come to power, as seemed quite likely. A rash of lectures and media interviews broke out, attacking the Manmohan Singh government and praising the 'Gujarat Model'. The list of economists enamoured with Modi, and critical of Singh, included Meghnad Desai, Arvind Panagariya and Jagdish Bhagwati (a close friend of Singh). They gave suggestions to the 'PM-in-waiting' (Modi) and expressed confidence in their public comments about how his leadership alone could put the economy back on the 8 per cent-plus growth path.

On joining office, Modi chose to indulge home-grown economist Bibek Debroy, who had had a brief and unpleasant association earlier with the Rajiv Gandhi Foundation. (A study on the economic freedom-rating of states he had done with economist Laveesh Bhandari in 2004 had ranked Gujarat as number one. Upon this he got a note from Mrs Sonia Gandhi saying that anything to be published by the Rajiv Gandhi Institute thereafter would be politically vetted, following which he resigned.)[155] On 10 June, barely days after being sworn in, Modi released a book, *Getting India Back on Track: An Action Agenda for Reform*, at the official prime-ministerial residence, 7, Race Course Road.[156] One of its editors, besides Ashley J. Tellis and Reece Trevor, was Debroy. Patnaik had authored the first chapter, 'Maintaining macroeconomic stability' in the publication.

Modi appeared visibly gung-ho about the book at the release, especially about the reforms vision it laid out.[157] After the formal release, he greeted Patnaik with 'Hello, Ila ji', but said no more. It was interpreted in government circles as encouragement for further development of the ideas Patnaik had been advocating in her writings.

She had been tasked with writing the Economic Survey to be presented in Parliament ahead of the budget in early July as the new government was yet to appoint a chief economic adviser, who normally authors the document.[158]

The economic system was broken and was no longer delivering for India's needs. The Economic Survey 2013–14 that Union Finance Minister Arun Jaitley tabled in Parliament in July 2014 proposed a bold new alternative that had little in common with the BJP's manifesto.

Free-market Leanings

'Issues and Priorities', the second chapter of the document, set out the Modi government's reforms agenda. It recommended bringing in legislative, administrative and regulatory changes required for transitioning to a market economy in which the state's role was proposed to be restricted to interfering only when there is market failure.

> The government faces the task of putting in place the legal foundations of a well-functioning market economy for India . . . there are fundamental differences between the legal and regulatory framework of a command-and-control economy and a market economy. In the former, economic activity is restricted to those activities that are permitted by the state. In a market economy, the economy thrives because the state

interferes only when there is 'market failure', i.e. monopoly power, asymmetric information or externalities . . . This reform agenda has three elements: short-term stroke-of-the-pen reforms, medium-term reforms that can be undertaken through executive decisions or the Finance Bill [a Money bill technically not requiring Rajya Sabha approval for passage], and long-term reforms for institutional change. Long-term reforms involve the challenging task of building capacity and institutions that provide the foundations of a market economy . . . Only the state can ensure provision of public goods such as defence, police, and judiciary. Only the state can address monopolies, externalities, and asymmetric information. In an environment of technologically sophisticated and internationalised firms, it requires considerable sophistication on the part of government to precisely address market failures. This requires state capacity. India needs greater expertise for establishing intelligent, efficient, cost-minimising government organisations that successfully address market failures.[159]

In other words, the Modi government should redefine the state's purpose and role, substituting markets for it. The state would intervene only if the markets failed. Monopoly power and asymmetric information would be market failures meriting intervention. All other roles would be delegated to market forces.

This was India's first official declaration of intent to embrace markets fully and restrict state functions drastically. The thrust since 1991 had been on freeing markets by withdrawing state controls and distortions. The Economic Survey of 2014 articulated in unambiguous and the strongest possible terms the intention of embracing the free-market economic model.

The sharp turn rightwards came at a time when the world was reaching the consensus that just as complete state controls fail, so do free markets.[160] Leaving all decisions to markets had not worked for advanced economies, which were now no longer valorizing free markets. Middle paths are increasingly being preferred around the world. After the global financial crisis, the focus even in the US is back on the fundamental question of whether the principles of market can be applied to development, equity, social justice and poverty alleviation.

In India, transition to the market economic model proposed in the survey, together with the Union cabinet's sanction a month later for scrapping the resolution that had set up the Planning Commission in 1950, signalled a complete inversion of Nehruvian socialism.

The announcement was greeted with caution by both Modi's supporters and detractors, although for entirely different sets of reasons.

The broad consensus had been that a break from the past demanded deep reforms, such as divesting political executives and bureaucrats of economic controls, privatizing the public sector, freeing land, labour, agriculture and other markets of distortions and controls, and establishing efficient and independent regulators. This was all a backlog of economic liberalization's unfinished agenda that had remained pending for twenty-five years after 1991, defeated by political pushback, ideological resistance, and the challenges and constraints of state capacity and vested interests.

Modi's backers wondered if he would be able to muster the political courage required to overcome resistance that could be expected not only from the left end of the ideological spectrum but even from the right, notably from the RSS. For the RSS, though culturally and socially 'right', often takes positions on economic matters that are anti-free market.

The survey's proposals, however, went unnoticed; there was hardly any public debate around what was said in the second chapter.

The government soon launched into decision-making. It did not engage with the fundamental issues laid out in the survey that can be determinants of success in any economy—such as state capacities and institutional robustness. The early decisions were made with a view to recasting the ecosystem for doing business with ease and to give industry a free hand. They seemed loosely aligned with the direction laid out in the survey.

Amendments to labour and land laws were drafted. A new insolvency law was in the works. The 'Make in India' initiative was launched. Natural resources, such as spectrum and coal, were to be allocated through auctions. The plan was that ease of acquiring land, hiring and firing labour, and running and exiting business would be improved. The faster growth thus produced would lead to quality jobs. Equally, the state's involvement would be reduced. Budget 2015 proposed to decontrol urea and diesel prices so that they would be market-determined.[161] It also proposed to withdraw kerosene from the public distribution system. Entitlements of subsidized cooking gas cylinders were cut. The review of subsidies was with an aim to remove price distortions and thereby strengthen markets.

Only some of these plans and announcements could be carried out. Before long, the Modi government would lose interest in carrying forward the 1991 reforms agenda.

If the survey was an early official document of the new government's intent for the economic future of the country, then, compared with the manifesto, it suggested that on coming to power the party's thinking had undergone a drastic change. If the manifesto leaned to the left, the survey's second chapter conveyed an inclination to veer the economy rightwards. But it was probably just an economic adviser's wish list.

Authored by Patnaik, the extraordinary chapter unveiling what might be the government's philosophical thrust got little attention outside Lutyens' Delhi. The only noticeable official endorsement it received was a tweet from Union Minister Piyush Goyal.[162] 'The "Issues and Priorities" chapter in the Economic Survey is particularly insightful. I encourage all to read it: http://indiabudget. nic.in/es2013-14/echap-02.pdf . . .'

The few in Lutyens' Delhi who noticed it read it as an early signal of an imminent turn to the right in economic policymaking, in line with Debroy, Panagariya, Bhagwati and Patnaik's ideological profiles. In these circles, besides corruption and inflation, the strongest criticism of the ten years of the Congress-led UPA's governance was that it had been infiltrated by the left. Ideologically driven policy directives seeped in from the NAC into the ministries, even as the centrists in the Planning Commission, the PMO and the finance ministry offered muted responses and resistance so mild it did not even register. The elite, as much as the non-elite, craved an alternative economic vision, a redirection, a correction. Before long, Patnaik exited the government.

The Imminent Death of the Planning Commission

18 June 2013

The Delhi Police had taken over the security of Yojana Bhawan, which housed the Planning Commission.[163] All entry and exit points were sealed, and there was heavy deployment of force in and around the premises. Yojana Bhawan resembled a fortress as Gujarat Chief Minister Narendra Modi arrived to discuss the Annual Plan for the state with Deputy Chairman Montek Singh Ahluwalia. Only still photographers were allowed in. All other media persons were denied entry. Only journalists accredited by the Press Information Bureau could attend the press briefing after Modi's meeting with Ahluwalia.

This was Modi's first visit to Delhi after his appointment as chairman of the BJP's election campaign committee for the 2014 general elections.

Addressing the packed conference room at Yojana Bhawan, he said, 'Dim the lights.'[164]

In the preceding years, Modi's annual presentations before the Planning Commission had been no less than performances.[165] He would proudly present his state's achievements in the past year, and its expectations from the next annual plan for fulfilling its aspirations.

The audio-visual started, but this time Modi's presentation was not about Gujarat. Beginning from the Nehruvian years, the presentation made a scathing attack on the Planning Commission: what it was, what it had done, or not done.[166] It went on to review the central government's economic policies and their impact— the rupee's depreciation, the foul-up of natural resources, the soured investment climate. Dumbstruck, the audience was trying to make sense of the show when the screen beamed a parting shot: Gujarat's economic potential was getting destroyed because of the Manmohan Singh-led government's economic mismanagement.

Modi did not speak at all. He let the brilliantly produced work of cinema, with its sound and music effects, convey how little he thought of the Planning Commission and its leadership, Singh and Ahluwalia, the most reputed policy economists of post-liberalization India.

There were many red faces in the room when the lights came back on.

'There were no lies or anything, but it was polemic . . . Modiji embarrassed everybody present,' recalls an official who sat through the rigmarole.[167]

No copy of the audio-visual presentation was received at the commission's secretariat despite numerous requests to bureaucrats in the state for one.

'The chief minister's officers were afraid to share the presentation,' says the official who coordinated with the state government.[168]

'Would you then like us to record that your chief minister did not intervene?' the Gujarat bureaucrats were asked.

'No, you just say that he made an audio-video presentation,' was their response.

That was not an option for the secretariat since the minutes had to be recorded. Minutes for all meetings with states are supposed to go up to the prime minister, the chairman of the commission.

'Later, I found out it was a very mundane reason: They were not sharing it because they didn't have it. My guess is that it was not produced by government machinery. They saw it [for the first time] with us . . .'

This episode was an indication of things to come.

More than once during Modi's prime ministership it would be impossible to pin down the faceless, nameless, invisible draftsmen of the official policies and communiques on important matters that would emerge from his office. The mystery would be accompanied by a need on his part to dazzle. The content would be seen. Its presenter would be visible. Its source, process, thinking, costing . . . would remain obscure. It was a style of functioning that betrayed a certain disregard for government rules on record-keeping and documentation. It would seek to escape review and inquiry. It would sidestep the Right to Information (RTI) system. The downside of the information filters was that there would be no way of deflecting responsibility. The accountability would become Modi's entirely. Initially, the enigma that he made of himself would add to his charm. But after the failures of demonetization, what had seemed enigmatic initially would begin to seem sly. His inscrutability would begin to subtract from his persona.

Modi's presentation in June 2013 would also be an early giveaway of the deep-seated animosity that he had come to harbour for the Planning Commission. As a chief minister he may have felt he had been treated inappropriately by the commission's members on occasion. He faced sharp criticism from them on his state's Human Development Index record that represented the deficiency in the 'Gujarat Model'. Commission members Syeda Hameed and Narendra Jadhav stood out in particular, the tone and tenor of their comments bordering on the abrasive.[169] His mistrust of the commission's expertise could only have deepened in response to the coarseness meted out to him; his prejudices probably thickened. (Although, to his credit, on becoming prime minister, Modi nominated Jadhav to the Rajya Sabha.)

Modi's disdain for the institution inhabited by economists and bureaucrats was shared, to a lesser degree, though, by chief ministers of other states. Over the ten years of UPA rule, the institution had been helmed by two non-politicians—Singh and his deputy Ahluwalia, under whom, many of the chief ministers held, the commission offered little by way of value addition. The commission's relevance had eroded also because at its meetings the Congress chief ministers said 'nothing of consequence', mindful of how their comments might be construed by 10 Janpath.[170] The opposition chief ministers, on the other hand, were relatively outspoken.

'They spoke sense. Critical or not, there was a sense of national purpose,' says a former high functionary of the Planning Commission.[171]

When Modi and Ahluwalia briefed the press later that summer afternoon in 2013, the mood was perceptibly frosty.[172]

'It has been our view that Gujarat needs—in order to bring its social sector performance up to its economic size—to have some special attention to this area,' Ahluwalia told the media.[173]

Modi stood by his side, scowling.

'[Gujarat] spends 42 per cent of its budget on the social sector, and has a motto of "*Sabka Saath, Sabka Vikaas*" [everyone's support, everyone's growth] . . . The funds would help uplift all sections of the society, including the scheduled castes, the poor, the exploited and the tribal. We want to ensure all sections of the society get the benefits of growth.'[174]

Gujarat's annual plan had just been finalized. At Rs 59,000 crore, it was Rs 2000 crore less than Modi's requisition, although 15.7 per cent more than the previous year's outlay.

'Ahluwalia had made sure to provide for raising the deteriorating child-sex ratio in about half of Gujarat's districts and the high infant and mother mortality rates too. Malnutrition, the deputy chairman of the commission reminded Modi, far exceeded the levels that the state's 'advanced economic level' should have warranted.

After departing from Yojana Bhawan, Modi later headed for his maiden poll strategy discussion with the BJP's general secretaries, where he issued a new commandment to his party:

'Be aggressive. We have one aim: A Congress-free India.'[175]

After the poll results' declaration in May 2014 showed the UPA had been voted out, Singh sent his resignation to President Pranab Mukherjee to enable the commission's reconstitution by the incoming government.[176]

Days later, members appointed by the Manmohan Singh-led UPA government submitted their resignations to the PMO.

In his farewell speech to the commission in late April 2014, also his last address as prime minister on a formal platform, Singh had made a case for reorienting the institution to retain its relevance.[177]

> With an increasingly open and liberalised economy with a greater reliance on market mechanisms, we need to reflect on what the role of the Planning Commission needs to be in this new world . . . I am sure it will subject itself to a critical review and will continue to play a leading role in the policy debate in government and in the development of our nation.[178]

Singh concluded by asking Ahluwalia to urgently answer four questions that ought to be weighed by the next commission (and by implication the new government):[179]

1. Are we still using tools and approaches which were designed for a different era?
2. Have we added on new functions and layers without any restructuring of the more traditional activities in the commission?

3. What additional roles should the Planning Commission play and what capacities does it need to ensure that it continues to be relevant to the growth process?
4. Governance issues being integral to economic growth, are these areas for the Planning Commission to delve into?

To them, Ahluwalia wrote a laboured twelve-page response.[180]

'All institutions should periodically rethink their purpose. Dr Manmohan Singh wanted us to ponder on what an institution like the Planning Commission should do to support government policy in the new economic environment. I had submitted a detailed note to the Prime Minister in the last months of UPA-II but I said action could be left to the next government . . . In the pre-reform era, about 80 per cent of the knowledge on most things was within the government and only 20 per cent outside. Today, it is the reverse,' Ahluwalia told me in an interview.[181]

A few months later, close to mid-August, Prime Minister Modi had still not named members for the Planning Commission. Notes had been moving back and forth between the PMO and the planning ministry about what the structure of the Planning Commission was, what its functions were, how its members were appointed, what their perks were, and so on.[182] But there was no movement on reconstituting the panel.

Around 13 August, the PMO asked the ministry to draft a note for the cabinet proposing that the prime minister be given all authority to take such decisions as may be necessary with regard to the Planning Commission. The note was readied within twenty-four hours.

The cabinet headed by Modi met on 13 August. The proposal was taken up. Sindhushree Khullar, secretary, Planning Commission, briefed the assembled ministers about why it was time for the Planning Commission to be 'transformed'.[183]

In the discussion that followed, nearly every minister present spoke. Harsimrat Kaur, Smriti Irani, Sushma Swaraj, Arun Jaitley . . .

'Each and every one of them spoke. Almost everyone said, yes, what a hopeless institution the Planning Commission was. They talked down to the officers,' recalls someone who was at the meeting.[184]

Two of the most experienced ministers, Arun Jaitley and Sushma Swaraj, said the matter should be put to Parliament.

Modi was quiet.

A suggestion was made to him, '*Aap pandrah August ko announce kar dijiye . . .* [You should announce this on 15 August.]'

That was it.

The cabinet approved the repeal of the cabinet resolution dated 15 March 1950 by which the Planning Commission had been constituted, and authorized the prime minister to take the further steps necessary.

The cabinet would go on to frequently and unflinchingly vest its authority in the prime minister and approve post facto the decisions taken by him, from easing of FDI caps to placement of orders for Rafale fighter jets. The bill for amending the Constitution to pave the way for the roll-out of the GST would be taken up for approval by the cabinet on a day the finance minister would be away on a private visit to Nainital. Urjit Patel's elevation as the RBI's twenty-fourth governor would be announced one August evening in 2016, when the finance minister was on board a Mumbai-Delhi flight.

15 August 2014

On India's sixty-eighth Independence Day, from the ramparts of the Red Fort, Modi sounded the death knell of the sixty-four-year-old commission, couching the announcement of its fate in sharp critique and the contraries of reverent gratitude and irreverent metaphor.[185]

I believe that when Planning Commission was constituted, it was done on the basis of the circumstances and the needs of those times.

So, I am saying from the ramparts of the Red Fort that it is a very old system and it will have to be rejuvenated, it will have to be changed a lot. Sometimes it costs more to repair the old house, but it gives us no satisfaction. Thereafter, we have a feeling that it would be better to construct a new house altogether and, therefore, within a short period, we will replace the Planning Commission with a new institution having a new design and structure, a new body, a new soul, a new thinking, a new direction, a new faith towards forging a new direction to lead the country, based on creative thinking, public-private partnership, optimum utilization of resources, utilization of youth power of the nation, to promote the aspirations of state governments seeking development, to empower the state governments and to empower the federal structure. Very shortly, we are about to move in a direction when this institute would be functioning in place of Planning Commission.

In a literal break from the past, Modi had dispensed with the bulletproof screen from behind which his predecessors had delivered their Independence Day speeches.[186]

Wearing a white kurta and flowing saffron turban that would become his trademark over the years, he spoke extempore and described himself as a Delhi 'outsider'; and not as the prime minister, but as the 'prime servant'.[187]

This national festival is an occasion to refine and rebuild the national character . . . whether it is the poison of casteism, communalism, regionalism, discrimination on social and economic basis, all these are obstacles in our way forward. Let's resolve . . . let's put a moratorium on all such activities for ten years, we shall march ahead to a society which will be free from all such tensions.[188]

He expressed gratitude to all previous governments and former prime ministers, and invoked the national leaders of the past, like

Mahatma Gandhi, Sardar Patel and Jai Prakash Narayan, but made not a single reference to Nehru.

Another slogan he raised in this speech for the first time was 'Make in India'—a precursor to an umbrella programme, which, he said, would bring together industry and government to craft a new future. He invited global companies to pick India to locate their factories in, promising to replace red tape with red-carpet welcomes. The jobs and incomes for Indians these factories would generate, he said, would in turn create the market for their output.

> We will have to lay stress on the manufacturing sector. I want to urge all the countries, come, make in India.[189]

Barring nagging conflicting views over the omission of Nehru and the allegory of 'an old house', the speech was well-received. Charmed, the country seemed suffused with a sense of hope, and on the cusp of a great new future.

26 August 2014

The process of building a new institution picked up pace and energy. Experts, ex-members of the Planning Commission and other eminent persons were invited to Yojana Bhawan to brainstorm on the role, functions and structure of the new institution. Discussions were conducted in two separate groups in two separate rooms.[190] In the first group, informally called the 'seniors', were N.K. Singh, the late Saumitra Chaudhuri, Yashwant Sinha, Bimal Jalan, T.N. Ninan, Vijay Kelkar, Y.K. Alagh, Nitin Desai and M.J. Akbar. Most of them submitted written papers. As did Montek and R.R. Shah, who were invited to the session but could not be present. In the other room were the nine invitees of the second group—the 'younger lot'—among them Rajiv Kumar. The group, and Kumar in particular, felt sidelined. But Kumar would, in time, become the most recognizable face of the new institution.

The main recommendation that emerged from this consultation was that elimination of poverty and provision of basic services should be the new institution's main focus.[191] Its role should not be limited to the financial resources of the government sector. Rather, it should provide policy inputs in the key areas of energy, water, land use, environment, transportation, urbanization, trade and investment. The institution needed to be conceptualized as an effective interface between the centre and the states.

The unanimous view was that allocation of annual plan resources to the states should be transferred to the finance ministry and that the devolution of funds to the states from the divisible pool of taxes collected by the centre must remain a function of the Finance Commission. At the same time, grave concerns were expressed over the limited capacity of the finance ministry for appreciating qualitatively the imperatives of development. The ministry tends to be focused on annual budget making and looks for the easiest options for slashing expenditure to manage fiscal imbalances. So transferring the allocation function to it would undeniably mean that the benefit of an independent and even adversarial perspective of prioritizing development expenditure would not be available to the prime minister. The Economic Development Board of Korea, the Planning Body of Singapore and the National Development and Reform Commission of China were suggested as role models.

The new institution, it was suggested, could be modelled on the National Security Council, with a national economic adviser serving in the PMO. The Economic Advisory Council could be subsumed into this body.

Among the suggestions for its name were: Development Commission, Sustainable Development Commission, National Development Advisory Board and Agency for Planning, Development and Reforms.

A consultation conducted on social media received more than 4000 responses, including suggestions for the logo.

There were consultations with senior members of the cabinet, with eminent personalities such as Yashwant Sinha and BJP President Amit Shah, who spoke very little, emphasizing the special needs of coastal states, including Gujarat.[192] His point was that clusters of states ought to be formed based on common geographical features for effective programme implementation. None of Sinha's or anyone's advice in the brainstorming influenced the course of decision-making.[193]

'After the government was formed, the only interaction for which I was invited was when they were abolishing the Planning Commission . . . I got a call from the prime minister's office saying that he was going to take a meeting. I was asked to submit my recommendations in writing, which I did, and none of the recommendations were [taken on board],' Yashwant Singh told me in an interview.[194]

7 December 2014

On this day Modi held a day-long retreat with chief ministers and Lt governors of union territories to discuss the role and responsibilities of the new institution.[195] Most of them were very critical of the by-now scrapped Planning Commission's processes, even though some of these grievances were extremely trivial. Their biggest complaint was that they were not given a place on the dais at the National Development Council (NDC) meetings while 'bureaucrats' got to sit beside the prime minister. The reference was to Montek Singh Ahluwalia, who has had the longest unbroken tenure as deputy chairman (July 2004–June 2014) of the Planning Commission, and was the only bureaucrat in its history to hold that position. The irritant was the seating arrangement for the NDC meetings held in the main auditorium of Vigyan Bhawan. On the dais would be seated the prime minister, who was the chairman of the Planning Commission, along with the deputy chairman, the finance minister and the secretary, Planning Commission. Sitting there, they faced the rest of the gathering, comprising state chief ministers, with their entourage, and central and state officials. 'The dominant feeling was that they [the chief ministers] were being looked down upon, and talked down to,' says a former high functionary of the Planning Commission.[196]

When a big institution cracks, it doesn't crack on its big failures. It cracks on bruised egos and status symbols. The format of the interactions was the issue with the chief ministers and not so much the substance. The processes could be changed. Fifty to sixty years of central planning had boiled down to objections to the seating layout.

Modi, a former chief minister himself, understood the resentment well. In all his meetings with chief ministers, every participant would be given a place at tables of the same height. '*Disha sahee hai* [the direction is fine],' Modi said in his concluding remarks at the meeting of the chief ministers during the day-long retreat.[197]

Unexpectedly again, immediately after Christmas, the planning ministry was told to draft the resolution for the setting up of the new institution. Sindhushree Khullar told B.V.R. Subrahmanyam, who was Prime Minister Manmohan Singh's private secretary in UPA-1 and joint secretary in his PMO in UPA-2 and had been retained by Modi in his PMO, 'The grandeur of the Nehruvian English of the Cabinet resolution for setting up the Planning Commission has to be matched . . . It is a model of Nehruvian vision.'[198]

On 29 December at 3 p.m., the cabinet met. Modi made a brief opening remark to his ministers about the *praroop* (draft) of the *niti nirdharak* (policy-determining institution) that would supplant the scrapped Planning Commission.[199] The resolution for setting up the new institution was thus approved.

Till then referred to as NI for New Institution, a name had to be finalized now. Many names had been floated in the PMO. Reforms Commission was the very first recommendation, but it was too close to the Chinese NDRC (National Development and Reform Commission). Nripendra Misra, principal secretary to the prime minister, had come up with Rashtriya Vikas Evam Navnirman Sansthan, the Hindi translation of National Development and Transformation Commission. He couldn't settle on an appropriate Hindi word for 'transformation', though.[200] Finally, the PMO settled on 'National Institution for Transforming India'. Or, in short, NITI, which struck the acronym-bedevilled and Sanskrit-obsessed regime as a name by itself. In Sanskrit, *niti* can mean morality, behaviour, guidance, politics, management, and so on.[201] But here it stood, quite appropriately, for policy. So, Aayog was added to the name, though having both 'Institution' and 'Aayog' or 'Sanstha' in the name was redundant.

On the last day of 2014, the planning ministry was told to speak to Arvind Panagariya, Bibek Debroy and V.K. Saraswat, and make arrangements for their appointment as vice chairman and members of the NITI Aayog, respectively.[202]

The resolution setting up the NITI Aayog reads like a fairly confused, hurriedly compiled patchwork, combining inspirational quotes with some of the ideas that had already been floated in the Modi government's maiden Economic Survey presented just a few months earlier (discussed earlier in this book).[203]

'What we got was all hotchpotch,' says an officer who was involved in setting up the NITI Aayog.[204] 'No one knows who had drafted it.'

The sloppiness in the resolution's drafting suggests that it could not have been prepared by an IAS officer, the PMO secretariat or even the think tanks closely identified with the government, such as Ram Madhav's India Foundation or the Vivekananda Foundation.

There would be more such specimens of inattentive drafting going forward. The draftsmen and draftswomen of the notes on policy pronouncements most important to the prime minister would remain a mystery even to the senior-most IAS officers in government.

'. . . told us, just do it, as it has to be immediately notified. So we called the PIB Chief and released it the way it was,' the official says.

The Rise and Fall of NITI Aayog

1 January 2015

On the first day of 2015, Modi approved the resolution setting up the NITI Aayog, which was to supplant the Planning Commission, the Nehruvian vestige that had witnessed the ups and downs of the economy, as too of the prime ministers who had led it. The new institution was tasked with the role of formulating policy and providing direction to the government.

The resolution invoked the words of Mahatma Gandhi, Swami Vivekananda and B.R. Ambedkar.[205] Modi tweeted that through the NITI Aayog, the country was bidding farewell to a 'one-size-fits-all' approach to development.[206] The body, he wrote, celebrates India's diversity and plurality.

The cabinet resolution for replacing the scrapped Planning Commission expanded on the ideological turn rightwards that had already debuted in the Economic Survey. Modi's cabinet resolved to adopt a 'Bharatiya' model for development and reform governance to diminish the role of the state as a player in industrial and service sectors, in particular. India needs an administration paradigm in which the government is an enabler rather than a provider of first and last resort, the resolution said. The Aayog, conceived as a think tank, was to recommend a national economic agenda. It was to provide strategic and technical advice, develop mechanisms for village-level plans and aggregate these progressively at higher levels of government. But what the 'Bharatiya' approach to development was going to be, how it would be a break from the past, and other such details were never fleshed out.

Like good '*chamchas*',[207] the first thing the scrapped Planning Commission's secretariat did was to get the signage 'Yojana Bhawan' outside its building on Parliament Street in Delhi changed overnight. It was pulled down and 'NITI Aayog' put up. New Delhi Municipal Council (NDMC) was asked to change the road signage urgently, which it did.

The main conference hall had a photograph of Nehru signing the Third Plan (all the Nehru Plans are signed.) Next to it, a photograph of the same size of Modi signing documents immediately after taking over as prime minister was hung up.

There was metaphor in the ritual. There would always be meticulous attention to detail in the bandobast by the Modi government. But the content and substance would rarely receive as much attention.

In early February, the first meeting of the NITI Aayog's governing council was held.[208] It comprised the prime minister, the chief ministers of all the states and of union territories with legislatures, the lieutenant governor of Andaman and Nicobar Islands, four Union ministers as ex-officio members and three Union ministers as special invitees. The council was tasked with evolving a shared vision of national development priorities.

A kitschy banner in dull white across which was written 'TEAM INDIA' in large deep-blue letters could be seen hanging on the wall behind the prime minister, who sat surrounded by central government officials and ministers, and the visitors from the states. The banner reminiscent of cricket, the seating arrangement and the brand-new slogan, 'cooperative federalism', that Modi gave at this meeting, were all part of his symbolic overture to staunch the chief ministers' shared animus against the paternalism of the Planning Commission.

The second meeting was called on 15 July, principally to orchestrate a view among states on the land acquisition law.[209] Land-owning farmers were upset over a bill introduced by the Modi government in Parliament to dilute the amendments to this legislation carried out by the UPA government in 2013. The move had left even the NDA's allies, the Akalis in Punjab among them, tied up in knots. Seizing initiative, Congress Vice President Rahul Gandhi had called the regime a *'suit-boot ki sarkar'* on the floor of the Lower House. The epithet had stuck.

Against this backdrop, to control the damage, a decision had been reached beforehand with the allies that dilution of amendments would be left to the states. The climbdown was dressed up as a consensus in response to the demands of the states at the platform of the governing council meeting. This was the first and the last time that there was even a semblance of a so-called meeting of the governing council.

A 'vision' document was unveiled at the third meeting on 23 April 2017.[210] After the day of its release, it was never heard of again.

The coup de grâce was long overdue.[211] From a highly centralized planning system, the transition to indicative planning had been made since the advent of the Eighth Five-Year Plan (1992–97). The halcyon days of centralized planning were over. The commission, as conceived by Nehru, had outlived its utility. No longer the exalted institution it once was, its relevance had been in question for long. The need for reimagining it had been expressed as early as in the 1980s, when Rajiv Gandhi famously called the commission members 'a bunch of jokers'.[212]

As prime minister, Manmohan Singh had asked Montek Singh Ahluwalia to make the commission relevant and responsive to the changed economic needs of the country. It must become a 'systems reform commission', an 'essay in persuasion', he had said.[213] In other words, the role he saw for it was of a change agent championing reforms.

In his Yojana Bhawan office, 'walking about in socks, without shoes, he [Ahluwalia] showed me cupboards full of reports. Then he told me that on every subject the Commission had the best know-how and yet it can't make things happen,' former commission member Arun Maira retold in 2011 Ahluwalia's frustration with the commission's ineffectiveness.[214]

Ahluwalia kicked off a process for arriving at what he called 'a new way of planning' in his second consecutive term. The failed redirection—the fifth or sixth such attempt since the 1980s—coincided with the preparation of the Twelfth Five-Year Plan.

It didn't help that the erudite Ahluwalia was no favourite of political leaders in the states or of the ministries at the centre. For instance, the minister for roads and highways, Kamal Nath, openly resented the plan panel as a set of nosy armchair advisers who were accountable to no one.

Nath, agitated over the panel's insistence on a certain standard for awarding contracts to road makers, said in early 2009, 'Certainly you can have a view but accountability rests with my ministry. People in Parliament question me, I have to answer them, not the Planning Commission.'[215]

The plan panel's release of funds to ministries and states had been made conditional on reforms, which was a sure way of devaluing the advice to carry out the recommended reforms. An 'I-give-you-money-you-do-this' sort of arrangement ran contrary to the real world of consultancy, where consultants and think tanks charge heavily for giving advice.

The panel's record with the states was no better. Bihar had to wait until November 2009 for Ahluwalia's maiden visit as deputy chairman to Patna. Chief Minister Nitish Kumar greeted him with sharp words over the controversy about the number of BPL (below poverty line) families in the state: 'You are the Deputy Chairman of Planning Commission and your little blessing will be of great help to this state . . . Now you tell me, you say there are 72 lakh BPL families, our survey says there are 1.5 crore BPL families . . . Is it possible to delete the names of families from our survey list?'[216]

The pressure to reform the commission, especially its fund allocation role, kept mounting. C. Rangarajan, chairman of the Economic Advisory Council to Prime Minister Singh, had been asked to head a High Level Expert Committee to look at better management of public expenditure, including a plan for the abolition of Plan and Non-Plan expenditure and a better structure for allocating funds from the centre to the states.

In July 2011, this committee said the Plan-Non-Plan distinction was 'dysfunctional and an obstacle in outcome-based budgeting'.[217] It recommended moving public expenditure from a single-year to a multi-year horizon for better results. Some of the committee recommendations were carried out by the Modi government.

It was clear that the commission had to move towards thought leadership, coaching and guidance of a quality that states would want to pay for. The relationship had to be as with clientele, like many other think tanks and research outfits Nehru had raised. The National Council for Applied Economic Research (NCAER) is one such example.

Ahluwalia could not deliver.

The task for the builders of the new institution, Modi and Panagariya, was clear. The economic reforms of the 1990s had transformed India from a low-income country to a middle-income one. But to become a high-income country, India needed to liberalize the economy much further. Sectors untouched by reforms, such as land, natural resources and labour, needed to be liberalized. The provision of public goods—police, judiciary, general administration, healthcare, education and infrastructure—had not kept pace with the rate at which improvements in economic performance were taking place. Capacities for governance and delivery in institutions needed to be strengthened, while administrative reforms were pending. The economy needed strategies for creating millions of jobs and the launch and implementation of second-generation reforms, because we were now ready to make a break with the past.

Globally, a number of aspiring market economies that had retained faith in planning had progressed impressively. After its market-oriented economic reforms began, China's planning instruments have become even more powerful. Its manufacturing success is backed by an industrial policy driven by its NDRC.

But the NITI Aayog's approach has been far too granular to perform any such role. It was tasked with defining a new poverty line but could not. In the absence of an accountability structure, and riddled with weak leadership, the NITI Aayog did not take off, illustrating the gap between the rhetoric in the speeches of Modi and his ministers and execution. The NITI Aayog could neither play a role in setting the agenda nor influence policies with long-term consequences: demonetization and the design of the rate structure and collection systems of the GST, for instance. Instead, it functioned as a public relations machine for the government, in particular for the prime minister, praising the political bosses, spinning the negatives into positives, and exaggerating the positives. This approach frequently landed it in controversies—such as in 2018 when it got involved in the computation of a set of GDP estimates by the Central Statistics Office drawing severe criticism[218] to itself, and in the process, lowering the credibility of the Indian statistics. These estimates (computed using new data sources and methodology and with an updated base year) showed lower GDP growth in the UPA years than previously estimated. Earlier, in 2015, the NITI Aayog had blocked the release of a similar computation for the same years that had showed faster growth in the UPA years.[219]

For a new institution to make its mark, two things are needed: direction from the chairperson and the choice of the person who will establish it. The NITI Aayog, like the Planning Commission, is not a constitutional body, which means it too is not accountable to Parliament. This made the role of the vice chairperson in shaping the institution's agenda all the more crucial. The builder of an institution has to compromise, juggle a whole lot of contradictory elements, and work with whatever is available in the beginning. If the vice chairperson is sidestepped, then it gets difficult for an institution to find its feet.

The direction, vision, philosophy and role of the institution were not planned in advance. Instead, the focus was merely on the bandobast of rolling it out. The prime minister never said what he wanted from the NITI Aayog. For the Aayog, it became impossible to figure out what the prime minister wanted. The mandate given through the prime minister's interactions with the officials involved was that the new institution should 'not look like Planning Commission, should not talk like Planning Commission, and should not walk like Planning Commission . . . So, the mandate was about what not to have,' says the functionary who was involved in setting up the NITI Aayog.[220] 'The best expression of intent was the prime minister's 15 August speech. "Get rid of the Planning Commission" was the single-line mandate.'

The choice of Panagariya to helm the institution as its vice chairman served a purpose. To have a big name from a reputed university head a new institution gave it credibility. Panagariya's access to the prime minister was restricted, whether on instructions from Modi or the controlling powers in the PMO one does not know. It did not help that he stayed at the Ashoka Hotel in the initial months, even as the government was trying to make up its mind as to whether or not the position of the vice chairman should be of cabinet minister rank, as was that of the deputy chairman of the Planning Commission, entitling him to a type VII or VIII bungalow and the attendant perks. Then, when Panagariya did finally move into an official residence, the first thing that happened was that his nameplate outside the gate was stolen, triggering a fresh round of decision-making about the category of security that should be accorded to him . . . how many guards and what sort of security . . .

Panagariya, an academic, could not build relationships in the bureaucracy and the circles of influence, which were necessary to float a new institution that would have to negotiate the complexities of the country's federal structure, multiparty political system, the growing economic and policy challenges. The skills required for this would go beyond the ability to apply the principles of market economy. In July 2017, Panagariya wrote to the prime minister requesting that he be relieved of his position.[221] Rajiv Kumar, who had been in the 'junior room' consultations for the institution, succeeded him.

Neither could give a purposeful direction to the stalled reforms process.

The Planning Commission, much like other institutions Nehru built, had brand recall. On retirement from the IAS, Amitabh Kant was brought in to build brand 'NITI Aayog', calculated to have been key to building the prime minister's image of being an 'institution-builder'. Before he arrived at the Aayog, Kant's record was of a tremendous marketeer who had built globally recognized brands, like 'God's own country', 'Incredible India' and 'Make In India'. 'NITI Aayog' as a brand could not make it to the Kant league, though. Perhaps because, to build a brand, the content of the brand must be clearly spelt out, which in this case just hadn't been.

The other reason NITI Aayog couldn't quite take off was Modi's disinterest in institutions and his disinclination for intellectual inputs. 'On the ground, he's very practical. He listens. But he has no patience with intellectual inputs or with a strategic forward-looking approach,' says a retired IAS officer who worked with him.[222] Economists and commentators have argued ad nauseum about why economics were not able to guide policy better during the Modi regime. Some blame it on the wrong choice of economic advisers. Others see a sheer absence of economics and a preference solely for politics. The story of the NITI Aayog is reduced, sadly, to a former chief minister coming to power at the centre and swiftly demolishing an institution that he felt had hampered, rather than supported, his state's growth. But he could not leverage the general disillusionment, shared even by Ahluwalia and Singh, with the commission, to formalize a new way of planning. Relegating the Planning Commission to history remains just a symbolic takeover of the set-up in Delhi. It could become the anchor for ideological policy, or even attitudinal change. But the new institution fails to convey what it even stands for, and what convictions guide it. Barring Modi's picture next to Nehru's in the conference room of the building, it bears no impression of Modi or his thinking.

Said economist Vijay Kelkar, who was formerly a finance secretary and chairman of the Thirteenth Finance Commission, on the setting up of the NITI Aayog,

> The Constitution and creative democratic politics addressed these [growth imbalances, the stock of physical and social infrastructure that gets accumulated over time] issues by creating the two institutions, the Finance Commission and the Planning Commission. The Finance Commission derives its raison de etre from Articles 275, 280 and their sub-clauses to meet horizontal and vertical imbalance [across states], whereas the political process had leveraged Article 282 to create the Planning Commission.[223]

In post-colonial India, these institutions were used to carry out systematic fiscal transfers in the nature of devolutions or conditional transfers. The Fourteenth Finance Commission headed by former RBI Governor Y.V. Reddy gave a sharp increase in the percentage share of taxes devolved to the states whilst virtually in effect eliminating conditional transfers via Planning Commission grants or grants under central sector/sponsored schemes. It recommended an increase in the share of states in the centre's tax revenue from 32 per cent to 42 per cent—the single largest increase ever recommended by a Finance Commission.[224] From a total devolution of approximately Rs 3.48 lakh crore in 2014–15, the total devolution to the states in 2015–16 shot up to Rs 5.26 lakh crore approximately.[225] Plus, it gave power to states to determine how they could spend this money.[226]

Said Kelkar:

> The collapsing of two different sources of transfers, aimed at differing objectives, is deeply problematic . . . There are different

types of imbalances . . . One has to do with the differing levels of per-capita consumption of basic public goods and services. The other has to do with the differing levels of stock of infrastructure leading the differential growth-accelerating potential. These are two distinct policy goals and warrant two distinct policy instruments . . . This approach, if not reviewed, can lead to a serious problem of increasing regional and sub-regional inequities.[227]

Eliminating the Planning Commission and replacing it with the NITI Aayog merely as a think tank leaves only one instrument; namely the Finance Commission. Kelkar recommended that the NITI Aayog be given significant levels of resources for allocation to states. The resource transfers, he argued, were required for mitigating growth imbalances and for reducing the developmental gap by promoting the accelerated growth of lagging states and subregions. Given the political economy, these grants need to be conditional and formulaic. The purpose of these grants would be to enable the lagging states to build capacities in infrastructure sectors such as roads, ports, railway networks, digital connectivity, supply of power, and access to credit and improving governance.

Kelkar said:

By nature of its mandate, the ministry of finance is primarily concerned not with structural transformation but rather with the issues related to short/medium-term macroeconomic stability, including managing balance of payments, inflation and business cycle.

Elsewhere he reiterated his view:[228]

I would argue that replacing the Planning Commission, which was promoting regionally balanced growth in India, by NITI Aayog, a Think Tank, has reduced the Government's Policy reach.

In 2014, the economy Narendra Modi inherited was recovering from severe macroeconomic shocks and a growth slowdown. As growth gradually bottomed out, there was fresh momentum, with the period from 2012–13 to 2015–16 witnessing annual growth rates of 5.5 per cent, 6.4 per cent, 7.4 per cent and 8.2 per cent.[229] The delays in addressing the banking sector's problems, in particular, and the debilitating impact of demonetization and the poorly designed GST rates and collection systems would start slowing down growth again from 2015–16 onwards.

The Modi wave had unleashed tremendous hope and energy, but it did not translate into a coherent plan of action for economic revival. The Union cabinet had sanctioned a sharp turn rightwards, articulated first in the Economic Survey, through its resolution to scrap the Planning Commission and replace the Nehruvian vestige with the NITI Aayog. The new institution was directed to formulate a 'Bharatiya' model in which the state would take on a curtailed role, with limited presence and influence in the industrial and services sectors.

The plan for unfettered markets would remain confined to its 'Section' chapter of the NITI Aayog. In early 2015, Modi's governance agenda began veering leftwards. His speeches took on a sharp pro-poor rhetoric too.

4

Another Recovery Destroyed (2016–18)

Modi had inherited a bad bank loans problem that he liked to call the 'phone-a-loan' scam. This referred to the flurry of investments that had been made on over-optimistic assumptions by companies, after the worst of the financial crisis had been dodged in 2008–09.

During Pranab Mukherjee's tenure as finance minister, not letting the economy slip into a slowdown had become a convenient excuse for North Block to issue oral instructions to PSBs.

North Block's mistake had been in pushing PSBs, untrained to assess long-term project finance, to lend, which they did somewhat indiscriminately, for infrastructure projects. The RBI's analysis showed that maximum NPAs were in fact in loans to industry and infrastructure.[1] Some of the bank losses and NPAs were also on account of fraud. In many cases, such as the Nirav Modi fraud that came to light as late as in early 2018, these were daylight bank robberies besides the wilful defaulters—companies that had defaulted on bank loan repayments even though they or their promoters had the ability to repay, or promoters who had siphoned off the money or put it to some other use than what was agreed on.

The lending was not all to dubious projects, although some may certainly have been out of malfeasance (yet to be established in a court of law). A majority of the projects that turned unviable had been hobbled by delays and depressed demand because of policy paralysis and slower-than-expected growth, including during the tenure of the Modi government. Banks' forbearance on the genuinely viable projects was a bet that growth would revive and they would come back on track. But corporate performance was rather bad in 2011 and 2012.[2] Despite Pranab Mukherjee's asset stimulus, corporate investments (as measured by growth of corporate gross capital formation) crashed from 29.6 per cent a year to virtually zero between 2008–09 and 2012–13. Slowing GDP growth, the delayed authorization of permits for infrastructure projects and the rising cost of capital were placing pressures on corporate profitability, which in turn had slowed down private investments.

Banks and Their Bad Loans

By 2013, the average corporate leverage and debt payment capacity were not markedly worse than during the global financial crisis, but default probabilities of the most vulnerable 10 per cent of firms were far greater than in 2009.[3] This vulnerability was further aggravated by concentration risk: banking-sector loans to the ten largest conglomerates added up to almost 100 per cent of the banks' net worth. The banking system was well capitalized (the capital adequacy ratio was 13.8 per cent in March 2013), but NPAs (4.2 per cent of total advances) and restructured loans (an additional 5.7 per cent of gross advances) were projected to continue to rise. The deterioration in credit quality was worse among public banks where lending is concentrated in the poorer-performing sectors of infrastructure, such as and especially power, aviation, agriculture, steel and textiles. New capital injections for banks (to meet Basel III requirements and additional capital requirements due to restructured loans being reclassified as NPAs) were likely to be manageable.

Besides the rupee's troubles and inflation management, in his September 2013 opening statement Rajan had also indicated that the RBI was studying the rising NPAs and the restructuring recovery process so that the corrective measures needed could be taken.

'The bad loan problem is not alarming yet but it will only fester and grow if left unaddressed,' he had said, announcing some of the steps he planned to take to avert a crisis.[4]

His initiatives will bring him into a simmering conflict with the habitual bank loans defaulters in India's big-businesses community.

To tackle the rising strain on the financial system and to improve the functioning of financial intermediation more broadly, the RBI tightened its monitoring and supervision of banks' credit quality in 2013 and asked banks to further increase provisioning. Incremental provisioning and capital requirements for bank lending to corporates with foreign-currency exposures were introduced.

It was soon discovered that, as had been suspected, banks were indulging in the classic behaviour seen in a banking system with balance sheet problems.[5] RBI discovered discrepancies between what banks had reported as NPAs and its own assessment. It was also found that a massive chunk of dud loans lay with just ten large borrowers, and that a significant portion of the NPAs at the PSBs pertained to projects that were still viable. These projects had not gone through to completion for reasons mostly extraneous, such as problems in land acquisition or environmental clearance. With restructuring and additional funding, they could have been completed and would create significant capacities, easing the supply-side bottlenecks in the economy.

The available recovery provisions[6] were proving ineffective, because of which bankers had very little power over large promoters. Of the outstanding debt of Rs 2,36,600 crore that needed to be recovered, barely Rs 30,590 crore was recovered by the Debt Recovery Tribunals (DRTs) in 2013–14.[7] That was just 13 per cent of the amount at stake. The law imposed a deadline of six months for disposal of cases before the DRT, but most cases went on for years. The rate of filing of cases was higher than the rate of disposal of cases, creating growing backlogs.

'Not only could they [promoters] play one lender against another by threatening to divert payments to the favoured bank, they could also refuse to pay unless the lender brought in more money, especially if the lender feared the loan becoming an NPA . . . Effectively, bank loans in such a system become equity, with a tough promoter enjoying the upside in good times, and forcing banks to absorb losses in bad times, even while he holds on to his equity,' Rajan wrote later in a note on NPAs to the Parliamentary Estimates Committee.[8]

In other words, while profits were private on the projects financed by these bankers, the losses were nationalized.

For sharper supervision of large exposures, the RBI created and shared a large database of borrowers, summarizing the status of each loan of over Rs 5 crore—whether it was performing, already an NPA or moving towards becoming an NPA. It served to flag early warning signs of distress. On the red flag going up on a loan, a Joint Lenders' Forum decided on an approach for its resolution. Incentives were built in for reaching quick decisions. Some improvement in the recovery mechanism for distressed debt was being attempted.

To stop the ever-greening of projects by banks who want to avoid recognizing losses, forbearance—the ability of banks to restructure a project without categorizing it as an NPA—was brought to an end in April 2015. Long-duration projects such as roads were restructured through a separate scheme.

India did not have a functional bankruptcy law. An efficient recovery system was not in place. So the RBI set up a resolution system comprising out-of-court bankruptcy processes. Through strategic debt restructuring (SDR), it allowed lender banks to convert debt into equity and displace weak promoters whose equity ownership was till then being protected by the judicial system, even when they did not bring in new funds. The idea was not that the banks would run these companies but that they would recover outstanding loans to the extent possible by selling the companies to new promoters.

Although Rajan and his team had effectively put in place a resolution system resembling an out-of-court system to deal with bankruptcy, and banks now had the power to resolve distress, the reluctance to conclude deals persisted.

So, while bad loans started getting recognized and showed up on the NPA account, resolution seriously lagged behind, leading to a pile-up of impaired bank balance sheets.

Banks still didn't write down the uncollectable loans, fearing that, in the atmosphere of heightened political attacks, activism in courts and the CAG, doing so would invite the attention of investigative agencies.

Instead, banks were simply extending bad loans by making additional loans so that the promoter could keep paying the interest and pretend it was not yet a non-performing loan. This was a convergence of everyone's interests; the promoter escaped adding equity, the bank avoided having to restructure and recognize losses or declare the loan an NPA and spoil profitability, and the government put off topping up the capital in banks.

In this way, as Rajan wrote, stalled projects continued as 'zombie'[9] projects, neither dead nor alive:

> In reality though, because the loan was actually non-performing, bank profitability was illusory, and the size of losses on its balance sheet were ballooning because no interest was actually coming in. Unless the project miraculously recovered on its own—and with only a few exceptions, no one was seriously trying to put it back on track—this was deceptive accounting. It postponed the day of reckoning into the future, but there would be such a day.[10]

The RBI's efforts were proving unequal to the task of getting the banks to recognize the full extent of the bad loans on their books. Even for loans that had stayed non-performing for a long time, banks were not provisioning adequately. Plus, they were slow to put projects back on track and had slowed credit growth. Without a clean-up, chances of their resuming credit were slim.

Finally, the RBI forced banks to comb their books for hidden bad loans. A dedicated team of supervisors completed the Asset Quality Review (AQR) in October 2015 and subsequently shared it with the banks. The Modi government was kept informed and consulted on every step. The AQR was initiated to stop the ever-greening and concealment of bad loans and force banks to revive stalled projects. The hope was that once the mass of bad loans was disclosed, the banks, with the aid of the government, would undertake the surgery that was necessary to put projects back on track.

Much of the hard work of repairing corporate balance sheets had to be done by the PSB bosses, and it included the restructuring and part-forgiving of loans. Many of the bank chiefs had inherited the mess from their predecessors. Many defaulting tycoons were politically connected, which was how they had landed the loans in the first place. Accepting that the defaulters were in no position to pay back, and waiving part of the debt, was sure to be seen as abetting crony capitalists and draw the eager attention of investigating agencies. It was easier for bankers to simply make no decision. Many of them extended the loans further to keep the borrower afloat so that interest payments would continue and the bank's balance sheets would not be soiled by a default. The losses in turn eroded their capital buffer.

Writing off loans would have been an option on the table if banks could foreclose on companies and convert unpaid loans into equity, which could then be sold to potential investors interested in good companies with bad balance sheets. But there was no proper bankruptcy code under which such resolutions could be carried out.

'Promoters do not have a divine right to stay in charge regardless of how badly they mismanage an enterprise, nor do they have the right to use the banking system to recapitalize their failed ventures,' Rajan had said in his opening speech.[11]

The intent was to ensure that everyone absorbed a fair share of the losses and that these did not fall entirely on the banks. Unfortunately, this process never played out as planned. It was bound to fail. Bankers still had no incentive to take decisions. Inaction precipitated the stress on the balance sheets of both banks and corporates. As NPAs age they require more provisioning, so projects that were not revived simply added to the stock of gross NPAs. A fair amount of the increase in NPAs was probably due to this ageing rather than as a result of a fresh lot of NPAs

In early 2014, ahead of the 2014 Lok Sabha elections, the annual Article IV consultations took place between IMF and finance ministry officials in Delhi and with Governor Rajan in Mumbai. Further measures in the areas of asset quality recognition and concentration risks were needed, the IMF had noted.

> The objective should be to fully recognize the true asset quality of banks' portfolios, with restructured loans counted toward non-performing assets immediately after a restructuring, and then moved to the performing bucket only after a period of satisfactory performance. This is of particular importance for the public sector banks. Moreover, all sectors of the economy (including infrastructure and real estate) should be subject to the same loan quality classification rules. This will require improvements in the legal and institutional insolvency framework, the regime for insolvency professionals, the functioning of the distressed asset market, and out-of-court settlement procedures.[12]

Although the NPAs were manageable, the IMF noted in that consultation, it was clear that the banks were going to require significant new capital injections over the next few years, based on the challenging operating environment, combined with the new Basel III capital requirements. The restructured advances were fast increasing. As of March 2013, they comprised 5.7 per cent of the banking system's gross advances, and 7.1 per cent of the PSBs' advances.[13]

'Restructured assets are usually not considered "non-performing" in India, and their rapid rise has led some observers to doubt the publicly displayed financial strength of many Indian banks,' the IMF had noted.[14]

The IMF stress-tested the banks' capital position for possibility of sudden deterioration in loan quality and evaluated the impact of Basel III requirements. It found the PSBs in particular to be vulnerable to a change in classification of a significant share of restructured loans to NPAs. Each bank's balance sheet was stressed individually, based on 45 per cent of restructured advances moving to NPAs, and it was assumed that both the PSBs' NPAs and their restructured loans would double. After this, three alternative provisioning ratio scenarios were assessed. In the most severe case, the government's share of the recapitalization cost was estimated at 5 per cent of the 2012–13 GDP.

A banking system staring at a possibility of capitalization needs growing to such a scale that it could not have powered a growth recovery. The stress in the banking system was, among other things, holding back the flow of credit. Stressed assets and unpaid loans had impaired the banks' lending ability. Because profits were eroded, PSBs, where the bulk of the bad loans sat, could not raise enough capital to fund credit growth. Without credit growth, the economy's return to a high-growth trajectory was difficult. It was crystal clear to the finance ministry that the bad-loan problem required urgent and effective resolution.

In the Article IV report in February 2014, the IMF had also cautioned that structural reforms were the only course of action available to India for anchoring an economic recovery and strengthening growth, since there was insufficient fiscal space for counter-cyclical stimulus. Its assessment would prove to be spot on.[15]

Twin Balance Sheet Crisis

When finance ministers rise to make budget speeches in the Lok Sabha, it is not widely recognized that these are a compilation of paragraphs drafted by various departments of government and autonomous regulators such as the RBI. Even if the initial ideas originate from the ruling political party or the PMO, or are the finance minister's, the drafting is done by bureaucrats and technocrats, from whom comes the substance of the budget speech.

For Jaitley's first budget, presented in July 2014, Finance Secretary Arvind Mayaram had drafted a paragraph with the aid of Additional Secretary K.P. Krishnan, Principal Economic Adviser Ila Patnaik and the IMF's Joshua Felman. Felman described the balance sheets of severely impaired banks and corporates as 'co-joined twins'.[16]

The economic consequences of the stress on the balance sheets of both banks and much of the corporate sector needed to be addressed on priority. Mayaram called this principal challenge to an economic rebound the 'twin balance sheet problem', an epithet Arvind Subramanian, who joined government a few months later, would popularize. A paragraph the economic affairs department prepared was included in the first draft of the finance minister's budget speech.

The political bosses, however, showed no appetite for the steps outlined in this paragraph.

And so a paragraph on this idea for dealing with MSME bankruptcy was smuggled into later drafts of the speech, through MSME Secretary Madhav Lal. Jaitley decided against restricting the bankruptcy proposal to only this category of firms. A Bankruptcy Law Reforms Committee was set up in August 2014 under T.K. Viswanathan, who had been law secretary in Vajpayee's government when Jaitley was the law minister. The Viswanathan Committee wrote the Insolvency and Bankruptcy Code within a month. By 31 October 2014 the first draft was in.

A sequence of events starting with the policy paralysis and the GDP growth slowdown to the Modi government's lack of interest in addressing the issues that were threatening to turn viable projects unviable, and therefore repayable loans into NPAs, had given rise to the spectre of the twin balance sheet problem. Resolving it needed a multipronged comprehensive policy approach. Speeding up of project approvals and building the GDP growth momentum was key to making sure that the projects would remain viable and the loans would continue to be serviced.

Each of the officials who had drafted the junked paragraphs for Jaitley's first budget speech was over time shunted out of the ministry. A high-profile IAS officer hand-picked to replace one of them was soon frustrated with the state of affairs. 'The government has no appetite for even small and easy-to-do reforms, forget the difficult ones . . . As far as I am concerned there are no half-reforms . . . But government is in "we-are-the-champions mode" and competing with the UPA in announcing schemes and programmes,' he told me in 2015.[17]

Although he later landed plum positions after retirement, at the time he expressed his exasperation with the prime minister's three-hour meetings on monitoring the progress of programmes and project implementation, though in a lighter vein. '[It was] really boring and the only thing to do was to polish off all the peanuts and chana! That's all that is served. I can vouch for the quality. They are the best.'

Then he added, 'All this incrementalism can't deliver 10 per cent growth.'

Another IAS officer who worked in the ministry of human development during Smriti Irani's tenure and had initially looked forward to coordinating with the RSS on their education agenda, within months found herself struggling with six questions that summed up the mood in the bureaucracy after their initial honeymoon with the new prime minister was over. These were:

'Why is the PM not in control? How is it possible?

'Why is he not fixing things?

'Why is he not getting rid of problematic people?

'Why is he not doing the obvious?

'Why are the most obvious policy decisions not taken?'

Every time officials were asked to list reforms that should be taken up, the department of economic affairs and financial services raised the NPA issue, but there was no buy-in from the political bosses. Bureaucrats were told in as many words that privatization of loss-making PSBs was simply out of the question, and committing too much tax money for bank recapitalization would be politically suicidal.

'Bank NPA reforms didn't sound sexy enough at the time. The minister would just lose interest the minute NPAs were talked about. There was no intent,' recalls an official then in the finance ministry.[18]

The government's attention would flit about and it would focus on other ideas instead. The agenda would soon be fraught with contradictions and gaps in thinking.

Barely two months after the cabinet sanctioned establishment of the NITI Aayog as a successor to the Nehruvian Planning Commission and directed it to formulate a 'Bharatiya' model, the 2015 budget was presented. It was the Modi government's second budget.

Modi Turns to a Nehruvian Strategy for Growth

The budget, trading in ideologies for pragmatism, reprised the Nehruvian strategy for growth: building physical capital with public investments.[19]

Finance Minister Arun Jaitley allocated Rs 70,000 crore for roads and railways. The Modi government had chosen to ignore the investment slowdown and the twin balance sheet problem that was guaranteed to blow up into an NPA crisis. It decided to concentrate its energies instead on an infrastructure push. The architect of this plan for accelerating growth was Chief Economic Adviser Arvind Subramanian.

Subramanian's infrastructure push was not altogether a new idea. The difference lay in its funding strategies. The UPA government too had wanted to focus on creation of physical capital as a source of growth, but with a role for the private sector. Its preferred model of financing infrastructure development, as enshrined in the Twelfth Plan document, were public-private partnerships (PPP). During Pranab Mukherjee's term in North Block in particular, PSBs were encouraged to lend for infrastructure projects. That 'asset stimulus' was, in part, responsible for the growing NPA problem and its economy-wide consequence—an investment slowdown. Now, balance sheets of both banks and borrowers were reeling under mountains of unpaid debt. The stress on corporate balance sheets ruled out PPPs. The challenge was that companies had no money to invest. The Modi government took recourse to tax money for its plans of infrastructure building—going against the counsel of the IMF that had cautioned of the ineffectiveness of a fiscal push for strengthening the economic recovery underway and recommended a strategy comprising reform instead.

Following Subramanian's proposition, the Modi government stepped up its public investments, even deferring fiscal deficit targets, but the decline in private investments was so sharp that the increases in government investments could not offset it. The stimulus Subramanian designed—Rs 70,000 crore of public investment for building infrastructure to stimulate private investments—proved insufficient to generate the growth impulses needed to kick-start the over $2 trillion economy and rekindle the animal spirits numbed by policy paralysis and corruption scandals during UPA's second stint.

The steps taken for improving the ease of doing business and the foreign investments regime proved insufficient for restarting the private investment cycle. Private investments remained unresponsive to the macroeconomic stimulus administered through budget allocations. Decreasing for the fifth straight year, the share of gross fixed capital formation in GDP shrunk to 27.1 per cent in 2016–17. It had been 34.3 per cent in 2011–12.[20]

No major growth push materialized, even as the investment climate soured further. The private investments could not have revived with the twin balance sheet problem remaining unresolved.

The brewing NPA crisis was being flagged in every review and agenda-setting meeting at the PMO and the finance ministry. Financial Services Secretary Hasmukh Adhia's presentation to the prime minister detailed in the strongest possible terms the crying need for corrective action in PSBs: the quicker the banking sector recovered its health, the speedier a pullback in the overall economy could be expected. It was clear that the stress, if unattended, would limit the effectiveness of the monetary support of lower interest rates—the Reserve Bank would go on to announce cuts adding up to 125 basis points in twelve months in its key interest rate.[21] The finance ministry officials, including the government's own publication, the Economic Survey, would routinely caution about the 'twin balance sheet problem'.

But the government was not moved to show the urgency needed to address the mess. The banks' capital buffers kept depleting as the loan defaults rose and NPAs aged. When capital is provided, there is enough to cover losses and finance credit growth.[22] Growth in credit, in turn, creates profit that can be ploughed back in to capital. But after RBI's AQR led to NPAs becoming unhidden, the government did not move swiftly to provide capital. In August 2015, it announced an infusion of Rs 70,000 crore over a four-year period. Next, as late as October 2017, it announced further infusion of Rs 1.35 trillion. Again, not in one go but spread over time. And therefore the infusions could only cover losses. In fact, 70 per cent of capital infusion was absorbed into losses. The recapitalization could not therefore provide for credit growth that may have generated profits. Banks and borrowers both lost out.

Bank lending to industry had grown in excess of 20 per cent year on year during 2006–11.[23]

The capital infusion announced by the government was a small fraction of the estimates the IMF and ratings agencies such as Fitch had said would be needed to get the banking sector on an even keel.

The projections quoted earlier in the IMF's stress tests for the banks' capital position in the event of sudden deterioration had thrown up startling numbers. But the peril of severe capital erosion of banks failed to move the government on the banks' problems. The government's dithering proved costly for the economy. Banks' lending capacities remained restricted. The credit crunch further choked private investments, and the economic recovery under way was stalled—the third time a recovery was destroyed.

The IMF's annual Article IV consultations report issued in March 2016 flagged the NPA issue:

> Public Sector Banks' capital needs are estimated to account for 2.9 per cent of (2018-19) GDP (cumulatively over the next four years) . . . Full recognition of risks on PSBs' balance sheets, adequate capitalization, and further governance reforms are critical for strengthening the banking sector going forward.[24]

Thankfully, the 'most severe case' scenario of the IMF's earlier projections had not materialized, but fundamental reform of the banking sector was needed on a war footing. Without reforms, any other action would have been like standing at Chernobyl and seeing they've restarted the reactor but still have the same old management.[25]

Rajan Calls Quits

Even before Modi was sworn in, the discomfort with Raghuram Rajan and his policies among the BJP and its affiliates was evident from statements issued by Subramaniam Swamy and a host of others. At the helm at RBI since 2013, Rajan had successfully brought stability to the free-falling rupee and brought double-digit inflation under control. He had demonstrated intent to get the NPAs-ridden banks' balance sheets cleaned up. Many of the concerns he was vocal about as an economist pertained to the impact of financial systems on the lives of ordinary people. He had identified the widening gap between the rich and poor as a big cause of the global financial crisis, and better education as a cure.

A former chief economist of the IMF, he exuded confidence, ambition and clarity. He was clear about what he wanted and what he didn't. In 2005, he had politely declined to be deputy RBI governor when approached by then RBI Governor Y.V. Reddy.[26] He was decisive and articulate, and was quickly making an impression on the urban middle class. For someone from the geeky world of the RBI, he was surprisingly popular among students.

As the new prime minister and his government got down to work, Rajan initially appeared to have succeeded in establishing harmonious working relationships in Delhi. He once described his relationship with Modi as one of 'complete understanding'.[27] Modi put on record his satisfaction with the convergence between the RBI and the government. When speaking at the central bank's celebration of its eightieth year, he heaped praise on Rajan, 'Raghuram explains [finance and economy] so perfectly I feel no need to ask questions':[28]

Raghuram and I meet every two months. With 3 or 4 slides he brings along, he explains matters to me so perfectly that he must be [the] best teacher? I find no need to ask any question, I understand so well what he tells me, what it means, what its results are, and this implies that perhaps the thinking in the government and the RBI are closely aligned. I believe this is very important and as the representative of the government I express my satisfaction in this matter.[29]

His influence may not have been similar to that of Montek Singh Ahluwalia's with Prime Minister Manmohan Singh, and he also may not have been the confidant that C. Rangarajan was to Finance Minister Manmohan Singh. But the quality of the Rajan–Modi relationship in the initial phase of Modi's prime ministership can be said to have exceeded its fame.

A fruit of Rajan's persuasive powers was the transition to the inflation-targeting monetary policy under which, for the first time, the government was formally telling the RBI how much inflation it wanted in the economy, essentially a political call. With this shift, elected governments accountable to the electorate were to determine inflation targets (in consultation with the RBI). The target level being aimed for in the RBI was formally and mutually agreed upon between the government and Rajan in February 2015.

Despite the reform, the perception in the BJP's business-class constituency was that Rajan was keeping interest rates too high for investments and growth to take off. At no point did the government clarify that he was doing what was necessary to hit the target inflation level given by the finance ministry.

Although the six-member MPC was set up immediately after Rajan left, the RBI had agreed under Rajan's leadership to relinquish the governor's singular powers of setting interest rates in favour of this committee, half of whose members were to be nominated by the government. This meant interest-rate decisions were not to be the governor's prerogative. To operationalize this, the RBI Act was amended in Parliament. Rajan seemed to have renounced, to an extent, the independence of the RBI, and ceded space to the government. Although the government soon figured out that influencing a committee would be tougher than nudging the RBI governor.

Guided by a committee that said the RBI's accumulated reserves had exceeded the needed buffer, Rajan for two consecutive years transferred the surpluses in totality to the centre, without keeping any for the central bank's statutory reserves.[30] In Rajan's three years, the RBI paid almost as much dividend to the government as had been paid in the previous decade.[31]

His record on reforms reflected expressed views. He did not do reforms by stealth. The financial plumbing was strengthened, the efficiency and fairness of the recovery system were improved, corporate promoters' tight hold over the system, which they were used to manipulating to suit their vested interests, was being loosened. These measures, a step forward in the direction India had embraced in 1991, divested promoters of their presumed divine right to stay in charge regardless of how badly they had managed an enterprise and used the banking system to recapitalize their failed ventures. Basically, it broke down the arrangement by which profits were private, but losses nationalized.

Business circles, naturally, had no love for what Rajan had unleashed on them. Most of all, they resented his communication skills. His speeches had firmly planted in the public discourse the politician-banker-business nexus. The resentment leaked from the business class to the political class, causing discomfort in the Modi government.

Rajan set up in the RBI a monitoring cell to coordinate the early reporting of fraud cases to investigative agencies. In 2015, he sent a list of high-profile fraud cases to the PMO, urging action to bring at least one or two to book so that a tough signal could be sent out.[32] He never heard of any progress on the front, although the matter ought to have been addressed with urgency. Rajan's initiative to crack down on fraudsters, it appears, went cold on reaching the PMO. The result, over the years, was that the system failed to bring to book or put behind bars even a single high-profile fraudster. In the absence of a deterrent, more and more cases of fraud tumbled out, even as many fraudsters, like Nirav Modi and his associate Mehul Choksi who escaped in 2018, succeeded in fleeing the country.

The PMO's inaction and silence in the matter strengthens the impression that Rajan's relations soured with Modi after his tough stance on NPAs in general and frauds in particular aggrieved big business houses. Indian industrialists are not used to being penalized for unpaid loans, and Rajan was bent on doing exactly that.

He had established his voice as one that could be relied upon to speak up if something was amiss—for instance, he got bank books combed for hidden bad loans that would have otherwise gone undetected. Because he was not seen cheerleading for New Delhi and was not shy of publicly expressing his misgivings on economic or political developments, though never recklessly, he commanded the trust of the markets and investors. His record of calling out bubbles early, dislike of policy adventurism and preference for caution and old-fashioned prudence, won him many fans. It produced tangible results too. India was one of the 'Fragile Five' economies when he was appointed governor in 2013. With three more months of his term still to go, India was being called a 'bright spot' in the gloomy world economy by the IMF.

All along, as his public standing kept rising, the credibility of bureaucrats and technocrats—who papered over economic issues, while spending a great deal of time lionizing the government and running down the RBI publicly—in Delhi took a beating.

'The least pleasant aspect of my job was dealing with bureaucrats over trying to undercut the Reserve Bank so as to expand their turf . . . Any public job involves undue praise and unfair criticism,' Rajan wrote later.[33] But even in his opening speech on his first day as governor, he had said, 'Some of the actions I will take will not be popular. The governorship of the central bank is not meant to win one votes or Facebook likes but I do hope to do the right thing no matter what the criticism even while looking to learn from the criticism.'[34]

The reforms undertaken in Rajan's term were guided by the need to increase the role of markets and improve competition, and to ensure that the right regulations were enforced in a predictable, transparent and non-disruptive manner so that the system could adjust accordingly.[35]

In 2016, even as speculation was rife as to whether Rajan would receive an extension at the conclusion of his three-year term in September, a toxic campaign was launched against him, questioning not only his competence, but also his Indianness and patriotism.[36] Besides his policy decisions, even his speeches, including the one emphasizing tolerance for dissent, were derided as being inimical to the national interest. He drew criticism from Minister of State for Commerce and Industry Nirmala Sitharaman for his description of the Indian economy as 'In the land of the blind, the one-eyed man is king'.[37] Better words should have been used, Sitharaman said.[38]

Rajan believed that the controversies arose out of an incorrect understanding of the overall context in which he made those statements.[39]

The diatribe from Rajan's detractors, both in and outside government, continued even after Prime Minister Modi expressed his disapproval of the public attacks on Rajan at a cabinet meeting on 23 June.[40] Whether or not there was in place an unstated approval for the campaign against Rajan, and the reforms he was pushing for, from Modi, one thing was clear. The agenda was being set by busybodies.

The BJP, when in the Opposition, had incessantly accused Prime Minister Singh of being the 'weakest prime minister'.[41] It was alleged that an executive government in office had completely surrendered its ability to act, even as the CAG, the judiciary, Sonia Gandhi, the anti-corruption movement led by Arvind Kejriwal, Anna Hazare and Baba Ramdev were setting the agenda. 'I don't remember any other time when the institution of the prime minister had become the butt of sarcasm and humour . . . The vestige of power in extra-Constitutional authorities outside the government has created an inability of the government to be decisive,' leader of the Opposition in the Rajya Sabha, BJP's Arun Jaitley said in 2013, on the fourth anniversary of UPA-2.[42]

'Manmohan Singh is the prime minister but neither a leader of the country nor the leader of his own party. Dr Singh's colleagues sit with him in the Cabinet and look towards the UPA chairperson for directions . . . The country had to face the consequences of this split leadership,' Jaitley's counterpart in the Lok Sabha, BJP's Sushma Swaraj said.[43]

But now, on many issues, busybodies and non-government actors in the BJP were setting the national agenda, while the government tried to cope, undo or pre-empt it.

Tired of the endless controversies, on 18 July Rajan announced that he would not be seeking a second term after the completion of his three-year tenure on 4 September, in an open letter to the RBI staff that was released on a Saturday.[44] It was a move that took investors and the government equally by surprise. It was a sign of the growing tensions that he chose not to inform top members of the government beforehand of his decision.[45] The vicious campaign that was allowed to be run against him is believed to be a factor that pushed him to the decision. He was upset that the government never defended him as effectively as it ought to have.

In the weeks preceding his letter to the RBI staff, Rajan had sent emails seeking clarity from the PMO and the finance minister on his second term, emphasizing that some of the tasks he had taken up were incomplete.[46] These included the setting up of the MPC and the bad loan clean-up process in the banking sector.

He never received any response from the government to these communications. So when Rajan decided to leave, he did so without warning and on his own terms, taking the Modi–Jaitley duo completely by surprise. He hit the government where it hurt the most. Their reputation of impatience with intellectual inputs and technical expertise never recovered after that. What was worse, he put them in a battle—one of public perception—which they would normally have won, but against him they lost. No individual is indispensable. And Rajan was not without his flaws and failings. His term at the RBI may have shown him how much tougher it was to manage crises than to foresee them. And yet the government simply had no comeback on why it had failed to retain Rajan as governor—a question that dominated the foreign investor circles the government so wanted to woo. He had them on the mat.

Even as his successor was being decided, there was a realization in government that its handling of the campaign against Rajan lacked assertiveness.[47] An immediate fallout was that the finance minister's first choice for Rajan's successor declined to be considered for the position.

'There could have been greater assertiveness in defending Dr Rajan, just as there was in defending the officials who came under attacks subsequently [Chief Economic Adviser Arvind Subramanian and Economic Affairs Secretary Shaktikanta Das]. No professional would want to work in the face of such attacks,' a highly placed official source told me at the time.[48]

'Exposure to and understanding of the complexities of the global economy are Dr Rajan's plus points—something the government rides on,' he added.

Rajan became the first RBI governor in liberalized India to not receive a five-year term. His four predecessors—D. Subbarao (2008–13), Y.V. Reddy (2003–08), Bimal Jalan (1997–2003) and C. Rangarajan (1992–97)—each had five-year terms.

Rajan would not be the first or last casualty of the Modi government, the BJP and its affiliates' distrust of economics and economists, especially those in the RBI. Over the years, the list of departures of qualified economists who had come under attack from some quarters of the BJP or its various affiliates kept growing. Ila Patnaik, Arvind Panagariya, Arvind Subramanian and Urjit Patel would also leave the government. A number of IAS officers with PhDs in economics would be shunted out of the finance ministry. The detractors would use every occasion possible to launch attacks on Jaitley and other officials in the finance ministry and on the investigative agencies, while Modi would just keep quiet. Finance Secretary Hasmukh Adhia, Modi's key appointee in the finance ministry, would become the focus of an intense campaign. Such was Modi's dependence on him that the final note on the bill for amending the Constitution for the introduction of the GST was moved by him before the cabinet, not by the minister in charge, Arun Jaitley, who was not in Delhi at the time. 'They are attacking Adhia's integrity . . . he is the kind of fellow who would put money on your table if he has a cup of coffee at your place,' an IAS colleague of his told me, expressing dismay at the handling of officers by the government.[49]

Banking Paralysis or a Full-fledged Banking Crisis

By 2016, banks had a full-fledged crisis on hand as more and more loans stopped being repaid. The losses on banks' books kept growing. Risk-averse bankers, seeing the arrests of some of their colleagues, were simply not willing to take the write-downs and push a restructuring to its conclusion without the process being blessed by the courts or someone higher up in the banking hierarchy.[50] The clean-up of the mess in banks called for setting up strong resolution and insolvency mechanisms. But the government preferred to play a passive role here too. It could be termed 'banking paralysis'.

With the hidden loans dredged out, NPAs went up from 4.62 per cent in 2014–15 to 7.79 per cent in 2015–16, and were as high as 10.41 per cent by December 2017 according to the RBI.[51] In other words, Rs 1.4 of every Rs 10 in gross advances was 'non-performing'.

The bulk of India's stressed debts problem was concentrated in fifty-seven corporate accounts that required banks to take haircuts of 75 per cent or more.[52]

The pressure to tackle bank NPAs had started mounting on the government. T.T. Ram Mohan, professor at IIM Ahmedabad, explained the challenge at hand.[53]

Once an asset is recognized as an NPA, banks must decide what to do with it. One, they can try to seize the assets pledged by the borrower and sell them. This typically involves large losses on loans as the assets have to be sold at steep discounts to their book value. Two, under the RBI's SDR scheme, they can convert their loans into equity, acquire a majority stake in the firm, dislodge the promoters or management and bring in new promoters and management. While this happens in advanced economies all the time, the SDR scheme had not taken off in India. Indian banks do not have the experience to run businesses till such a time as new promoters are found. Nor do they have experience in locating promoters and management who can take over stressed assets. Three, banks can restructure the loans so that borrowers are able to service them. This involves stretching out the period of payment, waiving a portion of the loans, reducing the interest rate on loans, or some combination of these. In any restructuring, banks incur losses on the loans they have made. At PSBs, managers are open to the charge that they have favoured borrowers in a restructuring scheme, which can invite action from investigative agencies. This resulted in virtual paralysis at PSBs.

A fourth option for banks is to sell the NPAs at a discount to an asset restructuring company. This again involves a significant loss on loans when the transaction is made. But it has the effect of getting an NPA off the books of the bank or of cleaning up the balance sheet. The bank's capital is eroded to the extent of the loss. However, since 100 per cent of the loan has exited the balance sheet, the ratio of regulatory capital to assets—or what is called 'capital adequacy'—improves, making the bank appear more attractive to investors.

Getting NPAs off the books would help the PSBs' management focus on new business instead of having to expend their energies on trying to effect recoveries.

By May 2016, the Insolvency and Bankruptcy Code (IBC)— based on the recommendations of the T.K. Viswanathan Committee report[54]—was in place for the resolution of sticky NPAs of banks and liquidation of companies that could not be revived. It was conceived as a big step to help lenders recover their dues within a fixed time frame. It gave rise to opportunities for funds to acquire borrowers' distressed assets.

According to World Bank estimates[55], the old law used to resolve insolvency and recover debt, the Recovery of Debts due to the Banks and Financial Institutions Act (RDBBFI) 1993 which had led to the setting up of the DRTs, used to resolve insolvency on an average in 4.3 years. Recovery was barely 25.7 cents per dollar. The hope was that the IBC would deliver bigger recoveries at accelerated pace.

The RBI's approach had been to aggressively push banks to first explicitly recognize the NPAs on their books and then actually set aside provisions for bad loans not earning returns. It now encouraged banks to initiate distress sales of assets, invoking the provisions of the IBC. Until the IBC was enacted, promoters never feared they could lose control over their firms.

Even after it was enacted, some did not give up trying to game the process and regain control through proxy bidders, at much lower prices. Many did not engage seriously with the banks. A second set of loans had become non-performing due to the economy's broader problems. The government dragged its feet on project revival—the unending problems in the power sector were an example. The proportion of stalled projects had risen to double digits in 2013 during the fag end of the UPA second term. But the change of regime had had no impact on the stalling rate of projects that shot up to hit a fifty-two-quarter, or a thirteen-year high of more than 20 per cent by mid-2017.[56]

Many of the large promoters filed frivolous appeals to beat the IBC. The idea behind the process was that while the defaulting promoter should have every chance of concluding a deal before the firm goes to bid, all such options should be closed once it does go to bid. The bankruptcy court is ideally a final threat, so that much loan renegotiation is done before an NPA reaches it.[57] This requires fixing the factors that make bankers risk-averse and promoters uncooperative. The judicial process was simply not equipped to handle every NPA through a bankruptcy process. Banks and promoters have to strike deals outside of bankruptcy, or if promoters prove uncooperative, bankers should have the ability to proceed without them. The last stage, of resolution of stress, was considerably delayed.

Finally, the Modi government tasked the RBI to get on with the job through an ordinance. In effect, the previous decentralized system empowering bankers in bad loans resolution was replaced with a more centralized one empowering their regulator.[58] Banks had shown no inclination to expedite resolutions. The Banking Regulation (Amendment) Ordinance, 2017 empowered the RBI to issue directions to banking companies to initiate an insolvency resolution process in respect of a default, under the provisions of the IBC. It also enabled the RBI to issue directions with respect to stressed assets and specify one or more authorities or constitute committees to advise banking companies on resolution of stressed assets.[59]

The hope was that the first would force banks to write down debt to match its economic value, while the second was to ensure that banks did not throw good money after bad on projects that have no future.

For bankers who feared that taking haircuts on loans—or settling them at a discount to their book value—would land them in the eager hands of overenthusiastic investigative agencies, this arrangement provided credible cover, since all decisions now had the RBI's blessings.

The choice of RBI as the agency to push for resolution seemed partly inspired by the US Fed's heavy involvement—of course, along with the US Treasury—during the global financial crisis of 2008, where the US central bank had gone beyond providing emergency liquidity. The new ordinance was expected to accelerate the resolution process, but the underlying challenges remained.

The first challenge was to find buyers for the distressed debt that banks may want to sell or for the assets of enterprises that were wound down under the bankruptcy law. The second challenge was that capital needs to be raised after banks take a knock after the inevitable loan write-downs. The combined bill for cleaning up banks as well as for meeting Basel III norms was estimated at around $100 billion.[60] The third big question, and a politically sensitive one, was to what extent corporate borrowers, rather than taxpayers, would bear the costs of bad-loan resolution.

The IBC was touted as the law that would extract the highest possible value from the asset within a specific time. But at least five of the first set of the twelve biggest insolvency cases extended well past the deadline. The respective National Company Law Tribunal (NCLT) benches approved the extension of timing in these cases— one of the reasons the new IBC would also suffer from delays, and within two years of its implementation be 'brought to the brink of irrelevance by the strain of resolving its most high-profile case: Essar Steel India Ltd', as senior banking journalist Tamal Bandyopadhyay wrote in January 2019.[61] 'The billionaire Ruia brothers used every trick in the book to ensure their prized asset stays in the family, despite owing financial creditors 508 billion rupees ($6.3 billion) in unpaid dues . . . lenders [State Bank of India primarily] themselves had started making a mockery of a fledgling insolvency law.'

He detailed the delays:

Under the new law, ICICI Bank filed the first case against a steel products maker which had Rs 955 crore debt in September 2016. At least 10,000 cases were filed in the next 28 months. But there are just 13 benches of the National Company Law Tribunal (NCLT) hearing these cases. Any default in excess of Rs 1 lakh can be dragged to the NCLT by creditors, financial or operational. The woefully inadequate infrastructure has meant cases have not been settled in the stipulated time of 180 days, or even 270 days. The RBI pushed bankers to move the insolvency court against 28 defaulters. But no settlements took place. The cases were all admitted by the NCLT . . . The RBI had listed . . . 28 defaulters against whom it wanted immediate bankruptcy proceedings invoked. These 40 defaulters account for half of the Rs 10 trillion bad debt in the banking system . . .

Although it could not deliver results as promised, at least in the early phase of becoming operational, nevertheless the Modi government deserves credit for at least laying out a bankruptcy system. The intent behind the reform was to disrupt the system of political capitalism that had only strengthened after 1991. Industries in sectors such as power generation, mining, telecoms and infrastructure had come to require, besides tremendous capital, huge clout within government. Many of the entrepreneurs who were able to build businesses were those with an edge, essentially connections, to win the necessary permits and to secure financing from state-owned lenders. Many tycoons could count on ministers to put in a word with a recalcitrant banker.[62] *The Economist* summed up the system as it exists, and the promise IBC held out of reforming it.

Some held political office themselves. Bankers were willing to extend repayment periods indefinitely in case things went awry. Clogged courts were in any case not equal to the task of enforcing contracts. Whether a business was profitable or not was not always material in this system, since the promoters could enrich themselves by securing assets without putting any of their own money in.

The bankruptcy code sought to dismantle this entire system of crony capitalism by making the seizure of businesses by banks easier. To smoothen this out, a new set of dedicated courts, backed by a cadre of insolvency professionals, was set up to help banks seize assets and sell them to fresh owners. The incentives structure was sought to be altered through the imposition of stringent deadlines. For the first time, promoters who had defaulted were explicitly banned from staying on as owners. A company found to be insolvent by a specialized tribunal was to have its board in effect fired, and an independent expert would be appointed to run it on behalf of its lenders. The new manager would then prepare the company for fresh investors. If creditors failed to reach a deal in nine months' time, the business was to be liquidated and its assets sold for scrap. Earlier, promoters could stay on as managers of stricken firms, and even drain them of cash. Their position at the helm also gave them leverage in negotiations with bankers, who often had little choice but to agree to debt reduction. Now, struggling tycoons faced the prospect of having their businesses seized from them.

The second setback to the so-far cosy system was the pressure on banks to recognize which loans were unlikely to be repaid, and to initiate insolvency proceedings in double-quick time.

But the early results were unsatisfactory.

Some aspects of the entire resolution process were particularly disturbing.[63] Buyers of the stressed assets were offered deep discounts. In effect, this meant that while the original borrower went scot-free after failing to repay the loans, the new entrant got the asset at a much cheaper cost.[64] While these two sets of private investors gained from the resolution process, the loss was borne entirely by the lending PSBs. The resolution of the NPA mess placed the entire burden of the adjustment on the banks rather than on the borrowers.

The PSBs registered their biggest collective loss in 2017–18, of Rs 85,369 crore.[65] This was a direct consequence of the aggressive push from the RBI, led by Rajan and kept up by his successor Urjit Patel, to clean up banks' balance sheets. For 2017–18, banks had made provisions amounting to Rs 2.7 lakh crore for losses in their loan portfolio. This was an increase of 57 per cent over the previous year. With such massive provisioning, there was no way the losses could be lower.

The financial stability report released by the RBI[66] in June 2018 warned that the gross non-performing assets (GNPAs) of scheduled commercial banks in the country could rise from 11.6 per cent of total assets in March 2018 to 12.2 per cent in March 2019, which would be the highest level of bad debt in almost two decades.

The GNPAs of banks under the prompt corrective action framework[67], in particular, is expected to rise to 22.3 per cent of total assets in March 2019, from 21 per cent in March 2018. The RBI believes that this will increase the size of provisioning for losses and affect the capital position of banks. In fact, the capital to risk weighted assets ratio of the banking system as a whole is expected to drop from 13.5 per cent in March 2018 to 12.8 per cent in March 2019.

No banking system so stressed could have supplied the credit needed to power high the GDP growth. Recapitalizing banks could have helped. Fitch ratings had put Indian banks' recapitalization burden, by 2019, at $90 billion, of which the government had committed only $10 billion in fiscal resources.[68] With NPAs rising sharply, the urgency for capital infusion—and the amount of fresh capital required—had risen commensurately.

As the discourse shifted focus to the Modi government's economic management, the latter fielded NITI Aayog Vice Chairman Rajiv Kumar in September 2018 to defend its record in interviews to the press. The DPhil in economics from Oxford, with a PhD from Lucknow University, sought to deflect blame for the state of affairs in banking on to Rajan, who was by then much hated in the Modi government's core support groups and no longer in the RBI. They blamed Rajan for inflicting a slowdown on the economy, which is what, according to them, spoiled the Modi government's performance record, by declaring loans NPAs.

'Under the previous governor, Mr Raghuram Rajan, who revised the mechanisms, the NPAs began to grow which is why the banking sector stopped giving credit to the industry. Never have we seen such a continuous and persistent year-upon-year deleveraging of credit. This is the cause of the economic slowdown,' said Kumar.[69]

But it was erroneous to blame the slowdown on Rajan and on the RBI's push for bringing out in the open the hidden bad loans on banks' books.

If loan classification was good accounting, the provisioning had forced banks to set aside a buffer to absorb likely losses. Where the losses did not materialize, the bank could write back the provisioning to profits. But where the losses did materialize, they were not unprovided for.[70] The banking system's vulnerability to unforeseeable shocks was thus reduced. Even when banks declared big losses, as a whole lot of them did through 2017 and 2018, they could set the losses against the prudential provisions they had already made. Bank balance sheets now represented a true and fair picture of their health. Institutionalization of the processes ensured that they were predictable and enduring.

All along, the government had ample advice and warnings to address head-on the issues of credit growth and banks' health. But it chose to ignore the follow-up action list. Instead, it toyed first with an investment push through a fiscal stimulus in its second budget and then with demonetization in 2016.

The government had two options: either to privatize the banks and allow their future solvency to be subject to market competition; or to design a radically new governance structure which would better ensure the banks' ability to compete successfully, as recommended in May 2014 by a committee the RBI had appointed.[71] Once banks had been encouraged to clean up their balance sheets, the government should have committed them to raising capital, or provided infusions from its own resources.

It did none of this, but continued with a policy of tinkering. It showed no courage to make drastic changes to aspects of operational autonomy and the ownership of PSBs. The steps to reform governance of PSBs were limited and ineffective. PSB boards are still not adequately professionalized, and the government still decides board appointments, with the inevitable politicization that follows. Banks are left leaderless for long periods of time, although the date of retirement of CEOs is well known, and the government should be prepared well in advance with succession.

The government did not capitalize the banks adequately. Nor did it undertake any reforms to free them of political interference and control in future. It was content to force bank managements to agree—often against their judgement—to mergers. Such as in the case of the Bank of Baroda, a large-sized bank; Vijaya Bank, a medium-sized bank with a relatively better NPA position; and Dena Bank, clearly the laggard in terms of its NPA position.[72]

The RBI's annual report in 2014 had flagged the NPAs in the infrastructure sector.[73] It stressed the need on the part of government to smoothen out the policy hurdles holding up these projects. In an interview, Urjit Patel, deputy governor of the RBI then, had told me how the Modi government could have prevented escalation in NPAs.

'If one goes behind the numbers on NPAs of the banking system in the infrastructure sector, it is important to note that these assets are real and can quickly bring in cash for the banking system if we just fix two-three things, such as power purchase agreements, fuel supply agreements. This should be the main task—to square that circle.'[74]

But neither stalled projects[75] nor the NPA crisis received speedy attention for resolution from the government, and its sheer inability to attempt banking reforms means future crises will be hard to prevent.

The Investment Slowdown

In the boom years during the UPA tenure, four engines had powered the economy: exports, government investments, private consumption and private investments. Of these, two were still running at the time Modi took office: government investments and private consumption. The other two, exports and private investments, were already sputtering, with no uptick following the regime change. The growth engine of private investments had begun stalling 2011–12 onwards.

Official statistics had captured the weakness consistently and unambiguously—in exports for three years, and in private investments for more than five years. Yet, the debilitating impact of this received inadequate policy attention.

Government investments depend on how well the economy is doing. As incomes improve, tax collections pick up. The scope for scaling up government investments was clearly limited.

New private investments remained on hold even after the change of governments in 2014. The returns-risk projections of projects were not favourable. Companies were not convinced that new factories would be sufficiently profitable. Among the variables that affect investment decisions are costs and availability of finance, land, labour, technology, logistics and taxation. Market price, or in other words, consumer price inflation, is a determinant of profitability on the revenue side. The Modi government, being politically sensitive, set a low target for consumer price inflation. For the same reason it made little progress on land and labour reforms, as the following subsections will show. The flow of credit in the economy had thinned to a trickle even as the government moved on bad bank loans belatedly and inefficaciously. Several wilful defaulters were absconding. More than a fifth of large companies did not earn enough in 2017 to be able to pay interest on their loans.[76] Naturally, the pace of new loans was the lowest in more than six decades.[77] Even if big companies could raise finance from alternative sources, the smaller ones could not. Most of the other factors that influence investment decisions escaped policy attention altogether. Additionally, in an environment of constant shocks and unanticipated policy changes, as happened with the land acquisition law amendments through 2015, the demonetization in 2016 and the GST 2017 onwards (all discussed in the following subsections), investment decisions tend to get postponed. If people feel unsettled, they are unlikely to invest.

Although the Modi government had inherited an investment slowdown, the economy had nevertheless been on a steady recovery path for four years. Macroeconomic stability had been restored. Global trends in oil and commodity prices had turned favourable. But the Modi government could not quite leverage these advantages to push growth. An appropriate growth strategy for the Modi government would have been to work to restore the stuck projects and strengthen the recovery. And simultaneously work on resolving the banking crisis and NPA problems. But that was not followed. The investment slowdown deepened with every passing year of Modi's tenure.

Decreasing for the fifth straight year, the share of gross fixed capital formation in GDP shrunk to 27.1 per cent in 2016–17. It had been 34.3 per cent in 2011–12.[78]

Arvind Subramanian's fiscal strategy for stimulating growth had failed. The glaring gaps in India's infrastructure financing strategy also became obvious. Eliminating infrastructure bottlenecks is of course critical to restoring the growth momentum, as public goods can help poor, unequal societies transition to relatively higher and more equal incomes. But this phase showed once again that India has not been able to come up with a sustainable funding option for building infrastructure. And that it focuses too much on physical infrastructure, neglecting human capital, the other essential ingredient of a just and prosperous economy.

Stagnating Exports

Along with private investments, exports were also out of steam. Export performance in 2016–17 was the worst since 1952–53.[79] India's growth is relatively more dependent on domestic factors, notably a big push in infrastructure and a revival in private investment, rather than exports. However, this type of growth nevertheless involves an increase in import. And so, better export performance was needed to manage the balance of payments.

The global economic downturn that followed the financial crisis of 2008 had dealt Indian exports a body blow. Before that, they had been growing smartly. When the global economy recovered, it lifted the exports scene in most Asian countries, but Indian exports kept on stagnating, their competitiveness eroded by the overvalued rupee. Aggressive cow politics hurt the related sectors' growth and exports.

Exports could have supplemented growth and jobs creation, but grew weaker than they were at the height of the UPA government's 'policy paralysis' phase. At the end of Modi's four years of governance, exports were down to $303 billion[80] from $312 billion annually.[81] As a percentage of GDP, they were down from 17.2 per cent to 12.4 per cent.[82] This, when exports from other emerging market economies were trending up, capitalizing on the pickup in global growth. In garments and textiles, India had been second only to China, but slipped to the fifth and third positions, respectively, in the two sectors.[83]

A government not shy of its business-friendly credentials should have picked up these stress signals early on and administered the remedies, but its mandarins were too excited: international agencies had declared that 2015 was going to be the year in which India would race past China (the Chinese economy is about five times as large as India's) to be the fastest-growing economy in the world. It was. But that this had probably more to do with China slowing down rather than India picking up, and their stark difference in size made the comparison irrelevant. However, the cheerleaders among the bureaucrats and ministers couldn't be bothered with technical minutiae—all that mattered was that India was a bright spot in a gloomy global economy.

The Disaster of Demonetization

'. . . Politicians are often required to square circles, which forces them to embrace dubious ideas. How does the governor go about his business in such situations? . . . The governor has to have enough tact and guile to have his say without putting him at the centre of political controversies.'

—I.G. Patel, fourteenth governor,
Reserve Bank of India [84]

On 8 November 2016, Prime Minister Narendra Modi went live in an unscheduled televised address at 20:00 Indian Standard Time (IST). The evening's pronouncement would become a defining moment of the prime-ministerial term. Wearing an unusually subdued expression, Modi began with greetings for the Diwali festive season that had just ended. He gave the messianic zip, the slogan slingers and usual wordplay that had come to characterize his speeches a miss, and stuck to standard fare about the poor, black money, and an incantation of schemes and programmes launched by his government. As the speech progressed, there were no signs of the adversity that was about to hit the nation, either in his tone or message.

My dear citizens,[85]

I hope you ended the festive season of Diwali with joy and new hope. Today, I will be speaking to you about some critical issues and important decisions. Today, I want to make a special request to all of you . . .

Our motto has been 'Sab Ka Saath Sab Ka Vikas': We are with all citizens and for development of all citizens. This government is dedicated to the poor . . . In our fight against poverty, our main thrust has been to empower the poor, and make them active participants in the benefits of economic progress.

The Pradhan Mantri Jan Dhan Yojana,
the Jan Suraksha Yojana,

the Pradhan Mantri Mudra Yojana for small enterprises,

the Stand-up India programme for Dalits, Adivasis and Women,

the Pradhan Mantri Ujjwala Scheme for gas connections in the homes of the poor,

the Pradhan Mantri Fasal Beema Yojana and Pradhan Mantri Krishi Sinchai Yojana to protect the income of farmers,

the Soil Health Card Scheme to ensure the best possible yield from farmers' fields,

and the e-NAM National Market Place scheme to ensure farmers get the right price for their produce . . .

In the past decades . . . The evil of corruption has been spread by certain sections of society for their selfish interest. They have ignored the poor and cornered benefits . . . On the other hand, honest people have fought against this evil . . . We hear about poor auto-rickshaw drivers returning gold ornaments left in the vehicles to their rightful owners. We hear about taxi drivers who take pains to locate the owners of cell phones left behind. We hear of vegetable vendors who return excess money given by customers . . .

There comes a time in the history of a country's development when a need is felt for a strong and decisive step. For years, this country has felt that corruption, black money and terrorism are festering sores, holding us back in the race towards development . . .

But have you ever thought about how these terrorists get their money? Enemies from across the border run their operations using fake currency notes . . . those using fake 500 and 1,000-rupee notes have been caught and many such notes have been seized . . .

The magnitude of cash in circulation is directly linked to the level of corruption . . .

High circulation of cash also strengthens the hawala trade which is directly connected to black money and illegal trade in weapons . . .

About fifteen minutes into his first televised address to the nation, at 8.15 p.m., Modi dropped the bombshell.

Brothers and sisters,

To break the grip of corruption and black money, we have decided that the 500 rupee and 1,000-rupee currency notes presently in use will no longer be legal tender from midnight tonight, that is 8th November 2016. This means that these notes will not be acceptable for transactions from midnight onwards. The 500 and 1,000-rupee notes hoarded by anti-national and anti-social elements will become just worthless pieces of paper. The rights and the interests of honest, hard-working people will be fully protected.

Taking the nation by surprise, Modi said invalidating these notes was a major assault on black money, fake currency and corruption. He implored the honest to bear with his plan for a thorough clean-up of the economy and promised to bring the corrupt to book.

The demonetization he had just announced was going to hit every individual, corrupt or not, and whether hoarding illegal cash or living on legal earnings. Officials in the know had stressed many times in their interactions with him that the currency shortage would be especially hard on the poor. Modi sought to prepare the vulnerable for the privation.

. . . there may be temporary hardships to be faced by honest citizens. Experience tells us that ordinary citizens are always ready to make sacrifices and face difficulties for the benefit of the nation . . . in this fight against corruption, black money, fake notes and terrorism, in this movement for purifying our country, will our people not put up with difficulties for some days? I have full confidence that every citizen will stand up and participate in this *mahayagna*. My dear countrymen, after the festivity of Diwali, now join the nation and extend your hand in this *Imandaari ka Utsav*, this *Pramanikta ka Parv*, this celebration of integrity, this festival of credibility.

Modi's confidence in his oratorical skills and his command of public trust was such that he did not hide the fact that the system had not been prepared in advance to manage the inevitable cash shortage or make the transition smooth for the non-corrupt.

> Secrecy was essential for this action. It is only now, as I speak to you, that various agencies like banks, post offices, railways, hospitals and others are being informed. The Reserve Bank, banks and post offices have to make many arrangements at very short notice. Obviously, time will be needed. Therefore, all banks will be closed to the public on 9th November. This may cause some hardship to you.

Before ending his speech, he announced that the cancelled notes would be replaced by newly issued Rs 2000 notes.

> RBI's recommendation to issue 2,000-rupee notes has been accepted. New notes of 500 rupees and 2,000 rupees, with completely new design, will be introduced. Based on past experience, the Reserve Bank will hereafter make arrangements to limit the share of high-denomination notes in the total currency in circulation.

He closed with an invitation to citizens to participate in the clean-up and contribute to the country's progress.

> Once again, let me invite you to make your contribution to this grand sacrifice for cleansing our country, just as you cleaned up your surroundings during Diwali. *Bharat Mata ki jai.*

Different classes of people responded variously to the broadcast. Some rushed to ATMs, others to jewellery and consumer durables shops. The process of converting black money into gold and other valuable products with a longer shelf life—longer than that of the cancelled notes—started immediately. Many stores across the country did not close for the night.

The prime minister's address was followed by an urgently called press conference by secretary, Economic Affairs, Shaktikanta Das, who warned, 'Banks will have video cameras for all transactions, people must be careful while exchanging legal cash.'[86]

It probably struck the authorities only later that scrutinizing all the video recordings would be humanly impossible.

In the weeks that followed, Shaktikanta Das became a household name. He addressed press conferences almost daily, bringing the nation up to date with the newest change in the fiat for the exchange of demonetized notes and the rationing of new notes. Sometimes the rules changed twice a day. Das, in his most memorable press outing, explained that any colour coming off the newly released Rs 2000 notes should not be a cause for worry, but was a security feature.

> The new currency notes, just as the old ones, will lose colour if rubbed with a piece of cloth wet because that's the nature of the dye used. If your note does not lose colour, it's one of the signs that it may be fake.[87]

After his initial address, Modi next spoke about the demonetization on 12 November in an address to an NRI audience in Japan. Back home, most Indians, barring those with resources who had managed to organize the exchange of cancelled notes, stood in queues outside banks. 'There's a wedding at home, but no money for it . . .' Modi taunted those who had lost access to their money, including honest, hard-earned, taxed money.[88] He warned of more measures in the fight against black money after the December-end deadline for depositing scrapped currency. The speech did not go down well. The government was belittling people, their honesty, their humanity. The prime minister was called out by many for his evident lack of empathy and regard for the honest and weak.

Chaos and anger at never-ending queues were being reported from bank premises across the country. Banks were struggling to exchange old notes and give out the new Rs 2000 and smaller-denomination notes. Hardly 40 per cent of ATMs were operating; within hours of being replenished they would run out of cash. The new Rs 500 note was available only in Delhi and Mumbai, and the RBI had started releasing soiled Rs 100 notes to cope with the demand.[89]

Hours after the PM's speech in Japan, Finance Minister Arun Jaitley addressed a hurriedly called press conference, his second in three days.[90] 'ATMs could not have been calibrated [before the announcement] because of secrecy issue. Thousands of people are involved in recalibration exercise [and] secrecy could not have been maintained. Recalibration takes at least two–three weeks.'

Modi changed track on 14 December. Speaking in Goa, he made an emotional appeal to the people.[91] In a choked voice, he reminded his audience: 'I was not born to capture power . . . I have left my home, my family, everything for the nation . . . how I was mocked inside the Parliament. They thought Modi would break down. But I won't even if I am burnt alive.'

He asked people to stand by him for fifty days as he battled it out with the corrupt.

If you face any difficulty after that, if you find me dishonest in my effort, you can punish me in whatever way you would wish to at any crossroads of the country . . . Once the country is clean during these fifty days, then we need not be worried even about a single corrupt mosquito.

He sneered at imaginary enemies, making exaggerated gestures at them (the imaginary enemies).

> You are now witnessing people accused of 2G scam and coal scam standing in queue to exchange their currency and get Rs 4,000. You can just imagine what kind of cases are surfacing. Those who didn't throw a penny in the Ganga earlier are now submerging bundles into it . . .

Organized Loot

On 24 November, Manmohan Singh rose to speak on the floor of the Rajya Sabha. The speaker allowed the impromptu intervention. Prime Minister Modi, who had made a rare appearance in the House, listened from across the treasury benches. Delivering one of his most memorable disquisitions, Singh rejected expressly and firmly Modi's theories about demonetization.[92] His persuasive and self-effacing demeanour contrasted starkly with the kitsch that had been on display since the announcement of demonetization on 8 November.

> . . . it is important to take note of grievances of the ordinary people who have suffered as a result of this imposition on the country overnight by the prime minister. And I say so, with all responsibility that we do not know what the final outcome will be.
>
> Prime minister has said that we should wait for fifty days. Well, fifty days is a short period. But for those who are poor and from the deprived sections of the society, even fifty days' torture can bring about disastrous effects. And that's why about sixty to sixty-five people have lost their lives, maybe more. And what has been done can weaken and erode our people's confidence in the currency system and in the banking system . . .

I would like to know from the prime minister the name of any country he may think of where people have deposited their money in the banks but are not allowed to withdraw their money . . .

In my opinion, the way the scheme has been implemented . . . will hurt agricultural growth in our country, will hurt small industry, will hurt all those people who are in the informal sector of the economy. And my own feeling is that the national income, that is the GDP, can decline by about 2 per cent as a result of what has been done. This is an underestimate, not an overestimate . . .

It is no good that every day the banking system comes with modification of the rules, the conditions under which the people can withdraw money. That reflects very poorly on the prime minister's office, on the finance minister's office and on the Reserve Bank of India. I am very sorry that the Reserve Bank of India has been exposed to this sort of criticism which I think is fully justified . . .

. . . the way this scheme has been implemented is a monumental management failure, and in fact, it is a case of organized loot, legalized plunder of the common people . . .

It is not my intention to pick holes . . . But I sincerely hope that the prime minister will at this late hour help us to find practical, pragmatic ways and means to provide relief to the suffering of the people of this country.

He who had until that day carried the appellation *maunmohan* (the silent one) was now voicing precisely what every honest Indian was now being made to feel. He did so with gravitas and without a trace of snark. Official statistics would, in course of time, bear out the prognosis. The speech rattled the prime minister. Singh was self-effacing and careful not to tread on Modi's toes or to challenge his ego. But the speech left Modi squirming.

By end-December, Rs 14 lakh crore of the Rs 15.4 lakh crore worth of the scrapped notes had returned to the system.[93] The worry now was that the quantum of notes returned would exceed the number that the RBI had said were in circulation. This would imply that either the RBI's statistics on notes in circulation had been an underestimate or, worse, that fake notes had been accepted undetected. In either case, the eventuality would have been an embarrassment. The daily updates by RBI on returned notes were halted.

Attorney General's High Expectations of Demonetization

A Supreme Court Bench presided over by Chief Justice T.S. Thakur and comprising Justice D.Y. Chandrachud heard a petition against demonetization on 15 November. The Bench refused to stay the notification demonetizing the Rs 500 and Rs 1000 currency notes.[94] While noting that it wanted to avoid interfering in the government's economic policy, the Bench asked the centre to take immediate measures to alleviate the hardships and sufferings of the traumatized common man who had been 'forced' to stand in queues to withdraw a little bit of his own hard-earned money.

'Carpenters, masons, daily-wage earners, maids, vegetable sellers are dependent on cash; we are only wondering if you are capable of doing anything to reduce the trauma of ordinary man?' Chief Justice Thakur asked Attorney General Mukul Rohatgi.[95]

Rohatgi argued that the only argument raised against demonetization was 'inconvenience'.[96] 'Some collateral damage will take place. I could not calibrate the 2 lakh ATMs, that would have brought the cat out of the bag. I could not print or keep the new money in godowns. . . . our objective is to wipe out black money and end terror financing. I have to say that for fifty years, when others were in power, we used to wait for our Fiat car, gas and phone connection . . . We waited. Now, people are willing to wait.'[97]

In his submissions on that day, Kapil Sibal, appearing for one of the four petitioners against demonetization, asked how banks, which are only trustees of a person's money, could restrict withdrawals. 'Under what right can you restrict my right to withdrawal?'[98]

He said the previous case of demonetization that had been carried out in 1978 dealt with high-denomination notes, which only comprised 2 per cent of the currency value in circulation. This was in stark contrast with the Rs 500 and Rs 1000 notes cancelled in 2016, which accounted for 86 per cent of the currency in circulation.

In what would ultimately prove to be a horribly wrong estimate, the attorney general submitted to the Supreme Court that he expected that Rs 4–5 lakh crore would not be returned to the banking system.[99] The expectation was that this sum, representing the hoard of black money, would get extinguished in the demonetization exercise. It would not be returned, out of fear of creating trails leading up to black money hoarders.

'After demonetization, the black money hoarders do not even have the money they once used to have in their pyjamas.'[100]

At final count, the notes that didn't come back added up to just Rs 10,720 crore.[101]

Shifting Goals

In the weeks after more than 80 per cent of the cash in circulation was removed in the quest, whether genuinely misguided or staged, to stifle the black economy, the discourse turned extreme and divisive. Economists critical of the move sparred with the ruling party's spokespersons over the undue costs of the move and its debilitating impact on the momentum of economic growth. An equal number sympathetic to Modi heaped insensate and uncritical admiration on demonetization.

A majority of the media, anxious to append the tag of 'genius' to the move, floated theories purely on the basis of Internet rumours and not rooted in verifiable fact, that the new Rs 2000 notes would have inbuilt chips that could transmit their location, and therefore their handlers, to income tax authorities, preventing the creation of black money.

The goals were shifted so fast by the government that getting a fix on demonetization became tough for the common people. A corpus of arguments that the prime minister had not listed in his 8 November broadcast was conjured up in support of demonetization—ranging from shrinking the cash economy and growing digitization to increasing tax compliance.

Many who misread demonetization were uninformed, unsuspecting. However, there were also those who understood well its economics but were keen to position themselves as aligned with the government, and so chose to add to the misinformation and confusion. In their public interventions, they insisted the government was clearly signalling its intention to move against illegal wealth, and that demonetization would immobilize and thus reduce the stock of black money held by tax evaders. Positive consequences over a longer period could be expected, they said, such as growth in the income tax base from increased income-tax compliance, reduction in tax evasion and bureaucratic corruption, switch in the financial holdings of households from cash to bank deposits, and an increased use of digital payments.

The government, for reasons best known to it, was reluctant to divulge how exactly it had planned for demonetization ahead of the 8 November announcement, or weigh in on the results achieved since then. Initially, the RBI was transparent. Details of the banned notes that were tendered were published at the end of each day on its website. It even gave a few replies to RTIs. But opacity soon set in, presumably following gag orders from the government.[102] All information related to demonetization was withheld on grounds of national security. Queries related to demonetization, including from the press, RTIs and parliamentary committees, were blocked by the government.

What was to be gained from this secrecy after the demonetization exercise was complete is not clear. Ideally, the government should

have laid on the floor of Parliament a white paper or statement on
the measurable results of the move.

After the First Fifty Days

It was expected that PM Modi would shed the veil of secrecy and
publicize the achievements of the demonetization exercise once
the initial fifty-day period was up.[103] Nearly every individual in the
country had been affected by it. Expectations of a pay-off in return
for the inconveniences endured had built up. An escalation in the
war against black money and corruption seemed imminent. The
sense of anticipation peaked when it was announced that the prime
minister would make another national broadcast. It was speculated
that he would share details of how the 'surgical strike on the black
economy'[104] would enter the next stage. The country waited for its
breath to be taken away—to see the obviously corrupt sent behind
bars, their ill-gotten wealth disgorged, and, hopefully, distributed
among the rest.

Modi's follow-up broadcast, a New Year's Eve address to the
nation marking the expiry of the first fifty days, however, contained
none of this. Belying hopes, he announced a relief package for
senior citizens, women, farmers and small businesses, essentially
those groups the demonetization had hit hard. Instead of reform,
Modi had chosen relief.

Relief is usually provided after calamities, accidents and
disasters, or during an economic slowdown. Relief for coping with
government policy is rare. If a policy needs follow-up relief, the
least one can say is, it was not well thought out. Relief for enduring
demonetization sounded less like part of an original plan and more
of an afterthought. The prime minister's address became the first
clear indication that things had not quite gone as desired.

The continuing caginess of the government, along with the
giveaways, suggested that the demonetization project was not
proceeding as desired, and that in the absence of measurable and

demonstrable achievements, the government had sought to buy time and support with sops to preclude, or at least postpone, an admission of failure.

Demonetization exposed the system. It also exposed Modi. In the days following his 31 December speech, hopes for a new wave of economic reforms receded. The government steered clear of reforms and opted for populism. Demonetization drained Modi's political capital. The severe hardships inflicted had been defended with statements such as, 'There is no magic wand; every policy has a stated goal as well as secondary consequences, some of which are unintended. Pay the price if you want a clean economy,' and so forth.

The exercise was presented as decisive action necessary to make long-term economic gains, even if at the cost of short-term pain—a project in nation-building. A bargain every individual had to make, in which the inconveniences and losses endured are to rid the foreseeable future of corruption and black money. By design, the enumeration of the impact of demonetization on such goals had to be postponed to the (undefined) future. But even the meagre disclosures from the RBI already suggested there was no need to wait for the future to understand whether the call to go ahead with the exercise had been a calculated risk backed by sound analyses, or a reckless experiment.

Some Unanswered Questions

With the slim evidence from the RBI, the few replies to RTIs and a parliamentary committee, a sketchy reconstruction of the demonetization decision is possible. Unless file notings from the PMO and the finance ministry can prove otherwise, the various written submissions by the RBI, when pieced together, suggest that the demonetization project was carried out in haste and without adequate application of mind, and possibly without a plan. It could well have been on a whim.

It appears that the RBI received a letter from the government on 7 November 2013.[105] This letter contained advice from the government that the RBI withdraw the legal tender of the Rs 500 and Rs 1000 notes in circulation. In other words, the government wanted the central bank to cancel or declare invalid currency notes of these two denominations. Three objectives had been stated in this missive: mitigation of counterfeiting, mitigation of terror financing and mitigation of black money. The government advised the RBI to place these matters of immediacy before its board for consideration.

The board hurriedly met the subsequent evening at 5:30 pm in New Delhi. No agenda was shared. The board members clearly knew that it was a meeting at an unusual time for an unusual purpose. The board was working on depleted strength. Due to vacancies, just three independent members attended this all-important meeting of 8 November.[106] The law provides for fourteen independent members on the twenty-one-member board of RBI. Governor Urjit Patel, Deputy Governors R. Gandhi and S.S. Mundra and two secretary-level bureaucrats from the finance ministry, Shaktikanta Das and Anjuly Chib Duggal, were present, bringing up the attendance count to eight.

The proposal before the board was in effect to cull more than 80 per cent of the notes in circulation. With full knowledge of the inadequacy of its stock of the new Rs 2000 notes that its presses had begun printing, the RBI board, functioning as a proxy for the Modi government, dutifully stamped its approval on the recommendation for demonetization. Hours later, the same evening, Modi obtained his cabinet's sanction, and by midnight, more than 85 per cent of the cash in the hands of Indians was turned into worthless paper.[107]

Whether a note for cabinet was prepared is not known. None appears to have been circulated or tabled at the cabinet meeting. Ministers who were present later admitted, privately, that they were 'told' at the meeting that high-denomination notes were being demonetized. Made to leave their phones outside and barred from leaving the venue immediately, they were allowed to depart only after the prime minister's live telecast had concluded.[108] Chief Economic Adviser Arvind Subramanian has persistently refused to say whether he had been consulted or taken into confidence. On 8 November he watched Modi's 'dramatic' nationally televised speech in his room in North Block.[109]

A number of questions remain unanswered with regard to the checks and balances that the institutions of the cabinet and the RBI board were supposed to provide in the case of the 2016 demonetization. These are:

- Did any of the ministers seek clarifications, pose concerns or in any way add value to the decision-making process?
- Did the checks and balances built into the government's decision-making machinery against arbitrary diktats kick in?
- Did the RBI board get only all of one day to calculate the associated risks and potential unintended consequences? To consider the extent to which demonetization could disrupt the economy? To weigh the costs and factors that might mitigate the potential pay-offs? To examine if there could be alternatives to demonetization?

The only other demonetization exercise undertaken in India had been in 1978 when the process followed was different.[110] The government then had promulgated an ordinance rather than taking the route of an RBI board decision. The move was enacted under the High Denomination Bank Note (Demonetization) Act, 1978, under which all high-denomination banknotes ceased to be legal tender after 16 January 1978. The Modi government's demonetization was done by the RBI board and cabinet approval, and thus bypassed Parliament. In 1978, all banks and government treasuries had to send to the RBI the total value of high-denomination banknotes held by them at the close of business on

16 January.[111] People were given till 24 January the same year—a week's time—to exchange any high-denomination banknotes.

'Given the way the RBI board works, I have no doubt that beyond asking questions, by way of seeking information, the members are unlikely to have actively protested. Materially, they won't have changed the proposal at all. I have seen how the board functions. Even if the government does not give formal instructions, and makes informal requests only, they get accepted,' says a former RBI governor on the Modi government's demonetization decision.[112]

In general, with the consolidation of power—and accountability—in the PMO, approvals under this government were swift, unlike in the UPA. The PMO's go-ahead was usually sufficient for making pronouncements. The cabinet's post facto consent was obtained later. The easing of caps on foreign investment announced in November 2015, two days after the BJP suffered a resounding defeat in the Bihar assembly polls, was one such decision.

'We have expedited these changes over the last couple of weeks. This exercise could have otherwise taken over a year and would have needed over 16 cabinet notes,' an official had said at the time.[113]

If the institution of the PMO had seemed enervated in the tenure of the UPA government, under Modi the institution of the cabinet suffered. The cabinet was informed about demonetization just a few minutes before its proclamation. A deal for the purchase of fighter jets was similarly announced by the prime minister while on a trip to France, and the cabinet committee on security's approvals were processed later. The policy paralysis Modi inherited was a thing of the past. But does speedy decision-making necessarily imply that quality decisions are made?

The window for turning in the demonetized notes closed on 30 December 2016. The government issued an ordinance to extinguish the RBI's liability towards honouring the returning notes. Months later, the central bank was still not done counting, and was unable to say how many notes were turned in. Not only was this tardiness, but it also held up evidence-based assessment of the extent of success or failure of the note ban. Without the data, how much black money was extinguished, if any at all, could not be estimated.

The first disclosure from the RBI came in its annual report released on 30 August 2017.[114] These were not final numbers, but the hope of a large surplus transfer from the RBI to the government was dispelled. The near-final numbers came in on 24 August 2018.[115] Far from a large surplus, the RBI reported collateral damage: the demonetization exercise had upset the RBI's balance sheet, with the cost of printing new notes more than doubling to Rs 7965 crore in 2016–17, from Rs 3421 crore in the previous year.[116] Higher printing and freight charges for notes and higher provisions for the contingency fund had escalated expenditures. RBI's income declined to Rs 61,818 crore from Rs 80,870 crore, while its total expenditure more than doubled to Rs 31,155 crore from Rs 14,990 crore.[117] The government had budgeted for a Rs 58,000 crore dividend from the RBI. But the bank could transfer just Rs 30,659 crore to the exchequer, which was less than half the Rs 65,876 crore it had paid to the government in 2015–16.[118] The lower dividend payout would create fresh tensions between the government and the RBI.

The biggest revelation of the disclosure in RBI's annual report for the year 2017–18 released on 24 August 2018 was, of course, that 99.3 per cent of the demonetized Rs 500 and Rs 1000 currency notes had returned to the central bank, with just a fraction remaining outside.[119] At final count, of the Rs 15.41 lakh crore of these notes in circulation, Rs 15.31 lakh crore had been returned.[120] Barely Rs 10,720 crore had remained unreturned.[121]

Even if all the unreturned notes were black money, demonetization had 'penalized' black money holders by immobilizing barely 0.7 per cent of the demonetized notes, a success rate poorer than that of the demonetization of 1978, when 1.8 per cent of the cancelled notes had remained unreturned.[122]

The attorney general had said that Rs 5 lakh crore was expected to remain unreturned, presumably by black money hoarders.[123] The Modi government had bet on the extinguished hoards representing a loss, and therefore a penalty on the corrupt. The reduced liabilities of outstanding money to be honoured as a consequence, it was assumed, would deliver a windfall to the RBI, which could then pass on a huge special dividend to the government. Spending the money so raised on welfare, the government had hoped, would make demonetization a sort of redistribution of wealth from the corrupt to the disadvantaged. The expectations had now proved a pipe dream.

Changed Tune on Demonetization

The near-term economic costs had outweighed the gains, if any so far, of demonetization.[124] The government's worst fear now was that if any more demonetized notes were returned to the central bank, and the figure crossed the total money in circulation in the demonetized notes, it would mean that demonetization had been used for money laundering. The limitations of the demonetization idea possibly dawned on the government at some point. From there on, it became a management exercise and a staging of inaccuracies and untruths. The Modi government now changed its tune. Confiscating money was never the objective of demonetization, said Jaitley.[125] Taking their cue from this, finance ministry officials too began giving statements saying that all scrapped banknotes were in fact expected to come back to the banking system.

The government abandoned the position it had taken in the Supreme Court. Asked about Attorney General Mukul Rohatgi's submission in the Supreme Court that an estimated Rs 4-5 lakh crore wouldn't be returned, secretary, Economic Affairs, Subhash Chandra Garg said it had been 'an opinion'.[126]

'The centre never said that it expects any currency not to come back. I don't think the government ever made any statement in Parliament or otherwise or as part of an affidavit.'[127]

The government's spokespersons would ascribe newer goals with passing time, only to have facts and data contradict their claims. Lauded initially as a master stroke, mounting a defence of demonetization became a Sisyphean enterprise.

Not willing to give in to emerging facts, the government celebrated the first anniversary of demonetization on 8 November 2017 as the first Anti-Black Money Day. Cabinet ministers dispersed to state capitals where they waxed eloquent on demonetization's numerous putative successes. The prime minister headed to Gujarat, which was soon to go to the polls. All day there was much speech-making. Rhetoric blended with half-baked analyses, and self-praise with fierce attacks on the Opposition.

Missing from the government's statements and presentations was conclusive proof of reduced corruption and evidence-backed answers to questions like: Were fewer bribes being paid and demanded than a year ago? Was corruption down? Were Indians evading tax less, post-demonetization?

Did the government know? Did it care to know?

An assessment of demonetization on reducing the black economy would be complete only if its deliverables on the state of corruption and the corrupt are established. Unmindful, the BJP nevertheless celebrated what had not—and possibly cannot—be measured. Ironically, the lavish celebrations of this unproven attack on black money hoarders were billed to the exchequer and footed by honest taxpayers. The bandobast details, released to the media in advance for maximum effect, suggested that the plan for unrolling the blitzkrieg had been meticulous. If only similarly exacting standards had also been applied to thinking through demonetization itself!

Urjit Patel: Bystander or Participant?

When Urjit Patel was elevated to the position of governor weeks before demonetization was announced, among the qualities that recommended him for the job were his orthodoxy, his technical competence and an evident indifference to the limelight (in contrast to his predecessor, Raghuram Rajan).[128] He had trained in macroeconomics at highbrow campuses, picking up BSc, MPhil and PhD degrees from the London School of Economics, University of Oxford and Yale University, respectively. His expertise on India goes back to the 1991 reforms that he had, as the IMF's deputy resident representative in New Delhi, monitored up close.

Deputy governor since 2013, he was well disposed towards maximum convergence with Delhi. Those acquainted with Patel's economic philosophy were somewhat surprised at the choice, though, for he had never once throughout his career demonstrated an inclination for adventurism and had enjoyed a reputation for conservatism. He was seen as a firm believer in institutional checks that force governments—even myopic and opportunistic regimes— to choose economically sound policies over those influenced by electoral calculations.

On out-of-turn interest-rate cuts and other wild expectations, it was thought he'd be no more likely to yield to the government than his high-profile predecessor. A lot of his time at the RBI had been spent reshaping and retooling monetary policy to insulate it from precisely such pressures. The manner of Rajan's exit from the RBI, after a high-pitch campaign questioning his integrity, suggested his replacement would be someone pliable, a trait Patel did not seem to possess.

Living up to expectations, Patel did not toe New Delhi's line on interest rates. On the rare occasion, he had spoken plainly, coldly and publicly to powerful politicians, advising against an ill-informed policy: his denouncement of loan waivers had come barely hours after Uttar Pradesh Chief Minister Yogi Adityanath announced that he would be going ahead with his party's poll promise to farmers. But Patel's governorship became an unusual one, and cannot be judged by the usual metrics. Demonetization put Patel in sharp focus.

Patel kept his public utterances to the minimum, making it impossible to guess whether he too saw demonetization as an ineffective policy tool to control black money and corruption, if he too found it unkind and unjust to the honest and the vulnerable, a diktat that was bound to inflict undue economic hardships on the people. In this, Patel's silence is puzzling. Demonetization does appear to be the sort of policy tool he might have tended to disapprove of. The power to say 'no' to government over demonetization may not be available to the RBI, as it is bound legally to manage currency, as many of his predecessors have also explained.

But did Governor Patel try to buy time to arrange supplies of new notes? His role in the demonetization of 2016 remains unclear. Was it of a bystander or a participant?

'There is no reason to presume that Governor Patel did not push back against the demonetization decision. In all probability he explained to the government, as indeed any of his predecessors would have, the policy challenges and operational difficulties of implementation. Could he have blocked demonetization? Not clear. The decision to recommend demonetization was that of the board of the RBI, not of the governor alone. We are not privy to the discussion in the Board,' a former governor told me.[129]

'Should Patel have resigned on the demonetization issue? Again not clear. It's a decision for an individual governor to make depending on how strongly he felt about the issue,' he added.[130]

Reddy wrote in his memoir (not in the context of demonetization, though):[131]

While interacting with the government, I had to sometimes take a firm stance on important issues. If there were persisting differences of views, I was prepared to annoy, or even irritate and frustrate the Sovereign, if necessary. But I was not inclined to defy . . . The law provides for the government to give written directives in public interest to the RBI. Prior consultation with the Governor, however, is mandatory. On critical issues where there is a difference of opinion, often the choice is for the Governor to concede to the sovereign with or without a written directive.[132]

Information available in the public domain so far makes it difficult to comment on the precise role Patel played in the run-up to the demonetization announcement on 8 November 2016. The experience of demonetization, and the indelible mark it left on the RBI's public image, though, may have deeply impacted him. Before long, he began to put his foot down on policy diktats from Delhi. His refusal to be pushed around cost him his job in 2018. The controversy leading up to his exit was nastier and uglier than in the case of Rajan's departure.

RBI's Unprecedented Credibility Crisis

Elections for the Uttar Pradesh assembly took place over seven phases in February–March 2017. Sifting gold from an otherwise muddy experience, the BJP reaped rich electoral dividends on the issue of demonetization, riding on its putative successes in penalizing the corrupt, in the UP polls. Voters, probably judging the policy in terms of intent rather than outcomes, handed the party a landslide victory. The BJP's rise in political popularity came alongside an erosion in institutional credibility for the RBI. The RBI took full blame for demonetization's messy execution and the missing numbers. Its public standing suffered. Patel's own reputation took a beating, with even senior parliamentarians unable to resist making fun of the governor publicly.

It was Manmohan Singh who stepped in to have MPs in a parliamentary committee spare Patel the ordeal of answering pointed questions about demonetization.[133] The idea of demonetization originated in government presumably, but the RBI got the flak for it. This is the context in which Patel's continued silence put the RBI, one of India's most respected institutions, at the centre of a political issue. By the time of the Gujarat polls in December 2017, the BJP's political gains from demonetization had either dissipated or had been neutralized by the GST-related disaffection. But the RBI's sullied image never fully recovered from the blotch of demonetization.

Demonetization: Who's to Blame?

A dial-back to August 2014 could have disabused the government of the notion that demonetization could resurrect its anti-black money plank. Asked about demonetization at the Lalit Doshi memorial lecture, Raghuram Rajan had made it crystal clear that killing black money is not as simple as killing high-value notes.[134]

> I am not quite sure if what you meant is demonetize the old notes and introduce new notes instead. In the past, demonetization has been thought of as a way of getting black money out of circulation. Because people then have to come and say, 'How do I have this ten crore in cash sitting in my safe?', and they have to explain where they got the money from. It is often cited as a solution. Unfortunately, my sense is, the clever find ways around it. Black money hoarders find ways to divide their hoard into many smaller pieces. You find that people who haven't thought of a way to convert black to white, throw it into the *hundi* in some temples. I think there are ways around demonetization. It is not that easy to flush out the black money.[135]

Focus on incentives that lead to the generation and retention of black money would be his advice to anyone asking, he added.

In his book *I Do What I Do* he clarifies that the matter had not been broached by the government at the time he responded to the question put to him. His views were sought eighteen months later, in February 2016. He gave his opinion orally, and, as is his wont, in no uncertain terms. The thrust of his arguments was similar to what he had earlier aired publicly.[136]

He was then asked to prepare a note, which the RBI put together and handed to the government. It outlined the potential costs and benefits of demonetization, as well as alternatives that could achieve similar aims. If the government, on weighing the pros and cons, still decided to go ahead with demonetization, the note outlined the preparation that would be needed, and the time that preparation would require. It flagged what could happen if the preparation was inadequate. The government then set up a committee to consider the issues. The RBI's deputy governor in charge of currency attended these meetings.[137]

At no point during his term was the RBI asked to make a decision on demonetization, Rajan notes, dissociating from the board's approval completely.[138]

The disclosure reinscribes the riddle of his exit: Did Rajan's stand on demonetization, in addition to his uncompromising policy on NPAs, render his position in the RBI untenable? The government and Rajan were evidently not on the same page on demonetization, and his keenness to distance himself from the decision is unmistakable. Whether it was these differences, or something else that sent him packing, cannot be said conclusively. Rajan has not fully disclosed the exact circumstances of his exit yet.

The other mystery that remains unresolved is who thought up the demonetization, and whether it was someone in government or outside. The idea did not originate in the RBI; it merely processed instructions from Delhi.

In light of Rajan's revelations, which the government has not refuted, what can be said conclusively is: one, the RBI's recommendation to the government was that demonetization would prove to be a weak weapon in its war on black money, and that superior policy alternatives were available for achieving the objective. Two, the government proceeded to overrule this expert advice. Three, demonetization's non-success subsequently confirmed that the RBI had been on point.

To characterize demonetization as a well-intended decision that got marred by poor implementation is to gloss over the fact that Modi pressed ahead resolutely with full cognizance of the RBI's misgivings. He had been apprised of what it could not do, what it would certainly do, and how woefully unready the banking system was for it. Incontrovertibly, there were forewarnings in the RBI's note on demonetization's potential for disruption. The improbability of success was also made known to him. Alternatives were recommended. The counsel in the note was rebuffed. Even after Rajan had explained the economics of demonetization, Modi persisted.

The accountability and the responsibility for the all-failure-no-victory stunt, then, wholly and solely rest with Modi, who turned a deaf ear to the RBI's written and the governor's oral advice. It wouldn't be unfair to conclude that he hurt the economy on purpose—like some medieval conqueror who could not be bothered about counting the costs.

The question is, in pursuit of what? The answer may lie in the politics, not the economics, of demonetization.

Suit-boot ki Sarkar: Power of a Slogan

Rajan received the government's call for his opinion on demonetization in February 2016, when the mood in the BJP could hardly have been peachy. It had suffered humiliating defeats in state assembly polls held in the run-up to this call. After the delirious unbroken high of the previous year, 2015 had opened dispiritingly for the BJP. In February, the party received a drubbing in Delhi at the hands of an upstart, the Aam Aadmi Party, winning just three of the seventy seats for the picking. The prime minister could not have been pleased about the turn of fortune. The magnitude of the loss stung. Up until this thrashing, the BJP had bagged every state that had gone to polls after the Modi government was sworn in in 2014: Haryana, Maharashtra, Jammu and Kashmir, and Jharkhand. But now, the capital that sits at the heart of the country's map, and was to be the crown piece in the BJP's conquest, instead of revalidating it, had resisted the 'Modi Wave'. The next assembly polls were lined up as late as November. No early redemption was possible.

By all accounts, the rout in Delhi was disorienting for the government and the prime minister. Modi did not fancy a challenger so early in his term. The initial energy and intent now gave way to incoherence and contradiction. Some party leaders interpreted the poll results as a resounding rejection of economic reforms. The Modi government's maiden budget in July had proposed decontrol of urea prices. Keeping fertilizer prices low was an election promise of the AAP in Delhi. The planned economic reform was hurriedly aborted. 'We are committed to keeping the policy pro-farmer,' late Ananth Kumar, fertilizer minister then, told me at that time.[139] Urea remains under statutory price control, which means its maximum retail price is fixed by the centre. Manmohan Singh's efforts to decontrol urea had similarly come to naught.

Adding insult to injury, that summer saw Rahul Gandhi give the government the epithet 'suit-boot ki sarkar' (a government for the wealthy), which stuck, finding resonance outside the political theatre. It negated Modi's pitch to voters of himself as a chaiwallah (tea-seller) rising against the odds through sheer hardship and dedication to become the prime minister of the country. To sharpen the message, he had repeatedly drawn contrasts between himself and Rahul Gandhi, who was born with a silver spoon in his mouth, to a family from which had come three prime ministers.

The unshakable tag of 'suit-boot ki sarkar' gave the Opposition a psychological upper hand. The Opposition was able to set the agenda. Modi's move to dilute the amendments to the land acquisition law passed by the UPA in 2013, an opportunity to present a reformist image, and a promise to BJP supporters in big business circles, became the first big setback for the government. The proposal was to dilute amendments the UPA government had introduced (discussed earlier in this book) as 'safeguards' into the land acquisition legislation. Farmers were restless over the move to empower industrialists to buy land without the owners' consent. Gandhi's 'suit-boot' barb was delivered on the floor of the House, during a discussion on the proposed amendments.[140]

Till then the government's focus had been on industry. 'Make In India' and 'Ease of Doing Business' dominated its policy agenda and publicity strategy. Its narrow ambition for farmers, traditionally not a constituency of the BJP, was that they needed to be somehow pulled out of agriculture and re-engaged in industry. It firmly believed that their land was better off with industrialists who could put it to more productive use.

Modi had launched 'Make in India' in the company of big capitalists, and had shared the stage on a couple of other occasions with owners of large corporations.[141] The imagery implied in the 'suit-boot ki sarkar' barb was of a prime minister so cosy with big business he was willing to suspend farmers' land ownership rights.

Barely two days before Gandhi's speech in Parliament, Jaitley had seemed confident about the Modi government's plans for the land acquisition amendment and public support for it. He had told me in an interview:

[The 2013 Act legislated by the UPA government] keeps rural areas poor in perpetuity. It prevents infrastructure development in rural areas. It prevents irrigation, rural roads, rural electrification, housing for the poor—for people from rural areas who want to migrate to suburban centres and have a better quality of life and for 300 million landless labour whose best prospects of getting a job is in industries set up in rural areas. It prevents the creation of industrial corridors . . . There is no sentiment [against Modi government's proposed amendments]. The power of acquisition of land is eminent domain. It is a part of the sovereign power. How would you get consent if the industrial corridor, let us say between Bangalore and Hyderabad, is to be created. Will you go in for consent of one lakh people? Therefore, you have to balance private interest with the larger interest of society. India has to take a decision whether it wants to keep its poor in poverty or whether it wants to urbanise, industrialise, wants to create urban-like facilities in rural areas or not . . . Ultimately, any form of development—townships are not going to be built in mid-air, railway stations are not going to be built in mid-air—they will require land. Ports are not going to be built in mid-air. National security requirements are not going to be satisfied with that. And for all national purposes including the welfare predominantly of rural areas, you will require some aspect of rural land . . . you have to balance private interest with the larger public interest.

Politically, Gandhi's epithet proved a master stroke. The BJP, probably still fighting the ghost of its 2004 'India Shining' debacle, was stung to the quick. Modi and his government took a while to recover from it. Starting that summer, and gradually over the course of that year and the next one, Modi redefined his economic agenda. 'Make In India' was allowed to slowly fade away from public memory. The land amendment was shelved. An ordinance through which farmland could be acquired for private projects without owners' consent had been repromulgated multiple times. It was allowed to lapse.

In his second Independence Day speech from the ramparts of the Red Fort, in contrast to the year before, Modi spoke of farmers, not 'Make In India'.[142] 'Start Up India' and 'Stand Up India' were announced to rebut Gandhi's charge of being a pro-business government.

By this time, Modi rarely addressed captains of industry. If on occasion he did, he made it a point to speak as a messiah of the poor, giving his voice to arguments that had a definitive leftist ring to them. In January 2016, he addressed the Economic Times Global Business Summit. He spoke of farmers, fertilizer subsidy, Mudra, Start Up India and Stand Up India. Even of khadi. But did not mention Make In India even once.

He told his audience comprising capitalists and investors:[143]

> I have been referring to cooking gas, fertilizer and kerosene subsidies. I must confess that I am surprised by the way words are used by experts on this matter. When a benefit is given to farmers or to the poor, experts and government officers normally call it a subsidy. However, I find that if a benefit is given to industry or commerce, it is usually called an 'incentive' or a 'subvention'. We must ask ourselves whether this difference in language also reflects a difference in our attitude? Why is it that subsidies going to the well-off are portrayed in a positive manner? Let me give you an example. The total revenue loss from incentives to corporate tax payers was over Rs 62,000 crores. Dividends and long-term capital gains on shares traded in stock exchanges are totally exempt from income tax even though it is not the poor who earn them. Since it is exempt, it is not even counted in the Rs 62,000 crores. Double Taxation Avoidance treaties have in some cases resulted in double non-taxation. This also is not counted in the Rs 62,000 crores. Yet these are rarely referred to by those who seek reduction of subsidies. Perhaps these are seen as incentives for investment. I wonder whether, if the fertiliser subsidy is re-named as 'incentive for agricultural production', some experts will view it differently.

Even as Modi was trying to carefully reinvent his image, a second setback followed in Bihar. The state assembly poll results were out on 9 November 2015. (Rajan's views on demonetization were asked for four months later, in February 2016.) The BJP lost again. Redemption, even after an agonizing wait and a strident campaign bordering on hysteria, was not to be. Worse, defeat had been dealt this time by a united Opposition. It was a personal setback; Modi had been the main campaigner. After collapsing on the shores of relatively urban Delhi, now the cow-belt state of Bihar had sent the 'Modi Wave' receding. The beating in Bihar could be ascribed to electoral arithmetic, but what of Delhi?

The winter session of Parliament was on; the BJP's lack of majority in the Upper House, in the face of a resurgent Opposition, had rendered the government's extensive legislative agenda difficult to achieve. In particular, to clear the Rajya Sabha, the constitutional amendment needed to roll out the GST needed support from the Congress's seventy members, as its passage required two-thirds of the votes. P. Chidambaram had made it clear even before the Bihar poll results were declared that nothing short of a call from the prime minister to correct course and reach out to the Opposition could save the bill and the session.[144]

The series of political blows left the government in shock. Following the twin debacles of 2015, 2016 brought more defeats. Out of five state polls held in 2016—in Tamil Nadu, Puducherry, Kerala, West Bengal and Assam—the BJP won only one: Assam. In response, it backtracked from its entire economic reforms agenda: putting on hold, diluting or stalling planned corrective measures for land acquisition, labour, insolvency and banks. Stunned at the unexpected directional shift, a key government economist hand-picked by Modi told me in a private conversation, 'Centre was already to the left in India. Now, even the right has shifted leftwards.'[145]

Post-demonetization, the BJP's electoral record was in fact resurrected, although the causality between demonetization and the electoral performances is for political observers to examine. It won Uttar Pradesh massively and the entire north-east. But by December 2017, the decline started once again with Gujarat, where it was handed a reduced majority, and Karnataka, followed by Chhattisgarh, Rajasthan and Madhya Pradesh.

Efforts were redoubled to ensure the passage of the Constitution Amendment Bill required for rolling out the GST that the Congress, its original architect, was supportive of. Modi hosted Sonia and Manmohan Singh for discussions.[146] Jaitley expressed his openness to discuss the GST with Rahul Gandhi and met him to extend an invitation to his daughter's wedding.[147]

Sonia nominated the Congress's senior Rajya Sabha leader Anand Sharma to coordinate with Revenue Secretary Hasmukh Adhia and Chief Economic Adviser Arvind Subramanian. Sharma had earned a reputation for delivering against odds. In the dying years of UPA-2, he had persevered to ensure the impact on exports of the global economic downturn would be minimal, and in the face of stiff opposition from the BJP, multi-brand retail was opened to FDI. Now he worked for the interlocution on GST with the government.

The BJP's strategists, meanwhile, returned to the drawing board to resurrect the 'Modi Wave' that seemed in danger of fizzling out prematurely. The narrative was spinning out of control. The government had failed to dazzle on the promise of recouping black money held overseas. The Modi government's black money disclosure schemes had yielded minimal results and even less political mileage.[148] After the drubbing the BJP received in Delhi in early 2015, the danger of the anti-corruption mantle being seized by the Aam Aadmi Party's Arvind Kejriwal loomed. A hunt was launched for a 'politically-saleable' scheme.[149] The return of the Manmohan Singh government in 2009 is attributed to its 'pro-poor' policies, among them a loan waiver for farmers and the Mahatma Gandhi National Rural Employment Guarantee Scheme. Eager to discard its 'pro-business' tag, the BJP decided to invest in a 'pro-poor' image too. The quest ultimately led to demonetization which, it was decided, would be marketed as an assault on the rich and on hoarders of black money. The political appeal of a scheme to sponge off the rich was irresistible.

Demonetization happened against the counsel received from bureaucrats and technocrats that it would not downsize the black economy or force-formalize the informal sector, and that there were better ways of achieving the same results at a lower cost. That Modi pushed full force on demonetization, ignoring the counsel, strongly suggests that the move was in fact a political one aimed at negating the 'big money' narrative and reviving his 'black money' narrative.

Demonetization held the promise of killing many political birds with one stone. It kept the black money rhetoric alive, gifted the government a brand-new pro-poor image and delivered rich electoral dividends in the Uttar Pradesh state assembly polls.

So effective was Modi's PR on demonetization that his government almost overnight transformed from being seen as a friend of the super-rich to a saviour of the poor and the downtrodden. Modi was successful in airbrushing his image. Demonetization served this purpose and checked off the necessary boxes. And yet, the politics of demonetization were to prove costly for the economy.

As was in fact expected, demonetization did not bring to book any well-known big-ticket black money hoarders. Nor did it substantially improve income tax collection. The direct taxes-GDP ratio went no further than 5.9 per cent in 2017–18,[150] significantly lower than the peak 6.3 per cent, achieved in 2007–08, the pre-global financial crisis year.

While the making and remaking of governance agendas was on, decreed by political calculations, the economy's growth engines started sputtering.

Originally, the Modi government had identified manufacturing as a growth engine for delivering its electoral promises, given its capacity to create jobs that can absorb the slack from the farms. That had been one of the main ideas behind the 'Make in India' push. Initially, following directions from the Supreme Court, a plan was put in place in 2015 to ensure coal supplies. FDI norms were liberalized. Through executive orders, there was an attempt to remove the bottlenecks to bring stuck and new projects on stream.

The hope was that the new incomes from new factories and ventures would generate purchasing power for products, completing a virtuous spiral. For this, the Skill India drive was to harness the demographic dividend.[151]

But soon the government's focus and energies had shifted to crafting a pro-poor image. It did not follow through with a well-thought-out strategy for easing the constraints and challenges that were holding back manufacturing. The economic growth engine could not be cranked up for delivering jobs. The twelve-fold jump in imports of electronic goods from $3.4 billion in 2011–12 to $42 billion in 2016–17 demonstrates the non-success of the flagship 'Make In India'.[152]

It's important to separate the policy failures of the incumbents from the legacy issues, though. The bad bank loans mess had been inherited from the previous government but had been allowed to worsen through inaction. The NDA government did not provide the necessary policy support to investments and exports, the two growth generators in the UPA years, or to manufacturing, its own choice of growth engine. Many of its policy decisions, in fact, added to economic hardships. Demonetization was a drag on an already slowing economy.[153] GST further dampened growth impulses. If demonetization led to demand destruction, the GST roll-out had disastrous effects on the supply side. The twin shocks compounded the problems of industry, big and small. The recovery stalled.

In rural India, despite bumper harvests, and despite Modi's utterances from the ramparts of the Red Fort, farm incomes crashed. Despite good rains and export controls, stocking limits for private traders and imports were managed poorly, resulting in gluts that sent market prices down, leading to farm loan waivers across states. Some IT and other companies cut a few thousand jobs, resulting in urban Indians being laid off. The RBI's analysis showed that wages in rural areas remained stagnant from 2014 onwards.

GST, a Problematic Approach

During the UPA's tenure, the BJP states had staunchly opposed GST on conceptual grounds. The spoilers ranged from insecurities that state legislatures may end up surrendering their fiscal sovereignty to concerns over loss of revenue, especially in the case of producer states, since unlike most of the taxes that the GST was to subsume, it would be collected at the point of consumption and not at the factory gate, for instance. There were reservations from some states who felt that a uniform rate of taxation would deny them the autonomy of imposing taxes, which they believed to be their sovereign right. All objections, however, were glossed over the day the BJP formed the government at the centre.

The recommendation for GST had first come in 2004 from a task force formed by the Vajpayee government under economist Vijay Kelkar.[154] Keen initially to craft a flawless GST, Jaitley had, in 2014, turned to Kelkar, the thirteenth Finance Commission chairman, for advice. The commission had in 2009 submitted a report recommending a single-rate GST.[155] Its calculations had showed that there would be no loss of tax revenue from the shift to GST if it were imposed uniformly across all goods and services at the rate of 12 per cent. In discussions with Jaitley, Kelkar endorsed a 'pure GST' that would exempt no goods or services at all, not even real estate, liquor and petroleum products, and would have a single rate—between 10 per cent and 12 per cent. This view eventually acquired the epithet, 'One nation, one tax'.

After the Bihar elections, on Manmohan Singh's advice, the Congress set aside its political differences with the ruling party to discuss the GST. Anand Sharma handled the back-channel talks with Jaitley, Adhia and Subramanian. Constitution (122nd Amendment) Bill, 2014, which was the bill to amend the Constitution and pave the way for the roll-out of GST, became a political football between the Congress and the BJP, and finally hit the goalpost in 2016 in the monsoon session of Parliament, with the main opposition party, the Congress, finally lending its unequivocal support.

The bill, approved by the Lok Sabha in May 2015, had got stuck in the Rajya Sabha, where the ruling BJP did not have a majority. At the culmination of weeks of back-room parleys between the government and the Congress, the Congress gave up its key demand for including a cap of 18 per cent on the GST rate in the Constitution. The government, on the other hand, agreed to address the Congress's concerns. The Congress had been insisting on the institution of an independent mechanism for dispute resolution. The stalemate ended after no less than seven rounds of discussions.[156]

Late in July, Jaitley and Arvind Subramanian held deliberations with leaders of the Congress, the Left, the Trinamool Congress, the SP and the JD(U) to garner support for the passage of the bill. CPI(M) general secretary Sitaram Yechury, former Finance Minister P. Chidambaram, who had just been elected to the Rajya Sabha, and Congress leader Anand Sharma were among those who participated in the separate rounds of discussions.[157] The government was also in touch with AIADMK leader and Tamil Nadu Chief Minister J. Jayalalithaa.

The Congress initially raised three demands in exchange for supporting the bill.[158] Jaitley placed these before the states, a large number of which were ruled by BJP governments, but they vetoed two of three—the demand for a constitutional cap of 18 per cent and an independent dispute resolution mechanism headed by a high court judge. Following this the Congress had no option but to change its stand.

Until then the Congress had been insisting that rather than be a purely executive body, the dispute resolution authority should have legally trained officials and the trappings of judicial authority. In the party's assessment, the sweeping changes set to be made to the indirect taxation system were bound to throw up issues of implementation.[159] It was inevitable that sooner or later disputes would arise between states, and that some, dissatisfied with the verdict of the dispute resolution authority, might go to the high court or the Supreme Court. And if and when states, unable to resolve disputes among themselves, did land up in courts, the power of judicial review would be with the high court and the Supreme Court. It is for this reason that the Constitution Amendment Bill introduced by Pranab Mukherjee, which had lapsed with the term of the previous Lok Sabha, had suggested a dispute resolution authority chaired by a retired judge. But that provision was now rejected by the states and the centre.

Chidambaram explained the Congress position on the GST rates thus: 'A higher rate will be inflationary. I am all for progressively reducing indirect taxes, which is what I did in 1997, which is what we did between 2004 and 2014. I would never support an increasing rate of an indirect tax. That is a policy approach. Indirect taxes, which are regressive, must be progressively lowered. Direct taxes, which are progressive taxes, must be gradually increased.'[160]

The Congress gave up its demand for a constitutional cap of 18 per cent in deference to the state governments, which had to ratify the Constitutional Amendment Bill passed by Parliament and which insisted against the cap in the bill.

'The state finance ministers, barring one or two Congress ministers, seem to have persuaded themselves to think that the cap should not be in the Constitutional Amendment Bill. So we had to necessarily defer to their opinion, but we are not giving up our basic demand that there must be a cap on the standard rate,' Chidambaram explained.[161]

His proposal was, 'The GST Council must enforce the rule that there can only be three rates: a standard rate, a standard minus rate [for wage goods], and a standard plus rate [for demerit or luxury goods]. The standard rate will fall on, say, 70–75 per cent of the goods and services, which doesn't derogate from the principle that there is "one nation, one tax".'

Before the bill was put to vote in the Rajya Sabha, the chief negotiator on the Congress side, Anand Sharma, disclosed that the party had agreed to let the rates be determined by the GST Council and was no longer insisting on 18 per cent as the GST rate, as the government, he told me, had assured it of 'legal ring-fencing' of GST tax rates, to be specified in the central GST law, the states' GST laws and the inter-state GST laws.[162]

The cabinet headed by Modi approved the sole Congress demand—of dropping a proposal for a provision regarding the imposition of a 1 per cent inter-state tax over and above the GST rate—that the states had approved.[163]

The constitutional amendment cleared the Rajya Sabha. Barely twenty-four hours later, the revenue secretary said it would be premature to expect the GST rate to be 18 per cent.

Parliament approved the constitution amendment in August 2016 to pave the way for the GST.[164] Only the AIADMK staged walkouts in both Houses ahead of voting on the bill. On the floor of the House, the government reached across the aisle, and the opposition and regional parties walked half the distance to see the constitutional amendment through. The political system set aside grudges and differences in the interest of the most significant tax reform in independent India.

Speaking in the Lok Sabha, Modi, while noting that all parties had risen above their ideological differences in support of the amendment, said: 'The GST could not be seen as the victory of a party or government . . . It is the victory for the democratic ethos of India and a victory for everyone.'[165] The bill would have been in trouble in the Rajya Sabha due to the BJP's lack of numbers and the reluctance of some states, but in the end all parties backed it, he said.

Lead speaker for the Congress in the Lok Sabha, Veerappa Moily, urged the government to acknowledge that 'If there was political consensus in 2011, this Bill would have been passed then.'[166] Several speakers, including Moily, Dharmendra Yadav of

Samajwadi Party and Congress leader Mallikarjun Kharge, sought to know why Modi had opposed the GST as the chief minister of Gujarat. While owning up to having had doubts over the GST as the chief minister of Gujarat when the bill was first introduced in the House in 2011, Modi said his misgivings about it had led him to speak several times to then Finance Minister Pranab Mukherjee, and as prime minister that experience had come in handy for him.[167]

Over the next few months, state legislatures ratified the constitutional amendment, and the necessary supporting legislations—the central GST Bill, the states' own GST Bills and the IGST Bill—were passed by Parliament and the states for rolling out the new tax regime.

After the legislative procedure was over, the GST Council, the all-empowered decision-making constitutional body on all issues including rates of the new tax, began giving shape to the new indirect tax regime. The council is chaired by the Union finance minister, but the centre's voting share is pegged at one-third of the total votes cast. The states' voting share taken together is assigned a weightage of two-thirds of the total votes cast. Decisions could be taken by 75 per cent majority. The council avoided voting, though, preferring to work through consensus.

Sixteen years in the making, the GST was finally rolled out on 1 July 2017, when at the stroke of midnight, taking a leaf out of Jawaharlal Nehru's book, Modi inaugurated the new indirect tax in Parliament's historic Central Hall.[168] 'A moment comes, which comes but rarely in history, when we step out from the old to new,' Nehru had said while ringing in India's independence. The two events were obviously not comparable—nonetheless, the GST's introduction could have been a rare transition for the country.[169] It turned out not to be so.

The Congress boycotted the midnight gala inauguration to protest the GST's suboptimal structure that had been decided in the GST Council in which the BJP-ruled states constituted a voting majority. Serious imperfections had in fact crept into the architecture. The GST rates for more than 1200 goods and services consumed in the country had been finalized by the GST Council. A fifth of these were to be taxed at 5 per cent or exempted. Another 17 per cent were to be taxed at 12 per cent. On 62 per cent of the items, the GST was to be paid at 18 per cent or 28 per cent, along with cesses to be imposed additionally in some cases. The extant taxation system was not given the boot. Electricity, real estate and alcohol remained in it, exempt from GST. Petroleum products were included in both the systems, old and new, but with zero-rate GST. Nearly eighty-three categories of services were exempted from GST.

More than sound economic, or political, logic, the GST seemed driven by the deciding authorities' discretion. The GST rate for gold, a luxury good, was set lower than that for matchboxes. The GST tax incidence was the same on environment-friendly hybrid vehicles and fossil-fuel-guzzling SUVs. In the extant system, the effective rate for guzzlers had been significantly higher than that for hybrids. This 'carbon tax' on SUVs, which are incidentally quite popular with politicians, was being withdrawn.

The GST was 18 per cent on soaps and washing soaps, but 28 per cent on detergents. To watch the same movie, some moviegoers paid 18 per cent GST and others 28 per cent, depending on the price of their cinema tickets—not exactly the promised 'one tax, one nation'. The basic principle of revenue collection is: the lower the taxation rate, the higher the compliance. But initially, more than half the items attracted 18 per cent or 28 per cent GST. An opportunity was lost to collect more tax revenues, while also taking a little load off the consumer's pocket.

The GST, to be collected on everything from matchboxes to gold, was to touch everyone. A modern tax system should be fair, uncomplicated, transparent and easy to administer. It must yield revenues sufficient to cover the cost of government services and public goods. India's GST did not pass these tests convincingly.

It was too complex. It needed to be collected at fewer and lower rates, and on a greater number of items.

Plus, the rates were a departure even from the BJP's own position. The party had in its manifesto for the 2009 Lok Sabha elections promised to strive for a GST rate of 12 per cent to 14 per cent.[170]

The roll-out was an outcome of a political process in which twenty-nine states and seven union territories agreed to give up their right to impose sales tax on goods (VAT), and the centre gave up its right to impose excise and services tax.[171] In the amended federal arrangement, each receives a share of the GST collected nationally. Instead of every state imposing a tax, they would now sit together and decide what that tax rate should be. Individually, states saw this as an erosion of their financial autonomy, although the finance minister, the chief architect of the consensus, described the amended federal arrangement as, 'the states and centre pooling their powers and sovereignty'. The centre and the states had become equal fiscal partners in sharing a common indirect tax base.

In effect, this was a 'grand bargain', with the centre undertaking to implement a commonly agreed-upon GST, which was designed and implemented by the GST Council in which the states and the centre were members. To dissolve the states' insecurities and win over their support for the new regime, the centre agreed to compensate them for any loss of revenue for a period of five years. But this constitutional guarantee—it was written into the constitutional amendment—of full reimbursement from the centre of any transitional losses, did not fully address the states' anxieties. To avoid revenue losses, the states insisted on keeping the GST rate structure as close as possible to the old system. A GST regime resembling the old tax system could not have been a low, single-rate GST.

The GST Council, working on the principle of consensus, conceded to every single demand put up by the states, whether it was justified or not. Consequently, imperfections crept into its architecture for rates and the collection system. Politicians, not tax experts, devised the GST. The GST Council, made up of ministers from state and central governments, scrambled elements from the current indirect taxation system into the GST, tinging the new with the old. They were guided by old habits, not a healthy appetite for reform.

The options narrowing to a delayed or an imperfect GST, the centre chose on each occasion to defer to the states' collective opinion. The compromise extracted a price. Far from being a 'good and simple tax', to echo the prime minister's words,[172] the new indirect tax was a multitude of rates, cesses and exemptions. The collection system became painfully complicated too. The deciding authorities' discretion was reduced, but not eliminated. Rates were tinkered with repeatedly, and the system was not allowed to settle down. As soon as the rates structure was announced, an assortment of manufacturers and sellers—of pickles, incense sticks, dry fruit and nuts, for instance—began lobbying to be included in lower rate slabs. Several demands found favour with the decision-making authority, the GST Council, leading to adjustments in the structure. Many backed by sound economic logic did not. The disregard for economic principles limited the GST's transformational potential. Increasing simplicity and reducing the complexities remains a promise made, not kept.

'On the GST, the political pressures from the states to keep rates low and simple were minimal. The general desire is for the structure to mimic the complicated status quo. There was insufficient concern for the implied consequences for efficiency and simplification,' Chief Economic Adviser Arvind Subramanian said, summing up the process that delivered the GST.[173]

The 'imperfections' limited the transformational potential of the 'second-best' GST.

Kelkar described the flaws in a lecture.[174]

- A full compensation guaranteed for five years had created a perverse incentive for the states and led to their not exerting enough to collect the tax revenues in an efficient fashion. A tapered form of less than full compensation would have avoided such an adverse outcome.

- Taxation policy has to be transparent, predictable and inclusive. A focus on these features would have maximized the favourable impact of the GST on investment and growth.

- Sweeping powers were vested with the GST Council, not unlike a regulator who also arbitrates. But the changes, how they were reached, and deliberations were not put out as discussion papers, so real consultations with the public could not take place. The GST Council ought to have been conceived as a twenty-first-century institution (The author's words, not Kelkar's. He said: 'Not enough emphasis was laid on capacity building. Politicians called the shots.')

- The flaws included the rates structure comprising multiple rates varying from 4 per cent to 26 per cent. And, different, rather than same rates for goods and services. Also, the exclusion from the coverage of GST of infrastructure sectors such as construction, and also immovable assets.

Kelkar projected high compliance costs arising out of the multiplicity of rates and a consequent need for classification of disputes. Lower compliance levels, due to the rates going up to as high as 26 per cent at the retail level, could be expected, he said. Most importantly, he warned of a potential slackening of tax-collection efforts by the states due to the promised 100 per cent compensation of shortfall in collections.

'The central government this week outlined its proposal for the GST rate structure . . . signals a disappointing beginning which could have been otherwise a thundering take-off to shock and awe the domestic and international community and capital markets . . . I feel that this approach adopted by the authorities robs the GST of its efficiency enhancing potentials.'[175]

A peculiar problem was posed by the IGST, which hobbled exports in particular.[176]

The states had succeeded in pressing through a GST made up of two types of levies, the central GST (CGST) and the state GST (SGST). The Constitution empowers the centre to tax sales anywhere nationally, but it allows a state to collect taxes only on sales within its territory. So, all twenty-nine states and the two union territories with legislatures separately enacted their respective SGSTs. The SGSTs have almost identical features and rates as the CGST—to prevent tax arbitrage across states—but in effect they are distinct SGSTs. This complicated the collection and refunds processes and system.

The GST is levied at the point of consumption, not the factory gate, unlike many of the levies it subsumed. Given the territorially limited tax jurisdictions of states, the collection of the SGST would have posed a problem every time goods and services got sold outside the state they were produced in. The solution worked out to overcome this problem is the IGST. It is imposed on inter-state sales.

Logically, the IGST ought to be imposed as a substitute for the SGST, such that the GST equals the SGST plus CGST for intra-state sales and IGST plus CGST for inter-state sales. In practice, needless complications were introduced into the IGST.

On inter-state sales, the IGST, at a rate equal to the applicable CGST and SGST, is levied. This means that despite its national tax jurisdiction, the centre confined levy of the CGST to intra-state sales.

A selling dealer in an exporting state collects the IGST from the buying dealer. The Goods and Services Tax Network (GSTN) credits it to the IGST account. Of this, the part corresponding to the CGST is transferred immediately to the centre. The balance is not all SGST revenue. It includes amounts to be refunded through a settlement process that takes months.

Some of the refunds are on account of input tax credits that the purchasing dealer in the importing state draws from this balance. (Tax paid on capital goods that go into making the final products is supposed to be fully set off. This is to avoid cascading taxation.)

The IGST collection and refunds system is ungainly. By design, the number of refunds required is more than necessary, such as in case of exports. To avoid exporting taxes, no GST is to be levied on exports out of India. In practice, despite their GST-exempt status, exporters first pay the IGST, which is then refunded to them. The excuse for this convoluted system is that it is a way to refund the input taxes exporters pay on components.

In effect, the GST system processes a whole set of IGST payments, only to refund them—not an international best practice. Suppliers to exporters and special economic zones are compulsorily required to register in the GST system even if they do not fall in the GST threshold. This needlessly increased the working capital and the burden of compliance costs on exports. The systemic loss of export competitiveness started showing up in the country's trade balance. Exporters and small companies ended up paying the cost of the incompetence of the designers of the GST systems. Exporters complained that it was taking quite some time to get reimbursements. The government put in place mechanisms to address these complaints and speed up refunds, but could alleviate only some of the pain.

Letters of undertaking or bonds can be submitted in lieu of IGST payments, but they increase exporters' vulnerability to bureaucratic rent-seeking. The IGST system is not compliant with global norms. Following global norms, the IGST could be simplified as a substitute for SGST in inter-state supplies, and exporters, while not subjected to the IGST, would be truly zero-rated.

In the summer of 2018, Adhia shot off a missive[177] to central tax officials over the lower number of returns filed under CGST, compared with the number filed under SGST. Alarmed by a nearly fourfold rise in GST compensation to states for June–July 2018 over April and May, the finance ministry started engaging with states to identify issues hindering collections and to craft strategies for shoring up their revenues.[178]

Over time, the GST Council announced a reduction in tax rates for over eighty-five goods, including consumer durables such as television sets, washing machines and refrigerators, from 28 per cent to 18 per cent. Some products from the employment-intensive sectors of carpets and handicrafts were also placed in lower tax slabs. The expectation was that these rate cuts will drive mass consumption, a fiscal stimulus of sorts, aimed at boosting sales and lifting the public mood ahead of the festive season and the state and parliamentary elections due in 2019. The GST Council virtually succumbed to populism, resulting in pretty negative impacts on the long-run functioning of the GST. Besides vote-bank politics, the main driver of the cuts was the hectic lobbying by corporates, saddled with underutilized production capacities, which the council could no longer resist.

On the first anniversary of its roll-out, West Bengal Finance Minister Amit Mitra said the GST was not performing up to expectations.[179]

The complexity of the GST was complicating collections and diminishing its potential benefits. The collection and payment systems were not being allowed to settle down. More than 200 items were tweaked in successive GST meetings, necessitating adjustments by assessees every single time. The compliance costs began to mount for the smaller businesses. Stuck refunds were blocking working capital, resulting in job losses.

Even big companies started complaining about the challenge of increased compliance. A biggish services-sector company told a group of journalists and economists[180] in late 2018 that while it used to file five service tax returns a year, this number had swelled to 975 GST returns immediately after the roll-out, which then dropped slightly to 575 GST returns filed and scrutinized in more than twenty tax jurisdictions across states. Service tax was under the centre, so each entity filed four quarterly and one annual returns a year. So in all, a company filed five returns a year. Under GST, two returns (GSTR 3B and GSTR1) had to be filed in every state the company did business in, every month. Plus, an annual return had to be filed in each state.

The compliance burden shot up. But what was tougher was that while for service tax, only central service tax administration authorities had to be dealt with, now all the states' tax administration authorities, as well as the centre, had to be dealt with. The scope of rent-seeking had shot up manifold.

In its twenty-eighth meeting, thirteen months after the new tax's imposition, the GST Council abandoned the principle of consensus to press ahead with impromptu rate cuts. State finance ministers called the proceedings in the council meeting, 'undemocratic, unpleasant, unfortunate and non-egalitarian'.[181] Council member and Punjab Finance Minister Manpreet Singh Badal left the meeting midway, saying that the rate cuts had not been listed on the agenda, rendering the process 'unfair and undemocratic'.[182] He followed this up with a letter to Piyush Goyal, who was taking care of the finance portfolio in the absence of Jaitley, who was recuperating from a kidney transplant. The GST Council's non-BJP members were especially vocal.

The economic hardships the messy GST imposed on smaller firms were explained away by the BJP as 'creative destruction'. What it really implied was that closure of informal-sector firms that had failed to cope with the burden placed by the badly designed GST was welcome as it had led to, in the party's view, greater 'formalization' of the economy.

Not Schumpeterian Creative Destruction

The only way the GST may have led to more formalization of the economy was by putting bigger companies at an advantage over smaller ones in coping with the burden of complying with its new—and constantly changing—system of compliance and collection. The GST was, after demonetization, another challenge in the operating environment that had proved to be a disadvantage for smaller firms relative to the larger ones.

In September, the BJP's national executive meeting passed a political resolution that sought to characterize the 'harsh action' taken by Modi as the sort of 'creative destruction' Austrian-American economist Joseph Schumpeter had described as the 'process of industrial mutation that incessantly revolutionizes the economic structure from within, incessantly destroying the old one, incessantly creating a new one'.[183]

The resolution listed demonetization and GST among the various kinds of 'harsh action' that Modi had taken recourse to.

This was, of course, an inaccurate reading—whether deliberate or out of ignorance is hard to tell—by the BJP of Schumpeter's 'creative destruction' principle that applies to innovation succeeding through competitive and well-regulated markets, not devastating disruptions induced by badly designed policies.

In truth, the reason for the destruction was that the Modi government had rolled out an unenviable series of ill-advised and conceptually flawed policies.

After the Congress's 'suit-boot' slogan forced the Modi government to retreat from the land acquisition reform, its focus shifted to schemes as reforms took a back seat. The GST rate structure and compliance were similarly bogged down by political messaging.[184] The GST, supposedly a 'one nation, one tax' reform, was treated like a populist scheme, a conduit for appeasing vote banks. The GST on Gujarati savouries was reduced before the Gujarat assembly polls after Congress President Rahul Gandhi issued the slogan 'Gabbar Singh Tax' and promised to reform the GST if voted to office in 2019.

The government was driven completely by politics. Economics did not seem to matter at all.

Dark clouds now loomed over the economy, not as a result of any 'policy paralysis', paradoxically, but due to hastily thought-out and insensitively implemented policy decisions, such as demonetization and GST, whose roll-out was hampered by its complicated and suboptimal design.[185] In fact, the inadequate concern for preparedness or attention to detail was discernible when a unique feature of the Indian GST, the proposal involving the matching of what the supplier says he sold to a buyer and what the buyer says he has bought from the supplier, was held in abeyance. It was kept on hold for fear of adding to taxpayers' transition pains. If that matching had begun to happen, evasion would have been checked.

The situation was compounded by the refusal of an increasingly populist Modi government to heed its own bureaucrats and advisers, including Chief Economic Adviser Arvind Subramanian, who consistently and diligently raised red flags over areas of concern, from bad bank loans, the investment slowdown and the distorted signals to farmers on what to grow and how much, to the suboptimal design of the GST and the never-ending delays in the reforms of land, labour and the public sector.[186]

The RBI had advised against going ahead with demonetization, but this too the government overruled. In fact, it seemed to view all and any feedback as adversarial. There seemed to be inadequate regard for sound economics and trained economists. The government remained inert even to the advice of its own economists; the analyses documented in successive editions of its own publication, the Economic Survey, influenced policy minimally. The government paid no heed to the warnings, the price for which was paid by the economy.

There was no policy paralysis. On the contrary, decision-making was speedy. But it was of poor quality. The ill-informed idea of demonetization and the half-baked GST roll-out demonstrated the growing disconnect between policy tools and objectives. They also betrayed Modi's abiding suspicion of qualified experts, disdain for expertise, rejection of evidence-backed analyses, valorizing of feelings of people and weakness for simple, quick but ineffective solutions.

The measures will prove beneficial over time, the government kept insisting. There was inexplicable reluctance to take decisions that would deliver speedier positive results and reverse the investments slowdown and exports stagnation. Difficult structural reforms simply fell off the agenda because of political calculations, among them: liberalization in land, labour and agriculture. These reforms, though painful in the short run, were necessary to change lives still mostly untouched by the reforms initiated in 1991. Unshackling these segments would have nudged the economy towards its full potential and development.

The economy could have still recovered and returned to the high-growth path with bold reforms, but the policy response remained feeble and missed urgency. The pain began to spread consequently to the rest of the economy. As a result, new jobs were not getting created, which meant consumption would grow only up to a point. The country had missed a third chance at a sustained economic recovery.

At the commemoration function of the eightieth year of the RBI, Prime Minister Modi had confessed to being an economics novice.[187] If a prime minister says he doesn't know economics and at the same time refuses to listen to those who do know economics, economic policymaking is bound to suffer. Modi appointed an Economic Advisory Council to the prime minister, an institution that served his predecessors, only in the fourth year of his term after columnists pointed out that even Prime Minister Singh, a distinguished economist himself, had relied for inputs on the council. Some of India's best-known economists were on it, hand-picked by Singh. Their advice received little weightage in policy decisions, but the collective wisdom of domain experts was available and informed the internal debates in government. As it turns out, during Dr Singh's tenure the number of people that exited poverty in that period is the maximum in post-1947 India.[188]

These empirical findings, which offered significant learnings for the Modi government, ought to have helped it focus on reviving the economy and creating jobs on the back of faster growth. During his 2014 prime-ministerial campaign, Modi had correctly identified joblessness as the single biggest worry in the economy. The anxiety over unemployment had stemmed from jobs lost after the global economic downturn hit growth. After his government was sworn in, Modi identified manufacturing as a growth engine with a renewed focus on the jobs-creating sector. The diagnosis was not off point, but the government failed to back it up with an effective strategy. In 2006, the UPA government had put out a national agenda for manufacturing, projecting 2006–15 as the 'decade of manufacturing in India'. The five-year period of 2005–06 to 2009–10 was one of smart growth for the sector, before the global economic downturn brought it to a halt. If, despite Modi's 'Make In India' push, manufacturing continued to languish, one of the main reasons is the poor health of banks and indebted companies. The resolution of bad loans that were haemorrhaging both the banks and the companies, spoiling their balance sheets, was a perquisite for the flagship umbrella scheme to make a difference.

Prime Minister Modi ought to have made a renewed effort for a less imperfect GST, and ought to have convinced states that the GST was not about to rob them of their financial autonomy, because the principle that guided the structure was of Revenue Neutral Rates (RNR). By definition, RNR meant that rates would be set such that there would be no loss of revenue. Add to that the efficiency gains that the GST would bring, the reduction in tax evasion and the fact that GST would promote growth and trade—these factors should have given states the confidence that in the medium to long term, GST will actually bring more revenues than the extant multiplicity of rates. These were exactly the kind of fears that the states had with VAT, but those fears were disproved in a matter of three or four years.

'If you believe in GST, then you must also believe that the GST is a more efficient tax. You must also believe that it will promote growth and trade. I believe that. If the finance ministers of states don't, then that means they don't believe in the concept of the GST,' said Chidambaram.[189]

Farm-sector Crisis

In the 2014 general elections that brought him to power, farmers—swayed by promises of higher crop prices—had voted overwhelmingly for Narendra Modi.[190] By December 2017, rural hope had completely soured. The incumbent BJP government suffered losses in the assembly elections in Gujarat and in the bypolls in assembly and parliamentary elections held in Rajasthan in January 2018, and later that year in the assembly elections in Madhya Pradesh, Rajasthan and Chhattisgarh.

Rural distress had turned the sentiment negative, and large-scale farmer protests were being reported from across the country: Maharashtra, Rajasthan, Uttar Pradesh, Chhattisgarh, Gujarat, and Madhya Pradesh, where five protesting farmers lost their lives in police firing in June 2017.[191] All through 2017, farmers from Tamil Nadu protested the government's indifferent attitude at Jantar Mantar, Delhi. They bit into mice, held mock funerals, drank their own urine and displayed vials of poison, and seventeen skulls and pairs of femur bones that they said were of farmers who had been forced to kill themselves because of drought and debt.[192] Through the monsoon, they braved the rains and scoured for meals at a nearby gurdwara.

In March 2018, a long, 40,000-strong farmers' march arrived in Mumbai, demanding a sensitive approach to land acquisition and implementation of the Forest Rights Act of 2006 in letter and spirit, including settling of all pending claims of ownership of the landless tribals who had received title areas that were less than what their eligibility entitled them to.[193] A majority of the protesters were poor landless tribals who had suffered decades of injustice in the absence of land titles. Having no land rights, the tribals are denied loans too.

In April 2018, in Charkhi Dadri, three hours' drive west of New Delhi, farmers dumped tomatoes on the road in protest after prices dropped to a quarter of a rupee per kilogram for a crop that had cost at least Rs 6 a kg to produce.[194] In July the same year, dairy farmers from Punjab emptied cans of milk, pouring litres on to Parliament Street in Delhi after a record produce saw prices crash.[195] The surplus milk produced could not be processed at costs competitive enough for the export markets.

Elsewhere, the political and economic consequences of the crude attempts by the government's ideological support groups to regulate the livestock market by imposing bans—both officially and illegally—on livestock movement hurt dairy farmers' profitability. Those accused of lynching suspected 'cow smugglers' were seen to receive the regime's protection. This had twin consequences—of higher costs and aggravation of the widespread problem of animals destroying crops.

A Kisan Kranti Padyatra that had begun from Tikait Ghat in Haridwar, and which farmers from as far as Gonda, Basti and Gorakhpur in eastern Uttar Pradesh and the sugar-cane belt of the state's western region joined, arrived in Delhi early October 2018.[196] Traffic restrictions had to be imposed in Delhi and schools were ordered shut in parts of the National Capital Region after 30,000 farmers attempted to march to Raj Ghat, Mahatma Gandhi's resting place, some on foot and many on tractors. On the morning of Gandhi Jayanti, the police stopped them at the border using batons, tear-gas shells and water cannons, injuring many.

The National Crime Records Bureau reported an eight-fold increase in farmer protests in just three years of the Modi government: from 628 in 2014 to 2683 in 2015 and 4837 in 2016.[197] The problem was not limited to marginal farmers, or to a specific crop or region. Farmers were angry even in the agriculturally advanced states. Traditionally landowning people and even dominant agrarian communities were up in arms, demanding reservations in government jobs because agriculture was no longer a stable source of livelihood.

The Jats are an agrarian middle-caste and a politically powerful community in Haryana.[198] In 2016, the more than decade-long demands for OBC status for Jats turned into a particularly fierce and hostile agitation, with protesters seeking to blockade the capital, which is surrounded by Haryana on three sides. The Patels, a dominant caste in Gujarat, held the quotas for SCs/STs as anti-merit and unfair. Violent agitations that demanded that quotas be scrapped had rocked the state in the mid-1980s. The community, also called 'Patidar', had led bloody protests, but abandoning its previous position in 2015, it was back on the streets, demanding to be classified as OBC. Similarly, the Marathas, a predominantly landowning caste and a politically and economically dominant group in Maharashtra, want to be included in the OBC category.

The demands for inclusion in quotas are actually a euphemism for access to government jobs. Research has shown that these communities already take up sizeable percentages of government jobs and face no access barriers. Yet there was unrest among Jats in Haryana and Uttar Pradesh, Patels in Gujarat and Marathas in Maharashtra. All of which suggested that in large swathes of the country, agriculture was becoming unviable and farm incomes were too unattractive. A deepening discontent with the state of agriculture was now spilling on to the streets.

At the root of the simmering tensions is the fact that agriculture is no longer remunerative. Structural and institutional weaknesses have long plagued the sector. For some time, the country has been in denial over the extent of the mess agriculture is in. Modi underestimated the gravity of the situation, and in fact policy failures in his term aggravated farmers' problems and contributed to rural distress.

The Modi government limited its response to the droughts in 2014–15 and 2015–16, when it revised the eligibility cap for compensation.[199] This was only the third instance of a back-to-back drought since Independence. The first was during 1965–66 and 1966–67, and the second during 1986–87 and 1987–88. Yet, no proactive measures were pressed for declaration of drought, improvement in rations delivery, or response to a drinking-water crisis specified in the central government's manual for drought management. The compensation amount was raised, but cuts were announced in the contribution from the National Disaster Relief Fund to States. The wholly lackadaisical approach of the government even attracted the Supreme Court's reprimand.[200]

Post-November 2016, demonetization had dealt a severe blow to agricultural markets on the whole, but especially to fruit and vegetable markets, just when the farmers were recovering from consecutive droughts. A sudden shrinking of cash led to demand contraction and a fall in prices and earnings.

Farm incomes, unlike business earnings, tend to be vulnerable to variables beyond farmers' control: weather conditions, floods and pest attacks can damage produce. Nearly half of Indian agriculture is still rain-dependent. Crop insurance cover remains limited across the country. Agriculture is also becoming unviable because of soil-nutrient stress, depleting groundwater, high input and capital costs, and shrinking landholdings. Moreover, farm incomes are rendered more unattractive by the absurdity of policies.[201] Crops can be insured against the vagaries of weather and pests, but the absurdity of state policies is the real unmitigable risk.

Agriculture pricing policies are set in India with a focus on keeping market prices stable. Agri-markets are not free. Governments seek to influence prices, to smoothen them out. In the absence of state intervention, prices soar in bad-weather years and plunge in good-weather years, hurting both consumers and farmers. The levers in the governments' hands are import and export controls, buffer stocks management and MSPs. The centrality of MSPs to vote-bank politics is well known, but the economics of it is not sufficiently appreciated. The MSP, the price at which the government offers to procure from farmers, is an economic policy tool which requires technical acumen.

A sensible policy is to buy from farmers when market prices are depressed and sell stocks in the open market when prices are elevated. In the first scenario, if the MSP is pegged higher than the market price, the procurement will raise the market price, boosting farm incomes. In the latter, by offloading its stocks at a price lower than the market price, the government can cushion consumers against excessive inflation. The buyers of subsidized sales (an efficient public distribution system) are directly benefited, but as the sales also lead to lower prices in the open market, all consumers gain.

There's a catch, though. Procurement works effectively only if trade controls and stocks management are aligned with it. Unfortunately, these tools are often deployed in a counterproductive manner, as became evident once again in 2017. Bumper harvests after good rains produced gluts in the market, sending the prices of many crops, and therefore farm incomes, crashing. Steep MSP hikes were announced to prevent a slump in market prices of agricultural produce. But at the same time, export controls and stocking limits for private traders were retained and, on top of that, a record volume of imports was allowed to be shipped in. The result was a glut in the domestic market that sent market prices crashing.

The MSP announced proved useless for putting a floor to the market prices. A bumper crop after two years of drought, and still farmers were staring at losses. All because procurement, trade controls and stocks management were used in a counterproductive manner. The looming losses set off farmer protests—including in Mandsaur, Madhya Pradesh, where police firing claimed five lives—seeking even higher MSPs. For several crops, the quantities procured were minuscule portions of the total produce.

Although the Commission for Agricultural Costs and Prices (CACP) announces MSPs for twenty-three crops, which excludes most vegetables and horticulture products that see large price fluctuations, noteworthy procurement is conducted for only three: paddy, wheat and sugar cane.[202] Sugar cane is procured by sugar mills, not the government, given that the cane must be crushed within a few hours of being cut, failing which it dries up, impacting sugar recovery drastically. Further, procurement of paddy, wheat and sugar cane frequently takes place at prices below MSPs, as, reports indicated, happened in 2017. Also, small and vulnerable farmers usually do not get paid MSPs at all, as they sell their produce to aggregators and not directly in mandis.

Of the economic tools available for protecting farm incomes—the price support scheme, the price stabilization fund, the market intervention scheme—none was employed to best advantage. Quick and precise adjustments to the export and import rules could have arrested the price fall by diverting excess supplies to overseas markets. But the changes required were not carried out in time. Instead, inflows of imports were allowed to go on, which worsened the price situation, forcing distress sales by farmers, especially by those in debt. Rural distress was now at a peak in over a decade.

It was reminiscent of the severe distress between 1998 and 2004, when another NDA government led by the BJP, under Atal Bihari Vajpayee, was in office.[203] The growth rate of agriculture during 1998–2004 was 1.76 per cent per annum. The rural economy had bounced back during the Manmohan Singh-led UPA government's tenure, with the growth rate of agriculture accelerating to more than double, to 3.84 per cent per annum, between 2004–05 and 2012–13. In the first four years of the Modi government's term, the agriculture growth rate declined to 1.86 per cent per annum, or almost half of what was achieved during the UPA period. Calculations by economist Ashok Gulati, professor with the think tank Indian Council for Research on International Economic Relations (ICRIER), showed that even if farm GDP were to grow at a targeted 4 per cent in 2018–19, the final year of the Modi government's tenure, the average farm growth for five years would still work out to 2.3 per cent, the lowest in two nearly two decades.[204]

The Modi government acquired the reputation of being anti-farmer. Modi's farm policy was so bad the proverb 'reap as you sow' wasn't true any longer.[205] A bumper crop was no different from a drought, for it too depressed farm incomes.

The gluts, depressed market prices and mounting farmer losses were a direct consequence of the malfunctioning of agri-pricing policies. Farmer support could have been provided through three alternative policy options: soaking up excess supply through procurement to add to state buffer stocks, diverting excess supply through exports, and building capacity for processing farm commodities into end products such as milled, dehusked pulses or vegetable oils. Most of these options would have required long-term structural changes.

But the Modi government remained steadfast in its pursuit of what can only be called anti-farmer trade policies.[206] The government systematically discouraged farm exports. For instance, it imposed minimum export price on potato and imported sugar from Pakistan. Agricultural exports declined from $43 billion in 2013–14 to $33 billion in 2016–17. At the same time, imports of lentil, chana, wheat and milk powder were allowed.

By early 2018, rural economic anxieties had acquired a strong political voice, turning Modi's attention to agriculture. Intermittently, the BJP and other governments in states, taking a leaf from the Congress party's national announcement in 2008, took recourse to loan waivers. While this may have provided relief to the distressed farming community in the short run, it was accompanied by a decline in investment across states in agriculture and rural development.[207] The government's commitment to reviving the rural economy and doubling farmers' income by 2022 lay in a shambles.

Gulati estimated that real farm incomes had grown just 2.5 per cent between 2012–13 and 2016–17 and would need to clock a compound annual growth rate of 10.4 per cent to double by 2022, as promised by Modi.[208] Farmer incomes had increased 5.13 per cent per annum during the ten years between 2004–05 and 2014–15, the highest since the beginning of economic reforms in

1991.[209] They had declined 0.55 per cent per annum during the Vajpayee years from 1999–2000 to 2004–05.[210] Generous increases in MSPs and a general shift in terms of trade in favour of agriculture after 2004–05 had led to a revival in farm incomes after 2004. After negligible growth between 1999–2000 and 2004–05, the MSPs for paddy and wheat were more than doubled by the UPA. As the terms of trade shifted in favour of agriculture, the growth rate of value-added goods in agriculture was high too.

But the neglect of structural factors over the years by successive governments and the indifference of the Modi government in particular ensured that from a situation of fastest rise in incomes and fastest reduction in poverty between 2004–05 and 2011–12, rural areas were plunged into extreme distress. After years of stagnation, investment in agriculture had risen 10 per cent between 2004–05 and 2012–13.[211] But from 2013–14 to 2016–17, it declined 2.3 per cent per annum.[212] Credit to agriculture, which had increased 21 per cent per annum, rising from Rs 1,25,309 crore in 2004–05 to Rs 8,45,328 crore by 2014–15,[213] slowed to 12.3 per cent between 2014–15 and 2016–17, rising only to Rs 10,65,756 crore in 2016–17.[214]

The sluggishness in investments and the supply of agricultural credit increased farmer vulnerability to price movements and, therefore, debt. Farmers became more dependent on non-institutional sources such as high-cost village moneylenders. This was more so because of the rise of horticulture, which is more investment-intensive, both in terms of traditional infrastructure such as irrigation, and also marketing and storage facilities.

According to the National Sample Survey Office (NSSO) estimates based on employment–unemployment surveys, real wages in rural areas increased by more than 8 per cent per annum between 2007–08 and 2011–12.[215] The sharp pickup in the rural non-farm sector, particularly construction, contributed to rising rural wages between 2008 and 2013, which in turn contributed to the sharp decline in poverty, the fastest since the economic reforms of 1991.

While there is no information from NSSO, the Labour Bureau series, Wage Rates in Rural India (WRRI), shows that the wage rate growth continued until 2012–13,[216] but decelerated thereafter. Real wages of agricultural labourers declined at 0.3 per cent per annum between 2013 and 2017, whereas non-agricultural wages declined 1.1 per cent.[217] The stagnation in farmer incomes coincided with a decline in real rural wages. Earlier, the non-farm sector helped diversify incomes and played the role of a shock absorber when the agrarian economy faltered. With incomes stagnating in the non-farm economy, including the self-employed and casual-worker population, rural demand collapsed.

The distress was further exacerbated by a slowdown in construction, a source of alternative employment.[218] The construction sector, which grew at 9.4 per cent during 1999–2000 and 2004–05, continued to grow at 7.9 per cent per annum between 2004–05 and 2012–13.[219] However, construction-sector growth decelerated to as low as 3.5 per cent between 2014–15 and 2017–18,[220] and was particularly hit by the cash crunch following demonetization.

By 2018, the historically high prices of diesel, used to run tractors and trolleys, and the rising tariffs of electricity, used to operate irrigation pumps, added to the farm sector's rising costs.[221] Earlier, in 2010, the UPA had decontrolled the price of complex fertilizers and introduced Nutrient Based Subsidy (NBS).[222] The subsidy reform had led to an increase in fertilizer prices, raising input costs for farmers.

Politicians strive to be seen as being farmer-friendly in election years but show little political will for agri-reforms during the rest of their tenure. The same happened with Modi. If the first year of his tenure had seen him bent on amending the land acquisition law by promulgating ordinances, by the fifth year his focus had moved to MSPs.

A Rs 7000 crore bailout was announced for the beleaguered sugar sector groaning under a cane arrears burden that had climbed to Rs 22,000 crore.[223] Notwithstanding the attempt at damage control, the sugar crisis was yet another consequence of the absurdity of policies followed for decades. The package announced did little to fix the structural flaws in the industry. Water-guzzling sugar cane should be grown only in water-sufficient lands such as the Indo-Gangetic plains, but with subsidized water, power, fertilizer and credit, governments promote its cultivation even in the arid regions of the Deccan.[224] The MSPs for sugar are fixed by the central government. Some states such as Uttar Pradesh, where cane farmers enjoy significant political clout, prescribe higher, state-advised prices that have little to do with the economics of the sugar sector. As a result, arrears, shortages and gluts recur, and the subsidies mount.

The Modi government had in February 2015 filed an affidavit in the Supreme Court that reneged on its manifesto promise of ensuring '50% profit over the cost of production' to farmers. This was on the grounds that implementing it would 'distort' the agricultural market.[225] But as the state polls in Rajasthan, Chhattisgarh, Madhya Pradesh, Telangana and Mizoram, and the 2019 Lok Sabha elections, drew close, the pressure to deliver on the 2014 poll promise of higher MSPs for all crops mounted. Over its nearly five-year period, the percentage increase in MSPs had been lower than the hikes announced by previous governments. Bonus over the MSPs announced by state governments had been stopped. Modi was forced to respond to the long-standing demand for remunerative prices. His government responded with the populist, short-term fix of higher MSPs without ramping up procurement.

The last full budget of the Modi government, in 2018, promised that the MSPs would be at least 150 per cent of the production costs, a long-standing demand of farmers and the recommendation of experts.[226] If the market prices fell below the MSPs, as they had for major kharif crops in 2017, the government promised to procure the entire produce on MSP. Or if procurement could not be done, it promised to provide a mechanism to ensure that payments, equal to the gap between the MSP and the market price, would reach farmers.

The assumption was that assuring farmers a 50 per cent profit margin over the cost of production would make farming remunerative. Farmer groups and the government were not on the same page as far as the formula for calculating production costs for plugging into the MSP formula was concerned. But it was clear that whatever manner in which production costs were calculated, simply announcing higher MSPs was not going to raise farmer incomes. The system was not geared for scaling up procurement. As was expected, by November, the prices of most crops had fallen to levels below the MSPs.

The government had announced in the budget its intention of taking recourse to payments compensating for the difference between market prices and MSPs to appear less farmer-unfriendly. In principle, it was only right and fair that the government paid reparations to farmers. The gluts, depressed market prices and mounting farmer losses were a direct consequence of the malfunction in agri-pricing policies. But the price-differential payments policy was not followed through—rightly so, for these payments would have distorted price incentives to farmers.

Instead, weeks ahead of the announcement of the 2019 general elections, the Modi government's Interim Budget in February 2019 rolled out a Rs 6000 a year income support scheme for farmers with up to 2 hectares of land.[227] Income supplements do not distort price signals to farmers. This peace offering was a small step in the right direction but bypassed landless cultivators, the most vulnerable class in the agriculture sector. Because of the design flaw, the scheme could even encourage further fragmentation of already much fragmented landholdings. Farming households holding larger land parcels will try to split holdings to qualify for the benefits under the scheme. Had the scheme been dovetailed with a replacement of the highly distortionary fertilizer subsidy with a direct benefit cash transfer, not only would a long-pending reform have been accomplished but the income support offered to farmers could have been nearly twice as much as has been announced. In India, MSPs and procurement often produce suboptimal results. Stocks pile up, even as prices spiral out of control. Or, farmers face heightened losses in years of bumper harvest. Pricing policies distort market prices and send distorted signals to farmers on what to produce and how much. The inept policy system fails to correct such situations, which then spiral out of control. The farmer is not unproductive. He is given wrong signals. There's no reason he won't respond rationally to the right price signals. The system—delivery mechanism, pricing policy, release mechanism—has evolved to be harmful to farmers, consumers and taxpayers. Market forces are not allowed to function, as a result of which price fluctuations don't get ironed out. Subsidies mount as governments procure when prices are high and hold stocks. Within the farm sector, there is an anti-small-farmer bias—in lending by banks, procurement and payment of MSPs. Big farmers corner the benefits. That's why there are farmer suicides. Small farmers may absorb one or two consecutives shocks, say adverse weather followed by rising input costs, but not a series of disruptions ranging from droughts, rising input costs, malfunctioning pricing policies and depressed demand owing to the cash crunch after demonetization.

Although farmers were better off under the UPA, the episodes of rising prices under the UPA and falling prices under the NDA show that the current farm crisis is purely because of policy failure. Price-influencing policies get deployed counterproductively.

Contrary to popular perception, farmers' economic viability is rarely the primary consideration, although political rhetoric would suggest otherwise.[228] The overriding objective of price stability, over time, has tilted the Indian farm policy in favour of consumers, the numerically larger vote bank. Gulati's calculations showed that even after the four years of systematically aggressive hikes by the Manmohan Singh government, Indian MSPs for rice and wheat remained below the farmer support prices in China, Pakistan, Bangladesh, Indonesia, Thailand and the Philippines, thus betraying the bias of Indian price policies in favour of consumers.[229] Trade and price controls in India are highly restrictive, and mostly anti-farmer. The farmer is forced to sell in the domestic market, where prices are usually lower than global agricultural prices. Protection afforded to the inefficient fertilizer industry keeps input costs high. Research papers such as Gulati's have quantified the degree of anti-agriculture bias in the system. Increasingly though, incompetence and politics have ensured that policies are failing to serve even consumers, as was the case from 2009 to 2013, as explained earlier in this book.

This bias explains why episodes of rural distress recur with alarming frequency. This bias also lies at the root of the deepening economic divide between the farm-dependent and the rest of the population, which reflects in the growing insecurities of even traditionally landowning people. Increasingly, the economic discontentment is getting expressed in political terms.

On the other side of the conundrum, advantaged Indians question the logic of fiscal support for farmers on the grounds that it is unfair to make the majority pay to keep afloat a high-cost, low-productivity, income-tax-exempt sector.[230] In doing so, they forget that agri-prices, and therefore farm incomes, are not free-markets driven. They are kept artificially low, through use of pricing policy instruments, so that inflation does not erode the rest of the population's purchasing power. Often it is assumed that MSPs and procurement benefit only farmers and those consumers relying on the subsidized PDS. They gain directly. But subsidized sales of government stocks, when they do take place, also dampen inflation in the open market prices, benefiting all consumers. If the government wants to have in place a mechanism where it will intervene to cushion prices for consumers during inflationary periods, and procure from farmers during deflationary phases, then it will have to incur some fiscal cost. This cannot be eliminated. It

can, however, be economized by fine-tuning policies. The leaky
PDS needs to be reformed, for instance.

The popular narrative is that the bulk of agriculture is not
sufficiently productive to be able to gainfully engage young rural
Indians, and so tax money going to farmers would be put to better
use in a more productive sector.[231] Policy attention, says this line
of thinking, must be on the building industry. China's experience
challenges such notions. The Chinese economic reforms were
kicked off in 1978 with an overhaul of agriculture. As farm prices
were decontrolled, real per capita incomes began rising and, in just
six years, Chinese poverty levels halved, from 33 per cent in 1978
to 15 per cent in 1984.[232] In contrast, India's 1991 reforms bypassed
agriculture altogether, and instead focused completely on industrial
liberalization. Indian poverty took eighteen years to halve, from 45
per cent in 1993 to 22 per cent in 2011.[233]

Based on the experience of developing countries over the past
twenty-five years, the World Bank's World Development Report
of 2008 concluded that GDP growth originating in agriculture is at
least four times more effective in raising incomes of extremely poor
people than GDP growth originating in non-agriculture sectors.[234]
It is this centrality of agriculture that India needs to recognize if it
wants to abolish poverty at a faster rate, given that half of India's
workforce is still engaged in agriculture and almost 75 per cent of its
poverty is in rural areas. Yet, bold and decisive reforms have eluded
the farm sector. While fiscal space must be found for providing
income support to the most vulnerable farmers at least, there is no
alternative to deep reforms over the longer term. Nothing short of
an overhaul of agriculture, resembling the industrial liberalization
of 1991, will work.

The Battle for Control over RBI

In August 2018, a chartered accountant and commentator with
significant influence in the BJP and a leading figure in its parent

organization, the RSS, Swaminathan Gurumurthy was appointed by the Modi government on the RBI's board.[235] The soft-spoken and mild-mannered former co-convener of the Swadeshi Jagran Manch, the economic wing of the RSS, shook up with his ideas the central bank long steeped in conservatism.[236] Gurumurthy, an ideologue keen to set India on a path of self-reliance, had always been a staunch critic of the RBI. Before Rajan's exit in 2016, he had criticized the former governor, and by extension the RBI, for being insufficiently aware of Indian conditions. 'Raghuram Rajan destroyed the RBI's independence by making it subservient to global thought rather than pursue India-centric solutions . . . The RBI can't now move away from that line for fear of going against global financial opinion. RBI has lost its capacity to think for India,' the *ET* quoted his tweets.[237]

Following his appointment to the central bank's board, its meetings turned into battles over RBI policy.[238] What had added to the RBI's disenchantment with the government was that Gurumurthy's appointment on the board had come through, even as a member, Nachiket Mor, was sacked from the RBI's central board a month later.[239] Such a sacking was a first for the RBI.

At the October 2018 and November 2018 board meetings, Gurumurthy pressed for the state-owned banks that were carrying mountains of NPAs on their books, to open their purse strings for lending to smaller enterprises.[240] This added a new dimension to already strained relations between the government and the RBI.

At the centre of the simmering controversy was the RBI's policy for determining how much statutory reserves it must maintain. Reserves are built from the RBI's surpluses, or the difference between its earnings and spending, as per technical formulae that have evolved over time. The balance surplus that remains after making allocations to the reserves is passed on every year to the government. Larger the reserves, the less the RBI can remit to government as dividends.

Like any central bank, the RBI earnings comprise interest income from its holdings of government securities, its overnight lending to commercial banks and the returns on its foreign currency assets. Expenditures range from the costs of printing currency, agency commission paid to commercial banks to act on its behalf for government transactions, and employee costs.

As on 30 June 2018, the RBI had accumulated Rs 6.91 lakh crore[241] in its currency and gold revaluation reserve fund that is meant for absorbing the losses from its interventions in money, securities and forex markets for conduct of monetary policy and management of exchange rate. The fund is also meant for absorbing all shocks to its assets' valuations arising out of variations in the foreign exchange rates and gold prices. In a second reserve maintained for meeting unforeseen contingencies, the RBI had Rs 2.32 lakh crore as on 30 June 2018.[242]

Every year in the weeks leading up to the preparation of the Union budget, the quantum of surplus to be transferred is negotiated intensely between the RBI and the government. The government insists year after year that the RBI is far too conservative in estimating its contingent liabilities and is building reserves in excess of reasonable requirements. The RBI, on the other hand, defends its reserves citing recommendations from technical committees on minimum levels of prudence necessary.

The as-yet unsettled question of how much reserves are adequate had heated up and was at the centre of the public feud between the two sides, as the Modi government prepared to woo various vote banks in the election year 2019, and was on the lookout for sources of funds to finance the largesse being planned.

Over the years, a number of committees have examined the question of the appropriate quantum of reserves for the RBI. Based on their recommendations, the RBI's contingency fund had been downsized from 12 per cent in 2008 to 6 per cent of the RBI's assets in 2018.[243]

The conflict over the reserves, and consequently, the dividends had deepened in the aftermath of demonetization. Governor Raghuram Rajan, guided by recommendations of a committee that had said the accumulated reserves had exceeded the needed buffer, transferred surpluses—Rs 66,000 crore each in 2015 and 2016—in totality to the centre without appropriation to reserves.[244] This was equal to the cumulative dividends paid to the government by the entire public sector.

Following demonetization, however, the costs incurred for printing new notes had pared down the surpluses, and, in turn, the RBI's dividend payments, which upset the government's fiscal deficit calculations.[245] The finance ministry started pressing the RBI to reset the formulae, so that larger surpluses could become free for transfer to the government.

By late 2018, the Modi government and the RBI had become gridlocked in an ongoing feud that soon took a turn for the worse, and soon spilled out into the public. The finance ministry sought to initiate consultations under Section 7 of the RBI Act on three policy matters: treatment of power-sector loan defaults, the quantum of dividends from the central bank to the government and the restrictions the RBI had placed on PSBs with high levels of bad loans.[246]

The rules require that the section's invocation must be preceded by consultation with the governor. If the two sides fail to find common ground still, the government can issue written directions to the governor in 'public interest'.

Section 7 is, thus, a 'nuclear' option that had never been invoked in the RBI's eighty-three-year history till then. Although disagreements were common in the past too, including on the very issues on which the two sides were sparring.

The Modi government's move to break convention and press ahead with the section on routine policy differences attracted a sharp public response from the RBI, when Deputy Governor Viral Acharya told a meeting on 26 October 2018, 'Governments that do not respect central bank independence will sooner or later incur the wrath of the financial markets, ignite economic fire, and come to rue the day they undermined an important regulatory institution.'[247]

While the Modi government was not the first government to engage with the RBI on the issue of its risk-capital buffer, never before had deliberations been conducted in an atmosphere of the kind of hostility seen in the unfolding public falling-out between the two sides. It became post-liberalization India's nastiest such rift—that too when the two sparring sides were led by non-aggressive personalities. If the finance minister, Arun Jaitley, is non-confrontational, Patel is scholarly and dignified.

Acharya's speech had stunned the government. Finance Minister Arun Jaitley's retort was to charge the RBI publicly with looking the other way when NPAs were piling up on government-run banks.[248]

On earlier occasions too, the government sought to lecture the RBI on its supervisory failures, advising it on keeping a 'third eye' unfailingly open, and suggesting that the burden of accountability is tilted against politicians, although regulators decide the rules of the game.[249] The reasoning was flawed, but the government was keen to deflect the public gaze away from its own inaction on bank frauds and loan defaults that has led to an NPA crisis and a banking paralysis.

Even after the RBI had taken the lead in forcing banks to comb their books for suppressed bad loans—on their own, they would not have disclosed the threat to the economy's stability piling up in the system—the government had proceeded slowly on the required follow-through. Fearing political backlash, it had spared stingy allocations for the recapitalization needed for restoring banks' impaired lending capacities. It had shown zero appetite for the reforms required, even as the rot spread and recourse to bailouts—such as the engineered LIC-IDBI Bank deal—grew.

Central bank–government tensions are a universal phenomenon. Governments and the RBI are rarely on the same page as regards interest rates. The new dimension seen for the first time in the unfolding rift between the Modi government and the RBI, though, was the disinformation campaign against the central bank and its governors—first Rajan was openly attacked, and now Patel, and Acharya, who had been hand-picked by the Modi government, were being targeted.

Gurumurthy, the unyielding ideologue, was quick to complain about Acharya's speech to Patel. Gurumurthy told the *ET* he had objected to 'Acharya going public on issues not discussed in or disclosed to the board which met just two days earlier . . . My public position is that the much-talked-about RBI's independence equals—not more or less than—the independence of its board of directors, and certainly not the independence of RBI officials from the board itself, as is being claimed and even widely discussed.'[250]

The attempt was to frame the conflict as one of the limits of the central bank's autonomy. A sizeable section of the ruling BJP and its various affiliates did in fact hold the RBI's independence to be a 'farcical' notion.[251] But the question at the core of the rift was, who was going to be held responsible for the outcomes, if the RBI acquiesced to the government once again, as it had for demonetization.

The tendency in the Modi government was to pass on disproportionate share of the blame for governance and policy failures, many of which had resulted from its own decisions or procrastination, to the RBI. This included, besides demonetization, the handling of the NPAs crisis. RBI risked irreversible reputation loss if the tendency was to be allowed to go on unchallenged.

Silence, as demonetization had shown, was not an option for the RBI any longer. A central bank constantly under attack from the government must fight back to preserve its credibility, not just its autonomy. Hence Acharya's raised pitch, which had sent tempers soaring in Delhi.

In initiating the Section 7 process in issues that had been settled in the past without so much bad blood, the Modi government had clearly overreacted and exhibited poor timing. Public interest is hardly served by undermining the RBI, a systemically vital institution that, barring its meek acquiescence on demonetization, commands the confidence of the markets and the public's respect. It was hard to miss that what the RBI did not have in good measure was the Modi government's trust and support.

Patel's fightback, not in the least by permitting Acharya's speech, had brought the struggle into the open.[252] It was clear that if the government persisted in pressing its point of view through invocation of the section, a situation unprecedented in the history of the RBI would arise. Governor Patel would be left with no option but to resign. For it would imply he had lost the confidence of the government, forcing routine policy issues of the central bank to be run by the 'nuclear option'.

After an unprecedented three-week-long acrimonious build-up, the two sides stepped back from the brink and averted a further showdown. At a marathon meeting of the RBI's board in Mumbai on 19 November 2018 that lasted nine hours, frameworks for conducting further deliberations so that decisions can be reached were put in place.[253] Urjit Patel, it was reported, had flown down to Delhi, where he met up with the prime minister and later also the finance minister, ahead of the board meeting.[254] Chances of further public spats were now slim, but the RBI–government relationship was far from repaired. The differences proved unbreachable.

After a brief ceasefire, during which the two sides calmed down, on 10 December, Patel, abruptly resigned, citing 'personal reasons'.[255] The resignation was made public on the RBI's website.

'On account of personal reasons, I have decided to step down from my current position effective immediately. It has been my privilege and honour to serve in the Reserve Bank of India in various capacities over the years. The support and hard work of RBI staff, officers and management has been the proximate driver of the Bank's considerable accomplishments in recent years. I take this opportunity to express gratitude to my colleagues and Directors of the RBI Central Board, and wish them all the best for the future.'

That he had not cared to put in a single word thanking the government, the finance minister or the prime minister in his resignation letter was a giveaway on how acrimonious relations had become between them. The rupee dropped by 1.8 per cent against the dollar on the news.[256] He was replaced by Shaktikanta Das, a career civil servant who had been central to the planning and execution of demonetization.[257]

Just like Rajan and Patel, Governor Subbarao too had asserted the RBI's independence with Delhi, in particular North Block. However, with the opposite outcome. The handling of Rajan's departure in 2016 and Patel's resignation in 2018 by Modi was remarkably different than that of Subbarao's extension in 2012 by Prime Minister Manmohan Singh.

A former RBI governor (1982–85)[258] himself, Singh, too had submitted his resignation to Prime Minister Indira Gandhi over a disagreement on a policy subject that would have vitally affected the powers of the RBI. He wrote about the implications of the decision to her, sought an appointment and explained the merits of the case to her in person as well. After which, Gandhi reversed the cabinet decision and Singh carried on as governor.[259]

Repeated impasses on the RBI and institutions accrued in the Modi government's tenure because differences, whether of policy or appointments, got framed internally as contests for supremacy, limiting space for serious discussion. The feuds were spun in popular discourse as ideological conflicts of home-grown versus 'imported' economists. But for the first time, a number of IAS officers holding PhDs in economics had been sent packing from the ministry. Already Ila Patnaik, Arvind Panagariya and Arvind Subramanian had left government as noted earlier in this book. In early 2019, the only two independent members on the National

Statistical Commission, P.C. Mohanan and J.V. Meenakshi, stepped down from their positions over differences, non-release of data inconvenient to the Modi government and issues of autonomy, especially with regard to the release of GDP estimates and estimation of the level of unemployment in the country.[260]

And, Raghuram Rajan's messily handled departure was followed by the sacking in 2018 of Mor from the RBI's central board. With the government placing low premium on qualified economists, non-technical actors and busybodies were routinely able to muddy the waters and set the agenda.

At the time of Rajan's exit, attacks had been stepped up by Swamy. This time, Gurumurthy's presence on the RBI board appeared to have increased tensions between the government and Patel.

Technically trained economists and statisticians are like tools in a policymaker's kit. To use or discard advice is a policymaker's call. Whereas Singh's government frequently ignored advice, Modi's government got rid of the advisers.

In 2016–17, GDP growth slowed for the first time in five years, to 7.1 per cent.[261] From there on, the economic recovery that had gathered pace in the past four years started losing momentum. The growth rate slowed to 6.6 per cent in the next year.[262] The demonetization announced in November 2016 had certainly hurt the economy, but growth impulses had already started weakening six months earlier, as the quarterly GDP estimates show.[263]

The investment slowdown, on since 2011–12, deepened with each passing year in the tenure of the Modi-led NDA government, as it remained blind to the urgency of reforming the decrepit public banking system. It kept putting off cleaning up the NPA mess, jamming the smooth flow of credit to investment projects.[264]

Not only did the Modi government not provide the necessary policy support to the economy, many of its policy decisions in fact added to the economic hardships that firms and people faced. If demonetization led to demand destruction, the GST roll-out had disastrous effects on the supply side. The twin shocks compounded the problems of industry, big and small, that had just begun to shake off a slowdown. In rural India, despite bumper harvests in 2017 and 2018 and the prime minister's lofty promises from the ramparts of the Red Fort, farm incomes crashed. Despite good rains, export controls and stocking limits for private traders and imports were managed poorly, resulting in gluts that depressed market prices, leading to farm loan waivers across the states. By the end of the first four years of NDA rule, some of the economic parameters, such as exports, had become weaker than they were at the peak of the UPA government's 'policy paralysis' phase.[265]

Although the economy was less unstable, also because the external shocks were relatively less fierce, the structural challenges to economic growth remained totally unaddressed. The focus initially was on macro stabilization, both on the fiscal and the monetary fronts. In the first couple of years of the Modi government's tenure, Arun Jaitley, longest-serving finance minister in the decade, improved the centre's finances. But by the fifth year, the oil bonanza of benign crude prices that had helped improve macroeconomic parameters such as the fiscal deficit was no longer available. The fiscal deficit for 2019–20 was estimated at 3.4 per cent, lower just about by a percentage point of GDP compared to when the government had been sworn in.[266] But revenue deficit remained above targets, below-the-line bond financing made a comeback and public-sector borrowings continued to add to the overall public debt burden.

If the UPA government resorted to off-balance-sheet financing of large expenditures to deal with subsidies by issuing oil and fertilizer bonds, the Modi government did the same for recapitalizing banks. Of the Rs 2.11 lakh crore in funds allocated for recapitalizing PSBs, Rs 1.35 lakh crore was planned to be raised through bonds.[267] It also got a rap on the knuckles from the CAG for the quality of the fiscal deficit estimation.[268] The current-account deficit had climbed up from 1.7 per cent of GDP in 2013–14 to a four-year high of 2.7 per cent of GDP in the first six months of 2018–19.[269]

In 2017–18, the government announced twenty-four[270] public-sector units, including Air India,[271] for strategic disinvestment. Only one—HPCL, which was bought by public-sector ONGC and therefore remained in the government sector—went through.

Since the economy had been on a smooth recovery path for four years until 2016, the slowdown 2016 onwards could no longer be ascribed to the policy paralysis that had characterized UPA-2. The fresh bout of pain in the economy was to a great extent a fallout of decisions—both taken, such as demonetization and ill-thought-out GST, and those not taken, such as treating NPAs on a war footing—of the Modi government.

The high growth in the years preceding the global financial crisis was driven by savings and investments. After the global economic downturn disrupted that trend, an investments famine followed. A big expectation was that with Modi in the driver's seat, investments would revive, but he could not pull the economy out of the investment slowdown. The cause for caution is that GDP growth continues to be powered by consumption, not investments. A recapitalization of banks was undertaken, but that did not measure up to the problem. The capitalized money more or less went towards provisioning—something like filling up petrol to take the car to the mechanic.[272]

The insolvency mechanism started functioning after much dithering and delay. Reforms, by removing bottlenecks, could have promoted growth. The government, in spite of its majority in Parliament, made little progress in reforming PSBs. Even the Nirav Modi scam could not shake it out of inaction. By January 2019, the total market value of all the PSBs was Rs 4.83 lakh crore, less than that of just one of the private-sector banks, HDFC Bank, which was Rs 5.69 lakh crore.[273] The question remains: Why did Modi not take up bank reforms? Probably because it's a difficult, painstaking operation that yields no political benefits.

Fiscal resources instead spent on schemes deliver bigger political dividends.

The challenges that confronted the Indian economy in 2008–09 will continue to do so in 2019–20. They fall into two parts: the short-term macroeconomic challenges of monetary and fiscal policy and the medium-term challenge of returning to the high-growth path. The former covers issues such as the trade-off between inflation and growth, the use of monetary policy versus use of fiscal policy, their relative effectiveness, and coordination between the two. The latter includes policy and institutional reforms necessary for sustaining quality growth.

The Triumph of Populism

Why didn't the Modi government leverage its majority in the Lok Sabha to accelerate the pace of reforms?

In an interview in 2015, I'd asked Arun Jaitley, the finance minister with the longest tenure in the lost decade, 2008–18, 'for long we heard of Manmohanomics. Please define for us Modinomics.'[274]

His answer was not very insightful:

You must know the road map on which you are travelling, on which you have to take the nation and the economy. You must have the leadership to take decisive decisions in that direction. You must be careful not to deviate from that direction. That's the policy that the present government is following. I think Dr. Manmohan Singh did extremely well on the economic front as Finance Minister. I am afraid I can't say that for his tenure as Prime Minister.

Not a word on Modi's economic philosophy.

I persisted: 'Let us look ahead for a second. What second- and third-generation reforms are you planning?'

India is now growing between 7 per cent and 8 per cent on its present momentum. What is it that can add further value to this growth? One, the net impact of all these steps which we have taken, particularly [foreign direct] investments coming into sectors such as insurance and defence, the unleashing of mining, coal—its impact on power generation and manufacturing. Two, my additional emphasis on infrastructure spending, particularly on railways, rural roads, highways, corporatisation of ports; that is the next step I intend bringing in. Three, the impact of taxation reforms and the major taxation reforms will be GST and bringing down corporate tax and both my measures with regard to domestic black money and undisclosed money abroad. If this can shrink the level of black money in society and bring it into the system its ability to add to the GDP. Four, progressive steps such as a public procurement policy which is transparent, a bankruptcy code, resolution of contractual disputes in big projects, faster clearances of pending projects, the possibility of replacing prior permissions with a regulatory mechanism . . . If you see the net impact of all these steps each one has an incremental value. If without these steps, we can grow between 7 per cent and 8 per cent, then this incremental value will take us further. There is an area where I want to do more when I get the next bunch of resources in my hand—the area I am going to focus on in future will be investment in irrigation. Our services sector is growing. The potential is to push agriculture up. The potential is manufacturing and infrastructure. That is where the productivity will come in. The space for growth is much higher in those sectors.

A couple of months later, Arvind Panagariya gave me an interview[275], laying down some conditions and ground rules, one of which was that it would be on email. Among other questions, I asked him: 'What is the economic thinking of the Government, which, in public discourse is sometimes referred to as "Modinomics"?

What is implied by "Modinomics", how is it different from "Manmohanomics"?'

It was one of the questions he said he would not answer.

Of the reform agenda spelt out by Jaitley, the liberalization of foreign investments amounts to incrementalism, not a big leap of the sort seen in 1991. Caps on FDI the Modi government eased could have been possible during the UPA government's tenure, had it not been for political opposition from its coalition partners and on occasion the BJP. The GST too could have been rolled out by the previous government had it not been for the BJP's resistance, voiced by the BJP-ruled state governments in Gujarat and Madhya Pradesh, discussed earlier in this book.

Public exchequer-funded infrastructure creation and corporate income tax cuts hardly count as reform. Even in this, Jaitley was clear that infrastructure investments in agriculture were not to be accorded top priority.

The auction of natural resources such as coal, a significant reform, was carried out under a direction from the Supreme Court. GST turned out to be a half-baked reform. The rather well-conceived bankruptcy code would be sought to be softened within two years of its introduction. After a series of unsuccessful experiments for unearthing black money, the Modi government would finally opt for demonetization, a bizarre move that betrayed a complete disregard for the dignity of ordinary and entirely honest Indians.

The government's record suggests Modinomics combines the worst elements of capitalism and socialism.

His faith in public-spending-funded investment push, rather than business or markets, for steering economic growth aligned Modi more closely to Nehruvian socialism than right-wing economists would have hoped for. There was no significant scaling back of government. Government is still running Air India for instance, and taxpayers are still footing bills for its losses.

Introduction of bankruptcy laws and reform of indirect taxes was pro-markets. Within years, however, the implementation framework of the few pro-market elements, bankruptcy laws, reform of indirect taxes, was compromised—in pursuance of populism in the case of the GST and under pressure from vocal business lobbies in the case of the IBC.

The introduction of electoral bonds for political funding dealt a body blow to any hopes of institutional reform and a clean-up of crony capitalism. The scheme, announced in the 2017 budget, covers donations made to political parties. Electoral bonds, issued in multiples of Rs 1000, Rs 10,000, Rs 1 lakh, Rs 10 lakh and Rs 1 crore, are designed to be a bearer instrument like a promissory note. They are similar to a banknote that is payable to the bearer on demand and free of interest, and can be purchased by any citizen of India or a body incorporated in India from specified branches of State Bank of India (SBI). Donors purchase them through a KYC-compliant account. The bonds can be donated to political parties that can then encash them via their verified account within fifteen days. The donors' identity remains known only to SBI.[276]

Jaitley did not mention it, but a difficult reform carried out successfully was a drastic reduction in fuel, particularly cooking gas subsidies, for the middle class. The minimal resistance it incurred should have encouraged the rationalization of other distortionary subsidies such as on urea. But Modi did not bite the bullet.

The speed of growth is one thing, quality quite another. Modi, who advocates 'development' in his electoral campaigns, did not pick any proposal on the poverty line from the options on his table. Neither the poverty line proposed by the C. Rangarajan committee nor the alternative proposal submitted by Arvind Panagariya caught the prime minister's attention.[277]

Modi's record on poverty reduction, therefore, remains unknown. The early shift towards 'pro-poor' policies, but with no emphasis on measuring poverty, in fact, places Modi among populists with little or no attention to detail. He gives the impression of carelessness, of not being discerning. GST is a good idea. But the problem is his government has been passing off a complicated, arbitrary tax as GST without being able to distinguish between a good, well-formulated structure and knee-jerk responses to demands.

A major promise made by the Modi government in 2014 was to end 'tax terrorism'. In the context of the UPA government, this referred to the phenomenon of amendments made to tax measures in an unpredictable fashion and with a retrospective effect. However, the term acquired new meaning, with the Modi government equipping tax officials with extraordinary powers, all in the name of fighting black money.

Modi clearly did not consider that coercive tax collection might itself become the fount of black money creation. In the final analysis, it would seem that Modi is not a reformer by instinct, conviction or persuasion.[278] Politics, not economics, drives him— much like Pranab Mukherjee. The economy under him is not significantly reformed; the high-growth path remains out of reach. Commentators may be overstressing his government's record on the macroeconomy and understating the policy slip-ups.

Of course, not all of India's problems are of Modi's making. Previous governments cannot escape accountability, and four years is too short a period to fix all that is broken.

But in four years, the Modi government did not spell out a workable strategy for the next generation of reforms (agriculture, labour, land, administration) and could not settle on a proper model for growth or an engine for recovery. Its economic agenda was bogged down by the need to control political messaging.

Initially, decision-making was hectic because files were in the pipeline. Inflation targeting, direct benefits transfers and GST were all ideas in the making when Modi was sworn in. Some more cooked, some less cooked. By way of original contributions, the Modi government could only come up with demonetization and electoral bonds.

The Modi government often gave the impression of groping in the dark; of not knowing the problem and, therefore, coming up with wrong solutions. The fiscal stimulus for infrastructure building was one such policy. But as balance sheets remained weak, and companies were slow to risk new ventures, the public investments push failed to stimulate private investments.

The Modi government all along over-relied on analyses, claiming that it was the cost of capital that was singularly responsible for de-growth in the manufacturing sector. When in fact, the more complex issues of haemorrhaged corporate balance sheets and weak bank positions, the 'twin balance sheet' problem, were holding back the manufacturing sector.

Modi's choices were limited also because of his style. He is not one to take on board suggestions or devote time to contemplating and planning strategies. He's a man in a hurry.

Yashwant Sinha told me: 'In the run-up to the 2014 election, no plan was prepared in the BJP for the economy should the party form government, although it was well known that the economy was in acute need of attention. Other than what was put in the manifesto, there was no blueprint. Spokespersons used to speak on behalf of the party on whatever they thought was important. After the swearing in, the Modi government went on its own trajectory.

'Modi felt there was no need for any one of us. He must be having something in his mind, which he never shared with us. After government was formed the only interaction for which I was invited was when they were abolishing the Planning Commission and replacing it with the NITI Aayog. I got a call from the prime minister's office saying that he was going to take a meeting. I was asked to submit my recommendations in writing, which I did, and none of the recommendations were [taken on board].'[279]

Modi's economic philosophy is to have the corporates on his side, so that they can give him money, extend their control over various fields of activities, including the media, Sinha added.

'He was deeply impacted by this "*Suit Boot Ki Sarkar*" [slogan] and he wanted to change that image. So he started mouthing things which was pro-poor. He again tried to connect with the masses and then came out with the number of schemes which he could then talk about. Demonetization is one, Jan-Dhan Yojana, Mudra Yojana all these are the renamed schemes coming from before. But he might not be saying those things that he said in the beginning, he is still very much . . . he went to Mumbai recently and interacted with the corporates, so the corporate link has not weakened. That is in place. Simultaneously, he is also trying to woo the masses by appealing to the pro-poor.'

But aren't corporates complaining, at least privately, about tax terrorism? I asked him.

'Tax terrorism is against whom? It is being very selectively used to discipline those who are not within the ambit. Those who are already with him. They are not suffering at all and nothing has happened.'

In terms of policy, what have corporates received from the government?

'Let me tell you, the corporate will be happy if through your policies you don't do any to harm them. So that's also another way of looking at this. He has done nothing to harm them.'

The economic slump Modi inherited was not as grave as the 1991 crisis, although the expectations were certainly greater. The country had handed him a decisive mandate for steering India towards quick and quality growth, by which more and more people could get quality jobs, health and education. In four years, the Modi government could not offer even a road map or a strategy for remaking the broken economic system. Even the GST's game-changing potential was frittered away because of its flawed rate structure and red-tape-ridden implementation.

In fact, till about the halfway point in its term, the Modi government did not even spell out what in its view was the precise nature of the economic slump. Not knowing the problem, it could not come up with the right solutions. Then it realized it was the investments problem. So it took up the insolvency problem, but not bank reforms. This was too little too late.

Worse, the systematic resurgence of communal groups further dampened the sentiment.

The renewed plan to make India shine had the same blind spot—the farm sector, employer to the bulk of India's poor, and in desperate need of structural reforms, received inadequate attention. Instead of harnessing the demographic dividend, India finds that its severely underemployed and increasingly insecure and frustrated youth are at risk of becoming a nuisance for themselves and society.

Growth without a Story

Today, India's GDP is growing at a world-beating rate, but little on the ground suggests that people are actually feeling better off or experiencing the promised future of '*Achhe Din*'.[280] There's no exuberance like before. Economic discontent and insecurity are on the rise, Dalits and farmers are restive, and traditionally land-owning classes are demanding quotas in government jobs. The middle class is palpably disaffected, the informal economy is struggling, big business is quiet, and the clamour for infrastructure and skill development has all but died. An over-leveraged corporate sector and bad-loans-afflicted banks remain stressed. Debt is still not getting repaid. Finding a job is not easy, setting up a business is difficult, savings earn little. To the average person, the GDP growth showing in the estimates put out by the official statistical apparatus seem out of sync with the day-to-day experience of unending economic hardships and struggles. People's frustration, anxiety and insecurities are finding expression in political terms.

In the ten years that have been lost negotiating political setbacks, external and self-made shocks and chronic policy failures, what was called the 'India Growth Story' has become 'Growth without a Story'.

India's star status in the global economy is fading, the growth potential is lower, the halo has crimped, the need for serious hard work is a lot more apparent than ever. The bulk of the pending backlog of reforms remains, well, pending. If this lost decade demonstrated the resilience of India's economic power, especially after the global financial crisis, its fragility was evident just the same.

The cost of failure for the non-rich is high. Be it for the small farmer, petty unorganized-sector unit or a small enterprise. The shock-bearing capacities of these segments, the true entrepreneurial powerhouse of the economy that generates jobs, are low. The system offers to them no real coping mechanisms.

Does India have ability to deal with another adverse global shock or to exploit new global opportunities? Business leaders quietly grumble about missing dynamism, wobbly infrastructure and tax terrorism.

In the gone decade, while Indians were taken in with intrigue, conspiracy, cults and charisma, the consensus for proper structural reform of the 1990s broke down.

Not a single strategic privatization was completed in the last ten years. No comprehensive labour reforms were taken up. Political meddling in the functioning of banks did not lessen.

Both the UPA and Modi governments accepted the generous pay and pension hikes the sixth and seventh pay commissions recommended, but did not move on introducing meritocracy, or reforms, into administration. The bureaucracy remains seniority-based, even sycophancy-based, rather than merit-based. Similarly, eyeing perks and power, non-experts pretending to be know-alls are able to worm their way into important positions in the government system. All it takes is a few friends in the bureaucracy and an ability to make some pro-establishment noises.

Macro-economic stability comes under threat every time oil prices or global capital flows turn. Market reforms for increasing competition remain incomplete. Institutional strengthening and modernisation have not been taken up. Our approach to social equity and inclusion remains piecemeal and ad hoc. There needs to be a fundamental reassessment of the roles of the state and markets and their failures.

In economic matters, a variety of dogmas and myths have captured popular imagination. Such as good jobs can only be generated in manufacturing, not in the farm and related sectors. That it is okay to kill informal firms overnight to meet the long-term goal of greater formalisation of the economy. Speed of growth matters, but not the quality of growth, which is its ability to reduce poverty.

Fact is, giveaways by themselves cannot end poverty. The safety net of NREGA, the direct benefit transfers or food grains of the National Food Security Act, the sewer-less, water-less unusable toilets of Swachh Bharat, the health insurance of Ayushman Bharat and the low-cost houses and cooking gas cylinders will not end poverty. Only sustainable livelihoods will. Pakora-selling[281] is not a poverty-defying sustainable livelihood. Nor is NREGA job work.

The last ten years have shown that half-baked, ill-thought-out measures produce uncertain results. Be it the land acquisition law, the national food security law, demonetisation or GST. The big-bang economic reforms agenda has plateaued. We need to rebuild consensus for a steady stream of reforms and revive the spirit of 1991. For a number of years, it defied time and ideology. Economic policy graduated from pro-business to pro-market. But a reversal has been underway in the last ten years. The relationship between state and capital is turning murky again.

The economic reforms of the 1990s transformed India from a low-income country to a middle-income one. But without new reforms, this momentum will not be sustained. To become a high-income country, India must liberalise the economy much further.

Accelerating the rate of growth is not sufficient. What sets apart successful from unsuccessful economies, is the duration for which fast growth is sustained. Often countries' growth rate collapses after a spurt of fast growth; they are shooting stars that burn bright for a short period. Neither the UPA 2 government nor the Modi government succeeded in defining an agenda for the type of policy reforms that are needed to sustain fast growth, and which are not necessarily the same as those needed to accelerate growth.

Acknowledgements

This book would not have been possible without the love and support of my parents, brother, aunts and uncles, cousins, friends, colleagues and professional associates.

My special thanks to Indu Mehra, Vijay Mehra, Shankar Mehra, late Indu Ahluwalia and Brig. J.S. Ahluwalia, Kamlesh Behl and Col. Surinder Behl, Gaurav Ahluwalia, Shalini Sehgal and Brig. Sandeep Sehgal, Dr Rathin Roy, T.C.A. Srinivasa Raghavan, B.K. Walia, Mini Kapoor, Smita Gupta, Vidya Subrahmaniam, Sunil Khatri, V. V. Krishnan, Varghese George, Dr Arvind Virmani, Dr Ashok Desai, Dr Vijay Kelkar, Dr V. Bhaskar, Dr D. Subbarao, Sindhushree Khullar, Dr Arunish Chawla, Praveen Khanna, Smriti Kak Ramachandran, Praveen Swami, Meena Menon and B. Muralidhar Reddy and all those of my sources who prefer to remain unnamed.

This book owes immensely to the experience and exposure I gained at *The Hindu* and my writings published by *The Hindu Centre for Public Policy and Politics* for which am grateful to Dr Malini Parthasarathy, N. Ravi, Jayanth V, Suresh Nambath, Mukund Padmanabhan and Dr V.S. Sambandan.

Swati Chopra, along with Saloni Mital, patiently accommodated the delay in completing the manuscript. Without Swati's encouragement, I might have abandoned it half-written.

I am eternally grateful to all my teachers, editors and mentors.

Disclaimer

This book is a work of non-fiction and is based on the evidence collected by the author from various sources and through interviews conducted by the author. The instances in the book are based on a variety of sources, including but not limited to the personal interactions of the author with various persons mentioned in the book. The views and opinions expressed in the chapters of this book are those of the author only and do not reflect or represent the views and opinions held by any other person.

This book is based on actual events and is based on the materials collected by the author with respect to the events enumerated. It reflects the author's representation of the events enumerated as truthfully as possible. All persons within the book are actual individuals.

The objective of this book is not to hurt any sentiments or be biased in favour of or against any particular person, political party, society, gender, creed, nation or religion.

Notes

Introduction

1. https://in.reuters.com/article/india-economy-worldbank/india-needs-8-percent-growth-for-30-years-to-join-middle-income-group-world-bank-idINKCN1GQ175
2. https://in.reuters.com/article/india-economy-worldbank/india-needs-8-percent-growth-for-30-years-to-join-middle-income-group-world-bank-idINKCN1GQ175
3. https://www.deccanherald.com/content/40703/every-third-indian-lives-poverty.html
4. https://www.ndtv.com/india-news/over-10-years-poverty-rate-in-india-reduced-to-half-un-report-1919756
5. https://data.worldbank.org/indicator/NY.GDP.PCAP.CD?locations=INs
6. https://www.indiabudget.gov.in/bspeech/bs199192.pdf

Chapter 1: The Shock (2008–09)

1. Y.V. Reddy, *Advice & Dissent* (HarperCollins Publishers India, 2017), p. 253.
2. https://rbi.org.in/Scripts/BS_PressReleaseDisplay.aspx?prid=15124
3. https://rbi.org.in/Scripts/BS_PressReleaseDisplay.aspx?prid=16995
4. https://www.federalreserve.gov/newsevents/speech/bernanke20070517a.htm
5. https://www.nytimes.com/2007/05/18/business/18fed.html
6. Sub-prime mortgages are loans made to borrowers in the US perceived to have high credit risk, often because they lack a strong credit history or have other characteristics that are associated with high probabilities of default.
7. https://www.federalreserve.gov/monetarypolicy/files/FOMC20070810confcall.pdf
8. https://www.nytimes.com/2007/09/19/business/19fed.html

9.   https://dealbook.nytimes.com/2008/03/17/fed-
        lends-30-billion-for-bear-deal/?mtrref=www.google.
        com&gwh=395E771528F87C741F0AB6AC7F0CF0BC&gwt=pay

10.   https://www.nytimes.com/2008/07/14/washington/14fannie.html

11.   In the US, in some states, corporations can be placed under conservatorship,
        as a less extreme alternative to receivership. Whereas a receiver is expected
        to terminate the rights of shareholders and managers, a conservator is
        expected merely to assume those rights, with the prospect that they will
        be relinquished. In September 2008, even as the sub-prime mortgage crisis
        was going on, the chief executive officers and board of directors Fannie
        Mae and Freddie Mac were dismissed, and the companies were placed into
        the conservatorship of the Federal Housing Finance Agency (FHFA).

12.   https://www.nytimes.com/2008/09/15/business/15lehman.html

13.   https://www.nytimes.com/2008/09/15/business/15lehman.html

14.   https://www.nytimes.com/2008/09/15/business/15lehman.html

15.   https://www.thehindu.com/todays-paper/tp-business/lehman-weekend-
        the-biggest-bankruptcy-in-american-history/article24906041.ece

16.   https://www.nytimes.com/2008/09/15/business/15lehman.
        html; https://www.thehindu.com/business/Economy/lehman-weekend-
        the-biggest-bankruptcy-in-american-history/article24903998.ece

17.   https://www.thehindu.com/business/Economy/lehman-weekend-the-
        biggest-bankruptcy-in-american-history/article24903998.ece

18.   https://www.federalreserve.gov/BoardDocs/Speeches/2003/20030508/
        default.htm

19.   The House Committee on Oversight and Reform is the main investigative
        committee in the US House of Representatives. It has authority to
        investigate the subjects within the committee's legislative jurisdiction as
        well as 'any matter' within the jurisdiction of the other standing house
        committees; https://oversight.house.gov/about

20.   https://www.wired.com/2017/04/dont-despair-big-ideas-can-still-
        change-world/

21.   https://www.nytimes.com/2008/09/19/business/19fed.html

22.   https://www.nytimes.com/2008/12/17/business/economy/17fed.html

23.   With all the advanced economies in a synchronized recession, global GDP
        was projected to contract for the first time since World War II, anywhere
        between 0.5 and 1.0 per cent, according to a March 2009 forecast of the
        International Monetary Fund (IMF). Para 1 in https://rbi.org.in/scripts/
        NotificationUser.aspx?Mode=0&Id=4936

24.   https://www.nytimes.com/2008/12/17/business/economy/17fed.html

25.   https://www.cnbc.com/2017/11/24/the-fed-launched-qe-nine-years-
        ago--these-four-charts-show-its-impact.html

26.   https://rbidocs.rbi.org.in/rdocs/PressRelease/PDFs/80961.pdf

27.   https://indianexpress.com/article/news-archive/web/how-they-saved-
        the-india-story/

28. D. Subbarao, *Who Moved My Interest Rate?* (Penguin Random House India, 2016), p. 14.
29. Author's interview with D. Subbarao on 18 January 2019.
30. https://indianexpress.com/article/news-archive/web/how-they-saved-the-india-story/
31. https://www.livemint.com/Money/voTni4e3CzmosdUB1T00hN/Banks-are-well-regulated-no-cause-for-alarm-FM.html
32. https://www.livemint.com/Money/voTni4e3CzmosdUB1T00hN/Banks-are-well-regulated-no-cause-for-alarm-FM.html
33. Ibid.
34. https://www.forbes.com/2008/09/30/banking-india-icici-biz-wall-cz_mb_0930icici.html#1541b6583232
35. 'Fake news' as a phrase was not yet invented at that time.
36. Author's interview with D. Subbarao on 18 January 2019.
37. http://www.icmrindia.org/casestudies/catalogue/Marketing/Communication%20in%20a%20Crisis%20ICICI%20Bank-Excerpts.htm
38. https://www.livemint.com/Home-Page/v41qflAbIEj7HgxXYk727L/Kamath-sees-agenda-says-bank-is-safe.html
39. Author's interview with D. Subbarao on 18 January 2019.
40. Author's interview with P. Chidambaram on 26 October 2018.
41. https://indianexpress.com/article/news-archive/web/how-they-saved-the-india-story/
42. Ibid.
43. Ibid.
44. Author's interview with P. Chidambaram on 26 October 2018.
45. https://uk.reuters.com/article/icici-deposits-idUKBOM12662720081013
46. Author's interview with P. Chidambaram on 26 October 2018.
47. D. Subbarao, *Who Moved My Interest Rate?* (Penguin Random House India, 2016), p. 15.
48. Ibid., p. 26.
49. https://indianexpress.com/article/news-archive/web/how-they-saved-the-india-story/
50. D. Subbarao, *Who Moved My Interest Rate?* (Penguin Random House India, 2016), p. 25.
51. Author's interview with D. Subbarao on 18 January 2019.
52. https://indianexpress.com/article/news-archive/web/how-they-saved-the-india-story/
53. D. Subbarao, *Who Moved My Interest Rate?* (Penguin Random House India, 2016), p. 15.
54. Author's interview with D. Subbarao on 18 January 2019.
55. Author's interview with D. Subbarao on 18 January 2019.
56. D. Subbarao, *Who Moved My Interest Rate?* (Penguin Random House India, 2016), p. 18.
57. Author's interview with D. Subbarao on 18 January 2019.

58.   D. Subbarao, *Who Moved My Interest Rate?* (Penguin Random House India, 2016), p. 22.

59.   Ibid., p. 16.

60.   RBI raised the cap on the interest rate that banks could offer to foreign currency deposits by NRIs. Norms for external commercial borrowing by corporates were relaxed substantially, and NBFCs and housing finance companies were allowed to access foreign borrowings. To mitigate the dent on export prospects, credit and refinance facility for exports were enhanced. The lendable resources available to apex institutions like the Small Industries Development Bank of India, the Export Import Bank of India and the National Housing Bank were expanded so as to expand the flow of credit to productive sectors.

61.   D. Subbarao, *Who Moved My Interest Rate?* (Penguin Random House India, 2016), pp. 23-24.

62.   Interview of P. Chidambaram to the author on 26 October 2018.

63.   Y.V. Reddy, *Advice & Dissent* (HarperCollins Publishers India, 2017), p. 381.

64.   Author's interview with Arvind Virmani on 20 June 2018.

65.   https://www.thehindu.com/todays-paper/tp-opinion/The-fiscal-stimulus-challenge/article16350302.ece

66.   https://www.rediff.com/money/2008/dec/07bcrisis-govt-announces-package-to-boost-economy.htm

67.   https://www.thehindu.com/todays-paper/Government-unveils-stimulus-package/article15356803.ece

68.   Para 6 in https://rbi.org.in/scripts/BS_PressReleaseDisplay.aspx?prid=19792

69.   https://www.thehindu.com/todays-paper/Second-stimulus-package-unveiled/article16344800.ece

70.   Paras 8–9 in https://rbi.org.in/scripts/BS_PressReleaseDisplay.aspx?prid=19792

71.   Ibid.

72.   Para 4 in https://rbi.org.in/scripts/BS_PressReleaseDisplay.aspx?prid=19792

73.   http://archive.indianexpress.com/news/govt-unveils-second-stimulus-package/405782/0

74.   Author's interview with P. Chidambaram on 26 October 2018.

75.   https://www.thehindu.com/todays-paper/Second-stimulus-package-unveiled/article16344800.ece

76.   https://www.thehindu.com/todays-paper/Second-stimulus-package-unveiled/article16344800.ece

77.   Economic Survey 2008-09 (tabled in Parliament in July 2009), https://www.indiabudget.gov.in/es2008-09/chapt2009/chap24.pdf

78.   Chapter 1 Economic Survey 2008–09, https://www.indiabudget.gov.in/es2008-09/seconomy.htm

79. https://in.reuters.com/article/india-economy-worldbank/india-needs-8-percent-growth-for-30-years-to-join-middle-income-group-world-bank-idINKCN1GQ175

80. https://in.reuters.com/article/india-economy-worldbank/india-needs-8-percent-growth-for-30-years-to-join-middle-income-group-world-bank-idINKCN1GQ175

81. In real terms, at 2011–12 prices. Para 11 in http://www.mospi.gov.in/sites/default/files/press_release/nad_PR_31may18.pdf

82. Chapter 1 Economic Survey 2008–09, https://www.indiabudget.gov.in/es2008-09/seconomy.htm

83. Economic Survey 2008–09 (tabled in Parliament in July 2009), https://www.indiabudget.gov.in/es2008-09/chapt2009/chap24.pdf.

84. Ibid.

85. At 2004–05 prices (old series) Table 5.2 in http://www.mospi.gov.in/sites/default/files/committee_reports/Report_of_the_committee_on_real_sector_statistics_2182018.pdf

86. Author's interview with P. Chidambaram on 26 October 2018.

87. D. Subbarao, *Who Moved My Interest Rate?* (Penguin Random House India, 2016), p. 15.

88. https://www.nytimes.com/2008/12/20/business/20nocera.html

89. Y.V. Reddy, *Advice & Dissent* (HarperCollins Publishers India, 2017), p. 288.

90. https://www.bloombergquint.com/lehman-financial-crisis/the-global-financial-crisis-and-all-the-prime-ministers-men

91. https://www.businesstoday.in/magazine/features/two-bullies-and-an-upstart/story/10565.html; https://www.hindustantimes.com/delhi-news/manmohan-singh-won-friends-abroad-but-can-he-influence-people-at-home/story-chn03mB2JgVl401Sgcqb2O.html

92. Author's interview with D. Subbarao on 18 January 2019.

93. D. Subbarao, *Who Moved My Interest Rate?* (Penguin Random House India, 2016), p. 37.

94. Y.V. Reddy, *Advice & Dissent* (HarperCollins Publishers India, 2017), p. 240–41.

95. Ibid., p. 240.

96. Governor of Reserve Bank of India from September 2013 to September 2016.

97. Governor of Reserve Bank of India from September 2016 to December 2018.

Chapter 2: A Recovery Destroyed (2009–12)

1. http://www.visvabharati.ac.in/files/6340200114_Manmohan.pdf

2. Ibid.

3.   Press Communique, Rashtrapati Bhawan, New Delhi, 23 January 2009. 'The President of India, as advised by the Prime Minister, has directed that Shri Pranab Mukherjee, Minister of External Affairs is assigned the additional charge of Ministry of Finance from 24th January 2009 until the recovery of the Prime Minister from Medical treatment.' http://pratibhapatil.nic.in/pr230109-1.html

4.   Author's interview with P. Chidambaram on 26 October 2018.

5.   Pranab Mukherjee, *The Coalition Years 1996–2012* (Rupa Publications India Pvt. Ltd, 2017), pp. 161–162.

6.   http://timesofindia.indiatimes.com/articleshow/4032363.cms?utm_source=contentofinterest&utm_medium=text&utm_campaign=cppst

7.   Interview of the former secretary being quoted to the author on 19 July 2018.

8.   Ibid.

9.   https://www.hindustantimes.com/delhi-news/manmohan-singh-attends-office-after-his-heart-bypass-surgery/story-e6p7RWrKAUrNRyJ1c5EoQM.html

10.   D. Subbarao, *Who Moved My Interest Rate?* (Penguin Random House India, 2016), p. 95.

11.   Author's interview with the former secretary on 19 July 2018.

12.   In the period 2003–04 to 2007–08, P. Chidambaram reduced the fiscal deficit from 4.5 per cent to 2.7 per cent of GDP and the revenue deficit from 3.6 per cent to 1.1 per cent of GDP. In the same period, the savings rate rose from 29.8 per cent to 37.7 per cent of GDP and the investments rate from 27.6 per cent to 39 per cent of GDP. The direct tax-GDP ratio improved from 4.1 per cent to 6.3 per cent.
      Pranab Mukherjee, *The Coalition Years 1996–2012* (Rupa Publications India Pvt. Ltd, 2017), p. 163.
      Table 1.4 in https://www.incometaxindia.gov.in/Documents/Direct%20Tax%20Data/time-series-data-2017-18.pdf

13.   Announced in two tranches, on 7 December 2008 and 2 January 2009, these response measures were tax reliefs to spur demand and increased public expenditure on infrastructure for generating employment and incomes. Between August 2008 and January 2009, the government approved thirty-seven infrastructure projects worth Rs 70,000 crore. The farm loan waiver, the expanded MGNREGA and the pay and pension hikes, in line with the Sixth Pay Commission award that was anyway in process, were also expected to add to demand and were also counted as part of the stimulus.

14.   http://www.rediff.com/money/2009/feb/25pranab-unveils-third-fiscal-stimulus-package.htm

15.   https://www.hindustantimes.com/delhi-news/manmohan-singh-attends-office-after-his-heart-bypass-surgery/story-e6p7RWrKAUrNRyJ1c5EoQM.html

16. Pranab Mukherjee, *The Coalition Years 1996–2012* (Rupa Publications India Pvt. Ltd, 2017), p. 160.

17. https://www.rediff.com/news/2009/mar/02ec-announces-5-phase-polls.htm

18. Pranab Mukherjee's allocations for the social sector: Rs 1,22,345 crore in the 2009–10 budget, which he raised to Rs 1,51,013 crore in 2010–11, Rs 1,62,227 crore in 2011–12 and Rs 2,14,400 crore in 2012–13; Pranab Mukherjee, *The Coalition Years 1996–2012* (Rupa Publications India Pvt. Ltd, 2017), p. 169.

19. https://www.business-standard.com/article/opinion/interim-budget-options-for-mr-jaitley-119011600052_1.html

20. https://economictimes.indiatimes.com/news/economy/indicators/fm-chidambaram-blames-pranab-mukherjee-for-the-dire-state-of-the-economy/articleshow/22107036.cms

21. Pranab Mukherjee, *The Coalition Years 1996–2012* (Rupa Publications India Pvt. Ltd, 2017), p. 164.

22. Author's interview with the former secretary on 19 July 2018.

23. Author's interview with Arvind Virmani on 20 June 2018.

24. Ibid.

25. https://www.indiabudget.gov.in/es2009-10/chapt2010/chapter02.pdf

26. Chapter 2 of Economic Survey 2008–09 (tabled in Parliament in July 2009), https://www.indiabudget.gov.in/es2008-09/chapt2009/chap24.pdf

27. Page 29 of https://www.imf.org/external/pubs/ft/wp/2012/wp12185.pdf

28. Chapter 2 of Economic Survey 2008–09 (tabled in Parliament in July 2009), https://www.indiabudget.gov.in/es2008-09/chapt2009/chap24.pdf

29. http://archive.indianexpress.com/news/arvind-virmani-gets-plum-imf-job/512934/

30. https://www.businesstoday.in/magazine/features/static-on-the-fm-channel/story/9505.html

31. From interview by the author on 19 July 2018 of the bureaucrat.

32. https://www.indiatoday.in/magazine/from-india-today-magazine/story/20101025-there-is-a-limit-i-have-overstayed-my-wicket-744472-2010-10-15 India Today magazine dated October 25, 2010

33. Paras 8 and 29 in https://rbi.org.in/scripts/NotificationUser.aspx?Mode=0&Id=4936

34. Paras 30 and 31 in https://rbi.org.in/scripts/NotificationUser.aspx?Mode=0&Id=4936

35. Author's interview with Arvind Virmani on 20 June 2018.

36. Ibid.

37. Ibid.

38. Author's interview with Arvind Virmani on 20 June 2018.

39. Ibid.

40.   Author's interview with Arvind Virmani on 20 June 2018.

41.   Y.V. Reddy, *Advice & Dissent* (HarperCollins Publishers India, 2017), p. 253.

42.   D. Subbarao, *Who Moved My Interest Rate?* (Penguin Random House India, 2016), p. 18.

43.   Ibid., p. 24.

44.   Ibid., p. 46.

45.   Ibid., pp. 47, 48.

46.   Ibid., p. 49.

47.   Ibid., p. 49.

48.   Ibid., p. 47.

49.   D. Subbarao, *Who Moved My Interest Rate?* (Penguin Random House India, 2016), p. 50.

50.   D. Subbarao's interview to the author on 18 January 2019.

51.   Vijay Joshi, *India's Long Road* (Penguin Random House India, 2016), p. 143.

52.   D. Subbarao, *Who Moved My Interest Rate?* (Penguin Random House India, 2016), p. 95.

53.   Interview of the official who attended these meetings to the author on 11 October 2018.

54.   Ibid.

55.   Ibid.

56.   Para 6 in https://www.rbi.org.in/scripts/BS_SpeechesView.aspx?Id=630

57.   D. Subbarao, *Who Moved My Interest Rate?* (Penguin Random House India, 2016), p. 53.

58.   Ibid., pp. 96, 61.

59.   Ibid., p. 52.

60.   Table 5.2 in http://www.mospi.gov.in/sites/default/files/committee_reports/Report_committee_real_sector_statistics_25july18.pdf

61.   D. Subbarao, *Who Moved My Interest Rate?* (Penguin Random House India, 2016), p. 52.

62.   https://www.business-standard.com/article/economy-policy/pranab-as-fm-a-tale-of-two-stints-112061600017_1.html

63.   https://economictimes.indiatimes.com/news/politics-and-nation/cag-submits-report-on-2g-spectrum-to-govt-vinod-rai/articleshow/6900822.cms

64.   https://www.thequint.com/videos/news-videos/2g-spectrum-scam-verdict-a-raja-cag-report-vinod-rai-kanimozhi

65.   https://economictimes.indiatimes.com/news/politics-and-nation/cag-submits-report-on-2g-spectrum-to-govt-vinod-rai/articleshow/6900822.cms

66.   https://timesofindia.indiatimes.com/india/Raja-cost-nation-Rs-1-7L-cr-CAG/articleshow/6898236.cms?

67.   https://www.thehindu.com/todays-paper/Parliament-stalled-over-spectrum-issue/article15684017.ece

https://www.thehindu.com/todays-paper/tp-national/2G-issue-Congress-feels-the-heat/article15683318.ece

68. https://www.ndtv.com/india-news/telecom-department-files-affidavit-in-supreme-court-defends-raja-438905

69. http://www.bjp.org/en/media-resources/press-releases/press-statement-issued-by-bjp-national-spokesperson-and-mp-sh-prakash-javadekar29

70. https://www.thehindu.com/todays-paper/Jayalalithaa-to-Manmohan-we-will-back-you-if-Raja-is-removed/article15684019.ece

71. https://www.thehindu.com/todays-paper/Alliance-with-DMK-stands-as-of-now-Manmohan/article15685375.ece

72. https://www.ndtv.com/india-news/the-phone-calls-that-led-to-raja-resigning-439323

73. https://www.indiatoday.in/magazine/cover-story/story/20101129-is-raja-the-scapegoat-744799-2010-11-20

74. https://www.thehindu.com/news/national/Telecom-Minister-Raja-resigns-from-Cabinet/article15687906.ece

75. https://www.livemint.com/Politics/mCzlRHTm2VEdpbZsr4RxgP/Telecom-minister-A-Raja-resigns-over-2G-scam.html

76. https://www.thehindu.com/news/national/Telecom-Minister-Raja-resigns-from-Cabinet/article15687906.ece

77. https://www.thehindu.com/news/national/Telecom-Minister-Raja-resigns-from-Cabinet/article15687906.ece

78. https://economictimes.indiatimes.com/news/politics-and-nation/cag-report-on-2g-spectrum-allocation-tabled-in-parliament/articleshow/6934808.cms

79. https://www.ndtv.com/india-news/full-transcript-kapil-sibal-on-the-2g-controversy-and-the-pms-court-case-439772

80. https://www.thehindu.com/opinion/lead/from-bofors-to-2g-the-same-fate/article4743570.ece
https://www.thehindubusinessline.com/blogs/blog-nramakrishnan/congress-i-and-the-cag/article4504238.ece

81. https://www.thehindubusinessline.com/blogs/blog-nramakrishnan/congress-i-and-the-cag/article4504238.ece;   https://frontline.thehindu.com/cover-story/an-audit-gone-awry/article10008334.ece

82. https://indianexpress.com/article/india/latest-news/2g-former-telecom-minister-a-raja-sent-to-tihar-jail/

83. https://www.thehindu.com/news/national/supreme-court-scraps-upas-illegal-2g-sale/article2853159.ece

84. https://scroll.in/article/862349/if-there-was-no-2g-scam-why-did-the-supreme-court-cancel-122-licenses-in-2012

85. https://www.newslaundry.com/2013/05/23/vinod-rai-the-uncaged-cag

86. https://www.livemint.com/Politics/PgVi4YqgvUXMpUfST9kr7I/Government-plans-1-trillion-spending-on-infrastructure.html

87.   https://www.thehindu.com/news/national/Manmohan-leading-the-most-corrupt-Govt-in-Indian-history-Jaitley/article15515626.ece

88.   https://www.washingtonpost.com/world/asia-pacific/for-indias-prime-minister-corruption-refuses-to-stay-at-arms-length/2011/08/02/gIQAmiGvpI_story.html?noredirect=on&utm_term=.611c3a8a13be
       https://www.theguardian.com/world/2012/sep/11/indian-leader-manmohan-singh-criticism

89.   https://frontline.thehindu.com/cover-story/an-audit-gone-awry/article10008334.ece
       https://www.mea.gov.in/outoging-visit-detail.htm?3104/PMs+interaction+with+newspaper+editors

90.   https://www.livemint.com/Politics/XwBXRyhEwFuLWhDGj9vEvN/Vinod-Rai-Auditor-or-crusader.html

91.   Table 5.2 in http://www.mospi.gov.in/sites/default/files/committee_reports/Report_committee_real_sector_statistics_25july18.pdf

92.   https://www.thehindu.com/news/national/supreme-court-quashes-allocation-of-all-but-four-of-218-coal-blocks/article6441855.ece

93.   https://www.frontline.in/cover-story/an-audit-gone-awry/article10008334.ece

94.   https://www.frontline.in/cover-story/an-audit-gone-awry/article10008334.ece

95.   Vinod Rai, *Not Just an Accountant: The Diary of the Nation's Conscience Keeper* (Rupa Publications India), 2014.

96.   https://www.frontline.in/cover-story/an-audit-gone-awry/article10008334.ece

97.   http://www.ptinews.com/news/9342137_2G-cases--Raja--Kanimozhi--all-others-acquitted.html

98.   Andimuthu Raja, *2G Saga Unfolds* (Har Anand Publications, 2018).

99.   http://epaperbeta.timesofindia.com/Article.aspx?eid=31815&articlexml=A-RAJAs-2G-BOOK-Manmohan-Failed-Me-Vinod-29082016001055

100.   http://epaperbeta.timesofindia.com/Article.aspx?eid=31815&articlexml=A-RAJAs-2G-BOOK-Manmohan-Failed-Me-Vinod-29082016001055

101.   http://pib.nic.in/newsite/PrintRelease.aspx?relid=109313

102.   https://www.newslaundry.com/2013/05/23/vinod-rai-the-uncaged-cag

103.   https://www.businesstoday.in/magazine/features/cag-report-coal-allocation/story/187398.html

104.   https://www.thehindu.com/news/national/did-joshi-try-to-influence-cag-on-2g/article2630896.ece

105.   Ibid.

106.   Ibid.

107.   https://www.indiatoday.in/india/north/story/former-cag-official-rp-singh-2g-audit-report-122436-2012-11-24

108. https://www.tribuneindia.com/2012/20121123/latest-news.htm
109. https://www.indiatoday.in/india/north/story/former-cag-official-rp-singh-2g-audit-report-122436-2012-11-24
110. https://www.livemint.com/Home-Page/PgZsUAgqoObpJc4YtxyTNM/Auditor-was-divided-on-2G-losses.html
111. Ibid.
112. Ibid.
113. Ibid.
114. http://www.rakeshmohan.com/Business_Standard_Economic_Reforms_in_Vajpayee_Era_Part_1.pdf
115. Ibid.
116. https://www.tribuneindia.com/2012/20121123/latest-news.htm
117. https://indianexpress.com/article/india/india-others/r-p-singh-former-cag-official-who-disputed-2g-loss-passes-away/
118. https://www.frontline.in/cover-story/an-audit-gone-awry/article10008334.ece
119. Author's interview with the witness on 11 October 2018.
120. Author's interview with Subbarao on 18 January 2019.
121. Ibid.
122. Ibid.
123. https://www.thehindubusinessline.com/economy/gsts-17year-timeline/article9743284.ece
124. Pranab Mukherjee, *The Coalition Years 1996–2012* (Rupa Publications India Pvt. Ltd, 2017), p. 177.
125. Ibid., p. 177.
126. https://www.governancenow.com/news/regular-story/-recalling-a-time-when-bjp-opposed-gst--
127. Ibid.
128. Pranab Mukherjee, *The Coalition Years 1996–2012* (Rupa Publications India Pvt. Ltd, 2017), pp. 177–78.
129. https://www.thehindubusinessline.com/economy/gsts-17year-timeline/article9743284.ece
130. Pranab Mukherjee, *The Coalition Years 1996–2012* (Rupa Publications India Pvt. Ltd, 2017), p. 179.
131. https://timesofindia.indiatimes.com/city/ahmedabad/Gujarat-opposes-GST-regime/articleshow/24559119.cms
132. https://www.governancenow.com/news/regular-story/-recalling-a-time-when-bjp-opposed-gst--
133. Interview of a participant in these meetings to the author on 1 August 2018.
134. https://www.indiatoday.in/magazine/from-india-today-magazine/story/20101025-there-is-a-limit-i-have-overstayed-my-wicket-744472-2010-10-15
135. Interview of Yashwant Sinha to the author on 6 July 2018.
136. Interview of Jairam Ramesh to the author on 16 June 2018.

137. https://www.livemint.com/Politics/n4zC41fejoQ7ObfL4Bue6N/VodafoneHutch-deal--Retrospective-change-to-IT-Act.html

138. Pranab Mukherjee, *The Coalition Years 1996–2012* (Rupa Publications India Pvt. Ltd, 2017), p. 186.

139. https://www.livemint.com/Politics/n4zC41fejoQ7ObfL4Bue6N/VodafoneHutch-deal--Retrospective-change-to-IT-Act.html

140. Pranab Mukherjee, *The Coalition Years 1996–2012* (Rupa Publications India Pvt. Ltd, 2017), p. 191.

141. https://www.livemint.com/Politics/n4zC41fejoQ7ObfL4Bue6N/VodafoneHutch-deal--Retrospective-change-to-IT-Act.html

142. Pranab Mukherjee, *The Coalition Years 1996–2012* (Rupa Publications India Pvt. Ltd, 2017), pp. 186–91.

143. Para 26 in http://pib.nic.in/newsite/PrintRelease.aspx?relid=105494

144. https://indianexpress.com/article/opinion/columns/union-budget-2016-17-is-an-opportunity-wasted-by-bjp-govt-chidambaram-across-the-aisle-coloumn/

145. Interview of P. Chidambaram by author on 26 October 2018.

146. https://www.businesstoday.in/magazine/features/static-on-the-fm-channel/story/9505.html

147. Interview by author on 19 July 2018 of an official privy to the conversation.

148. Ibid.

149. Y.V. Reddy, *Advice & Dissent* (HarperCollins Publishers India, 2017), p. 384.

150. Interview given to the author on 19 July 2018 by an official privy to the conversation.

151. Ibid.

152. http://pib.nic.in/newsite/PrintRelease.aspx?relid=69449

153. Interview given to the author on 19 July 2018 by an official privy to the selections and ACC proceedings.

154. https://faculty.chicagobooth.edu/raghuram.rajan/research/papers/Parliamentary%20note.pdf

155. Vijay Joshi, *India's Long Road: The Search for Prosperity* (Penguin Random House India, 2016), pp. 144–45.

156. https://faculty.chicagobooth.edu/raghuram.rajan/research/papers/Parliamentary%20note.pdf

157. Vijay Joshi, *India's Long Road: The Search for Prosperity* (Penguin Random House India, 2016), pp. 144–45.

158. https://faculty.chicagobooth.edu/raghuram.rajan/research/papers/Parliamentary%20note.pdf

159. https://www.tribuneindia.com/news/nation/upa-phone-a-loan-scam-led-to-npas-claims-modi/646563.html

160. Interview of the RBI source by author on 11 October 2018.

161. https://timesofindia.indiatimes.com/india/ED-sees-political-push-behind-Vijay-Mallyas-Rs-950-crore-loan-from-IDBI-Bank/articleshow/51522930.cms

162. https://www.bloombergquint.com/business/lic-board-approves-proposal-to-buy-51-stake-in-idbi-bank#gs.BVXrEVA
163. https://www.thehindu.com/news/national/vijay-mallya-has-left-india-centre-informs-sc/article8331337.ece
164. https://www.facebook.com/notes/arun-jaitley/the-factual-situation/878476325674250/
165. Ibid.
166. https://www.thehindu.com/news/national/vijay-mallya-has-left-india-centre-informs-sc/article8331337.ece
167. Ibid.
168. Ibid.
169. Ibid.
170. https://www.thehindu.com/news/national/vijay-mallya-has-left-india-centre-informs-sc/article8331337.ece
171. Ibid.
172. Ibid.
173. https://timesofindia.indiatimes.com/india/Vijay-Mallya-flew-Jet-first-class-to-London-with-7-heavy-bags/articleshow/51352449.cms
174. https://m.timesofindia.com/business/india-business/CBI-altered-Vijay-Mallyas-lookout-notice-from-detain-to-just-inform-Agency-sources/amp_articleshow/51348532.cms?__twitter_impression=true
175. https://www.thehindu.com/news/national/vijay-mallya-loan-default-case-ex-idbi-bank-chairman-among-8-arrested/article17082954.ece
176. https://timesofindia.indiatimes.com/india/ED-sees-political-push-behind-Vijay-Mallyas-Rs-950-crore-loan-from-IDBI-Bank/articleshow/51522930.cms
177. https://timesofindia.indiatimes.com/india/ED-sees-political-push-behind-Vijay-Mallyas-Rs-950-crore-loan-from-IDBI-Bank/articleshow/51522930.cms
178. Ibid.
179. Ibid.
180. Ibid.
181. https://www.indiatoday.in/india/story/vijay-mallya-kingfisher-airlines-cbi-idbi-bank-loan-fraud-957505-2017-01-28
182. https://www.thehindu.com/news/national/vijay-mallya-loan-default-case-ex-idbi-bank-chairman-among-8-arrested/article17082954.ece
183. https://www.indiatoday.in/india/story/vijay-mallya-kingfisher-airlines-cbi-idbi-bank-loan-fraud-957505-2017-01-28
184. Ibid.
185. Ibid.
186. https://www.indiatoday.in/india/story/vijay-mallya-kingfisher-airlines-cbi-idbi-bank-loan-fraud-957505-2017-01-28
187. Ibid.
188. Ibid.

189. Ibid.
190. Ibid.
191. Ibid.
192. Ibid.
193. Ibid.
194. Ibid.
195. Ibid.
196. https://www.thehindu.com/news/national/vijay-mallya-loan-default-case-ex-idbi-bank-chairman-among-8-arrested/article17082954.ece
197. https://www.thehindu.com/news/national/vijay-mallya-loan-default-case-ex-idbi-bank-chairman-among-8-arrested/article17082954.ece
198. https://www.thehindu.com/news/national/vijay-mallya-loan-default-case-ex-idbi-bank-chairman-among-8-arrested/article17082954.ece
199. https://www.thehindu.com/news/national/vijay-mallya-declared-a-proclaimed-offender/article22369015.ece
200. D. Subbarao, *Who Moved My Interest Rate?* (Penguin Random House India, 2016), p. 176.
201. Ibid.
202. On the basis of an interview given to the author on 10 September 2018 by an IAS officer close to Manmohan Singh's PMO.
203. On the basis of an interview by the author on 19 July 2018 of an IAS officer (now retired) close to Manmohan Singh's PMO.
204. Ibid.
205. Ibid.
206. Ibid.
207. D. Subbarao, *Who Moved My Interest Rate?* (Penguin Random House India, 2016), pp. 202–07.
208. Ibid.
209. Ibid.
210. Ibid.
211. Ibid.
212. Table 5.2 in http://www.mospi.gov.in/sites/default/files/committee_reports/Report_committee_real_sector_statistics_25july18.pdf; and Table 3 in http://eaindustry.nic.in/key_economic_indicators/Key_Economic_Indicators.pdf
213. Quote from an interview of the former secretary by the author on 19 July 2018.
214. https://www.thehindu.com/news/national/pranab-lays-stress-on-economic-equity/article3681618.ece
215. Ibid.
216. Ibid.
217. Ibid.
218. Quote from an interview to the author given by the retired IAS officer on 27 August 2018.

219. Quote from an interview of the former secretary by the author on 19 July 2018.
220. Quote from an interview of the former secretary by the author on 19 July 2018.
221. Ibid.
222. Ibid.
223. Ibid.
224. Ibid.
225. Ibid.
226. Ibid.
227. Ibid.
228. Ibid.
229. Ibid.
230. Ibid.
231. Ibid.
232. Ibid.
233. Ibid.
234. Ibid.
235. Ibid.
236. Ibid.
237. Ibid.
238. Ibid.
239. Interview of P. Chidambaram by the author on 26 October 2018.
240. https://www.businesstoday.in/magazine/features/static-on-the-fm-channel/story/9505.html
241. Ibid.
242. Ibid.
243. Ibid.
244. Interview of the official to the author on 11 October 2018.
245. https://www.businesstoday.in/magazine/features/static-on-the-fm-channel/story/9505.html
246. Ibid.
247. Ibid.
248. Interview of P. Chidambaram to the author on 26 October 2018.
249. https://www.indiatoday.in/magazine/from-india-today-magazine/story/20101025-there-is-a-limit-i-have-overstayed-my-wicket-744472-2010-10-15
250. https://www.thehindu.com/todays-paper/tp-opinion/the-man-who-would-be-president/article3643967.ece
251. The Enforcement Directorate in October 2018 filed a charge sheet against P. Chidambaram in the Aircel–Maxis money-laundering case, accusing him of conspiring with foreign investors to clear their venture. He is contesting the case in court. The first charge sheet in the case was filed against Chidambaram's son, Karti, in June 2011. It claimed that he

controlled two firms which allegedly received Rs 1.16 crore as bribe money in the Aircel–Maxis money-laundering case; https://indianexpress. com/article/india/aircel-maxis-money-laundering-case-ed-files-charge-sheet-chidambaram-5418216/

Chapter 3: A Slow Recovery Again (2012–15)

1. https://www.livemint.com/Home-Page/7mxwqgZnZsLCEV2E3UaOSK/Government-keen-to-cut-red-tape-PM.html
2. http://content.time.com/time/covers/asia/0,16641,20120716,00.html
3. https://www.indiatoday.in/india/north/story/p-chidambaram-chief-troubleshooter-upa-ii-government-113319-2012-08-15
4. https://www.livemint.com/Politics/51z75ifGO3wJXtMvWFVK1H/Chidambaram-revamps-finance-ministry.html
5. https://www.moneycontrol.com/news/business/economy/-2006319.html
6. https://www.indiatoday.in/business/india/story/retail-fdi-reforms-at-full-throttle-anand-sharma-116587-2012-09-21
7. https://www.thehindubusinessline.com/economy/policy/nod-for-49-fdi-in-aviation-51-in-multi-brand-retail/article20502628.ece1
8. https://in.reuters.com/article/india-economy-sptext/text-sp-on-indias-sovereign-credit-rating-idINDEE89904K20121010
9. Ibid.
10. https://in.reuters.com/article/india-economy-sptext/text-sp-on-indias-sovereign-credit-rating-idINDEE89904K20121010
11. http://pib.nic.in/newsite/PrintRelease.aspx?relid=181001
12. Ibid.
13. https://www.financialexpress.com/opinion/the-amended-prevention-of-corruption-act-is-good-sense/1259951/
14. Ibid.
15. https://www.rediff.com/money/2007/jan/31ratings.htm
16. https://in.reuters.com/article/india-economy-sptext/text-sp-on-indias-sovereign-credit-rating-idINDEE89904K20121010
17. Interview of P. Chidambaram by author on 26 October 2018.
18. Daman Singh, *Strictly Personal: Manmohan & Gursharan* (HarperCollins Publishers India, 2014, 2017), pp. 370–71.
19. Ibid.
20. 'Twenty-five Years of Policy Tinkering in Agriculture', by Ashok Gulati and Shweta Saini, from the book *India Transformed, 25 Years of Economic Reforms*, edited by Rakesh Mohan (Penguin Viking).
21. Kaushik Basu, *An Economist in the Real World: The Art of Policymaking in India* (Penguin Random House India, 2016), Chapter 6.

22. Ibid., p. 108.
23. Ibid., p. 47.
24. D. Subbarao, *Who Moved My Interest Rate?* (Penguin Random House India, 2016), p. 47.
25. Kaushik Basu, *An Economist in the Real World: The Art of Policymaking in India* (Penguin Random House India, 2016), p. 47.
26. Ibid., p. 101.
27. Ibid., p. 102.
28. Ibid., p. 112.
29. https://www.thehindu.com/opinion/op-ed/agriculture-needs-a-reforms-package/article22406693.ece
30. Interview of P. Chidambaram by the author on 26 October 2018.
31. https://www.nytimes.com/2011/04/28/business/economy/28fed.html
32. https://blogs.wsj.com/economics/2011/04/27/live-blog-bernanke-holds-first-postmeeting-press-conference/
33. https://www.nytimes.com/2011/04/28/business/economy/28fed.html https://blogs.wsj.com/economics/2011/04/27/live-blog-bernanke-holds-first-postmeeting-press-conference/
34. Ibid.
35. Ibid.
36. https://www.nytimes.com/2012/09/14/business/economy/fed-announces-new-round-of-bond-buying-to-spur-growth.html
37. https://www.nytimes.com/2013/06/20/business/economy/fed-more-optimistic-about-economy-maintains-bond-buying.html
38. https://www.nytimes.com/2013/06/20/business/economy/fed-more-optimistic-about-economy-maintains-bond-buying.html
39. Ibid.
40. D. Subbarao, *Who Moved My Interest Rate?* (Penguin Random House India, 2016), p. 116.
41. https://economictimes.indiatimes.com/news/economy/indicators/fm-chidambaram-blames-pranab-mukherjee-for-the-dire-state-of-the-economy/articleshow/22107036.cms
42. Ibid.
43. Ibid.
44. http://archive.indianexpress.com/news/fiscal-deficit-at-5.8--india-worst-in-brics/956287/
45. https://www.thehindu.com/business/Economy/fiscal-deficit-lower-at-489-in-201213/article4769686.ece
46. Table 3 in http://eaindustry.nic.in/key_economic_indicators/Key_Economic_Indicators.pdf; and https://economictimes.indiatimes.com/news/economy/finance/p-chidambaram-bids-farewell-to-finance-ministry/articleshow/35152260.cms
47. D. Subbarao, *Who Moved My Interest Rate?* (Penguin Random House India, 2016), p. 118.

48. Ibid.

49. D. Subbarao, *Who Moved My Interest Rate?* (Penguin Random House India, 2016), p. 119.

50. Ibid.

51. Raghuram G. Rajan, *I Do What I Do* (HarperCollins Publishers, 2017), pp. 3–11.

52. Ibid., pp. 3–4.

53. https://finmin.nic.in/sites/default/files/Report_CompDevState.pdf; and https://www.livemint.com/Politics/Fl0Vfa3tMG3UiCO3aeXHQL/Rajan-committee-formula-for-central-funding-may-trigger-Unio.html

54. https://www.thehindubusinessline.com/economy/rajan-panels-new-pecking-order-for-states-has-some-surprises/article20665389.ece

55. https://www.thehindu.com/opinion/op-ed/the-gujarat-middle/article5993938.ece

56. http://planningcommission.nic.in/reports/genrep/rep_fr/cfsr_all.pdf; and Planning Commission, *A Hundred Small Steps: Report of the Committee on Financial Sector Reforms* (Sage India Pvt. Ltd, 2009).

57. Y.V. Reddy, *Advice & Dissent* (HarperCollins Publishers India, 2017), pp. 201–04.

58. Raghuram G. Rajan, *I Do What I Do* (HarperCollins Publishers, 2017), pp. 12–14.

59. https://www.imf.org/external/pubs/ft/scr/2014/cr1457.pdf

60. https://www.imf.org/external/pubs/ft/scr/2014/cr1457.pdf

61. https://www.imf.org/external/pubs/ft/scr/2014/cr1457.pdf

62. https://www.imf.org/external/pubs/ft/scr/2014/cr1457.pdf

63. https://www.thehindu.com/business/Economy/india-off-fragile-five-list-says-international-monetary-fund/article6535530.ece

64. https://www.thehindu.com/business/budget/economy-to-cross-5-mark-survey/article6194692.ece

65. Interview with P. Chidambaram by the author on 26 October 2018.

66. Ibid.

67. As told to the author in interviews on October 12 and 15, 2018 by an official present at the meeting.

68. Ibid.

69. Interview on 12 October 2018 to the author by the retired bureaucrat being quoted.

70. Ibid.

71. http://www.thehindu.com/news/national/we-lost-the-perception-battle-in-2014-salman-khurshid/article24038464.ece?homepage=true

72. Interview of P. Chidambaram by the author on 26 October 2018.

73. https://www.thehindu.com/opinion/lead/why-the-government-is-paralysed/article3670191.ece

74. Interview of the former bureaucrat by the author on 11 October 2018.

75. Interview of P. Chidambaram by the author on 26 October 2018.

76. Saurabh Chandra's (IAS) email to the author on 22 October 2018.
77. Interview of a secretary present at the meeting by the author on 12 October 2018.
78. Ibid.
79. Interview of a secretary present at the meeting by the author on 12 October 2018.
80. Ibid.
81. Ibid.
82. Ibid.
83. https://www.thehindu.com/news/national/plan-to-scrap-income-tax-gets-highlevel-hearing/article8206478.ece
84. Interview of a secretary present at the meeting by the author on 12 October 2018.
85. Interview of a senior IAS officer by the author on 10 August 2018.
86. Interview of a secretary present at the meeting by the author on 12 October 2018.
87. Ibid.; copy of the presentation accessed by the author.
88. Copy of the presentation accessed by the author.
89. Vijay Joshi, *India's Long Road* (Penguin Random House India, 2016), p. 22.
90. Interview of a secretary present at the meeting by the author on 12 October 2018.
91. https://www.bbc.com/news/business-35782239
92. Y.V. Reddy, *Advice & Dissent* (HarperCollins Publishers India, 2017), p. 238.
93. Ibid.
94. Y.V. Reddy, *Advice & Dissent* (HarperCollins Publishers India, 2017), pp. 249–50.
95. D. Subbarao, *Who Moved My Interest Rate?* (Penguin Random House India, 2016), pp. 3–8.
96. Ibid.
97. Ibid.
98. Ibid.
99. Ibid.
100. Ibid.
101. http://planningcommission.nic.in/reports/genrep/rep_fr/cfsr_all.pdf; Planning Commission, *A Hundred Small Steps: Report of the Committee on Financial Sector Reforms* (Sage India Pvt. Ltd, 2009).
102. https://www.prsindia.org/sites/default/files/bill_files/bill128_20070621128_Report_of_the_High_Powered_Expert_Committee_Percy_Mistry.pdf
103. D. Subbarao, *Who Moved My Interest Rate?* (Penguin Random House India, 2016), pp. 73–74.
104. https://nipfp.org.in/blog/2018/04/05/book-review-fiscal-consolidation-budget-deficits-and-macro-economy/

105. D. Subbarao, *Who Moved My Interest Rate?* (Penguin Random House India, 2016), pp. 73–74.
106. Raghuram G. Rajan, *I Do What I Do* (HarperCollins Publishers, 2017), pp. 3–11.
107. Ibid., p. 5.
108. Ibid., pp. 5–6.
109. Ibid.
110. Ibid., p. 16.
111. https://rbidocs.rbi.org.in/rdocs/PublicationReport/Pdfs/ECOMRF210114_F.pdf
112. Raghuram G. Rajan, *I Do What I Do* (HarperCollins Publishers, 2017), p. 20.
113. https://www.thehindu.com/business/Economy/rbi-adopts-new-cpi-as-key-measure-of-inflation/article5859713.ece
114. https://rbi.org.in/scripts/PublicationsView.aspx?id=15734
115. https://www.thehindu.com/news/national/interview-with-raghuram-rajan/article7110808.ece
116. Page 21, https://rbidocs.rbi.org.in/rdocs/PublicationReport/Pdfs/ECOMRF210114_F.pdf
117. https://www.thehindubusinessline.com/economy/macro-economy/fiscal-deficit-at-45-of-gdp-in-2013-14/article20787143.ece; https://www.livemint.com/Politics/MnCWYH7KLMzth6uugVVJDO/Budget-2015--RBI-Act-to-be-amended-inflation-to-be-kept-be.html
118. https://economictimes.indiatimes.com/news/economy/policy/fiscal-consolidation-with-quality-focus-crucial-rbi/articleshow/29517827.cms
119. Interview of an official handling the policy by the author on 12 December 2018.
120. D. Subbarao, *Who Moved My Interest Rate?* (Penguin Random House India, 2016), p. 80.
121. https://www.federalreserve.gov/faqs/money_12848.htm
122. https://www.thehindu.com/opinion/op-ed/comment-modernising-the-monetary-policy/article6549345.ece
123. https://www.financialexpress.com/archive/the-philosophy-of-dr-reddy/1108592/
124. Interview by the author on 12 December 2018 of the official handling the policy.
125. Ibid.
126. Ibid.
127. Ibid.
128. Ibid.
129. https://www.finmin.nic.in/sites/default/files/MPFAgreement28022015.pdf
130. https://www.thehindu.com/news/national/interview-with-raghuram-rajan/article7110808.ece

131. https://www.thehindu.com/opinion/lead/we-need-to-talk-about-this-manifesto/article5879871.ece

132. https://www.thehindu.com/business/Economy/changing-scene-shifting-tunes/article5905909.ece

133. Page 10, http://www.bjp.org/images/pdf_2014/full_manifesto_english_07.04.2014.pdf

134. Page 15, http://www.bjp.org/images/pdf_2014/full_manifesto_english_07.04.2014.pdf

135. Page 18, http://www.bjp.org/images/pdf_2014/full_manifesto_english_07.04.2014.pdf

136. Page 33, http://www.bjp.org/images/pdf_2014/full_manifesto_english_07.04.2014.pdf

137. Page 33, http://www.bjp.org/images/pdf_2014/full_manifesto_english_07.04.2014.pdf

138. Page 32, http://www.bjp.org/images/pdf_2014/full_manifesto_english_07.04.2014.pdf

139. Page 21, http://www.bjp.org/images/pdf_2014/full_manifesto_english_07.04.2014.pdf

140. Page 31, http://www.bjp.org/images/pdf_2014/full_manifesto_english_07.04.2014.pdf

141. Page 31, http://www.bjp.org/images/pdf_2014/full_manifesto_english_07.04.2014.pdf

142. Ibid.

143. Page 28, http://www.bjp.org/images/pdf_2014/full_manifesto_english_07.04.2014.pdf

144. Page 40, http://www.bjp.org/images/pdf_2014/full_manifesto_english_07.04.2014.pdf

145. Preface, http://www.bjp.org/images/pdf_2014/full_manifesto_english_07.04.2014.pdf

146. Page 27, http://www.bjp.org/images/pdf_2014/full_manifesto_english_07.04.2014.pdf

147. Page 19, http://www.bjp.org/images/pdf_2014/full_manifesto_english_07.04.2014.pdf

148. https://www.thehindu.com/business/Economy/rajan-has-failed-will-have-to-go-says-swamy/article5994079.ece

149. Ibid.

150. https://www.thehindu.com/business/Economy/only-55-who-earn-are-tax-payers-economic-survey/article8286548.ece

151. https://www.thehindu.com/business/Economy/rajan-has-failed-will-have-to-go-says-swamy/article5994079.ece

152. https://www.thehindu.com/business/Economy/rajan-has-failed-will-have-to-go-says-swamy/article5994079.ece

153. Interview of a source close to Ila by the author on 17 July 2018.

154. https://www.thehindu.com/business/Economy/finmin-appoints-ila-patnaik-as-principal-economic-advisor/article5933985.ece

155. https://www.huffingtonpost.in/2015/11/05/bibek-debroy-intolerance_n_8477332.html

156. Renamed Lok Kalyan Marg in 2016, https://www.thehindu.com/news/national/PM%E2%80%99s-new-address-7-Lok-Kalyan-Marg/article14992026.ece

157. Interview of a source close to Ila by the author on 17 July 2018.

158. Ibid.

159. https://www.indiabudget.gov.in/es2013-14/echap-02.pdf

160. https://www.thehindu.com/business/Economy/free-market-model-has-failed-kaushik-basu/article6713739.ece

161. https://www.thehindu.com/business/budget/bigticket-reforms-unstated-in-jaitleys-budget-speech/article6201647.ece

162. https://twitter.com/PiyushGoyal/status/486920992602599425

163. https://indianexpress.com/article/india/india-others/as-narendra-modi-arrives-montek-singh-ahluwalias-office-turns-into-fortress/

164. Interview of the official by the author on 12 and 15 October 2018.

165. https://www.indiatoday.in/magazine/nation/story/20140915-planning-commission-narendra-modi-montek-singh-ahluwalia-805189-2014-09-05

166. Interview of the official by the author on 12 and 15 October 2018.

167. Ibid.; https://www.pressreader.com/india/hindustan-times-gurugram/20130625/282256663070123

168. Ibid.

169. Interview of the official by the author on 12 and 15 October 2018.

170. Ibid.

171. Ibid.

172. https://www.dailymail.co.uk/indiahome/indianews/article-2344114/Modi-Montek-odds-Gujarat-model-Planning-Commission-raises-concerns-social-sector.html

173. Ibid.

174. Ibid.

175. Ibid.

176. https://www.thehindu.com/news/national/planning-commission-members-submit-resignation/article6026076.ece

177. https://www.thehindu.com/business/indias-growth-story-is-work-in-progress-manmohan/article5962552.ece; https://www.thehindu.com/todays-paper/tp-national/pms-farewell-speech-today-at-plan-panel/article5961430.ece

178. https://www.thehindu.com/business/indias-growth-story-is-work-in-progress-manmohan/article5962552.ece

179. https://indianexpress.com/article/opinion/columns/dr-manmohan-singhs-different-strokes/

180. https://economictimes.indiatimes.com/opinion/et-commentary/planning-omission-the-hydra-headed-monster-of-yojana-bhavan/articleshow/38085652.cms

181. https://www.thehindu.com/opinion/interview/%E2%80%9CIndia%E2%80%99s-changed-faster-since-1991%E2%80%9D/article14483507.ece

182. Interview of the official by the author on 12 and 15 October 2018.

183. Ibid.

184. Ibid.

185. http://pib.nic.in/newsite/PrintRelease.aspx?relid=108819

186. https://www.livemint.com/Politics/Nd6VqNJvOGOULnL6IUu1iP/On-68th-Independence-Day-Narendra-Modi-vows-to-fix-govt-mud.html

187. http://pib.nic.in/newsite/PrintRelease.aspx?relid=108819

188. Ibid.

189. Ibid.

190. Interview of the official by the author on 12 and 15 October 2018.

191. Ibid.

192. Author's interview with Sindhushree Khullar, then secretary, Planning, on 13 November 2018.

193. Author's interview with Yashwant Sinha on 6 July 2018.

194. Ibid.

195. Interview of an official present at the meeting by the author on 12 and 15 October 2018.

196. Ibid.

197. Ibid.

198. Author's interview with Khullar on 13 November 2018.

199. Interview of an official present at the meeting by the author on 12 and 15 October 2018.

200. Ibid.

201. http://www.mainstreamweekly.net/article6484.html

202. Author's interview with Khullar on 13 November 2018.

203. http://pib.nic.in/newsite/PrintRelease.aspx?relid=114268

204. Interview of the official being quoted by the author on 12 and 15 October 2018.

205. http://pib.nic.in/newsite/PrintRelease.aspx?relid=114268

206. https://indianexpress.com/article/india/india-others/niti-aayog-replaces-planning-commission-prime-minister-to-be-chairperson/

207. Interview of the official being quoted by the author on 12 and 15 October 2018.

208. http://pib.nic.in/newsite/PrintRelease.aspx?relid=115246

209. http://pib.nic.in/newsite/PrintRelease.aspx?relid=123274

210. http://pib.nic.in/newsite/PrintRelease.aspx?relid=161240

211. https://economictimes.indiatimes.com/opinion/et-commentary/planning-omission-the-hydra-headed-monster-of-yojana-bhavan/articleshow/38085652.cms

212. Daman Singh, *Strictly Personal: Manmohan & Gursharan* (HarperCollins Publishers India, 2014, 2017), p. 324.
213. https://indianexpress.com/article/opinion/columns/dr-manmohan-singhs-different-strokes/
214. https://www.businesstoday.in/magazine/features/montek-singh-ahluwalia-and-planning-commission/story/12523.html
215. Ibid.
216. https://www.businesstoday.in/magazine/features/montek-singh-ahluwalia-and-planning-commission/story/12523.html
217. Preface (page iii) in http://planningcommission.nic.in/reports/genrep/rep_hle.pdf
218. https://www.financialexpress.com/economy/gdp-back-series-niti-aayogs-role-raises-eyebrows-over-data-revision/1398054/
219. https://indianexpress.com/article/india/key-statistics-panel-revised-upa-growth-up-niti-aayog-rejected-it-5482457/
220. Author's interview with the official on 12 and 15 October 2018.
221. https://www.thehindubusinessline.com/news/national/panagariya-quits-niti-aayog-headed-to-us/article9796838.ece
222. Author's interview with the official on 12 and 15 October 2018.
223. The Shankar Aiyar Memorial Lecture: 'Fiscal Reforms in a Federal Framework' by Vijay Kelkar on 22 October 2016 in Chennai.
224. https://www.thehindu.com/business/Economy/all-you-need-to-know-on-finance-commission/article6928860.ece
225. https://www.thehindu.com/business/Economy/all-you-need-to-know-on-finance-commission/article6928860.ece
226. https://www.thehindu.com/todays-paper/tp-national/states-will-have-more-spending-freedom-cea/article6943065.ece
227. The Shankar Aiyar Memorial Lecture: 'Fiscal Reforms in a Federal Framework' by Vijay Kelkar on 22 October 2016 in Chennai.
228. https://nipfp.org.in//media/medialibrary/2019/01/WP_252_2019.pdf
229. http://eaindustry.nic.in/key_economic_indicators/Key_Economic_Indicators.pdf

Chapter 4: Another Recovery Destroyed (2016–18)

1. https://rbi.org.in/scripts/BS_SpeechesView.aspx?Id=1023
2. Vijay Joshi, *India's Long Road* (Penguin Random House India, 2016), pp. 144–45.
3. Para 33, https://www.imf.org/external/pubs/ft/scr/2014/cr1457.pdf
4. https://rbi.org.in/scripts/BS_PressReleaseDisplay.aspx?prid=29479
5. https://faculty.chicagobooth.edu/raghuram.rajan/research/papers/Parliamentary%20note.pdf
6. The Debt Recovery Tribunals (DRTs) were set up under the Recovery of Debts Due to Banks and Financial Institutions (RDDBFI) Act, 1993,

to help banks and financial institutions recover their dues speedily without being subject to the usual lengthy procedures of the civil courts. The Securitization and Reconstruction of Financial Assets and Enforcement of Security Interests (SARFAESI) Act, 2002, went a step further by enabling banks and some financial institutions to enforce their security interest and recover dues even without approaching the DRTs.

7. https://faculty.chicagobooth.edu/raghuram.rajan/research/papers/Parliamentary%20note.pdf

8. https://faculty.chicagobooth.edu/raghuram.rajan/research/papers/Parliamentary%20note.pdf

9. 'Zombie' is a technical term used in the banking literature and means a state in which a project/loan/bank does not respond to incentives, positive or negative.

10. https://faculty.chicagobooth.edu/raghuram.rajan/research/papers/Parliamentary%20note.pdf

11. https://rbi.org.in/scripts/BS_PressReleaseDisplay.aspx?prid=29479

12. Para 35, 36, https://www.imf.org/external/pubs/ft/scr/2014/cr1457.pdf

13. Box 5, https://www.imf.org/external/pubs/ft/scr/2014/cr1457.pdf

14. Ibid.

15. Page 8, https://www.imf.org/external/pubs/ft/scr/2014/cr1457.pdf

16. Interview of an official privy to that year's budget preparations by the author on 12 December 2018.

17. Interview of the official by the author on 1 July 2015.

18. Interview of the official by the author on 17 July 2018.

19. https://www.thehindu.com/opinion/lead/nehruvian-budget-in-the-corporate-age/article6959755.ece

20. https://www.thehindu.com/opinion/op-ed/need-for-corrective-action/article18718848.ece

21. https://www.thehindu.com/opinion/op-ed/A-tale-of-two-economists/article14005267.ece

22. https://www.business-standard.com/article/opinion/banking-where-do-we-go-from-here-119011601200_1.html

23. https://rbi.org.in/Scripts/BS_SpeechesView.aspx?Id=1055

24. Paras 14, 15, https://www.imf.org/external/pubs/ft/scr/2016/cr1675.pdf

25. To borrow from journalist Joris Luyendijk, who used the quote in 2013 to describe the London financial sector. https://www.wired.com/2017/04/dont-despair-big-ideas-can-still-change-world/

26. Y.V. Reddy, *Advice & Dissent* (HarperCollins Publishers India, 2017), p. 339.

27. https://www.thehindu.com/opinion/columns/A-governor-with-gumption/article14424159.ece

28. https://www.narendramodi.in/text-of-prime-ministers-remarks-at-the-inaugural-session-of-rbi-conference-on-financial-inclusion-2968

29. Ibid.

30. Raghuram G. Rajan, *I Do What I Do* (HarperCollins Publishers, 2017), pp. 219–22.

31. Ibid.
32. https://faculty.chicagobooth.edu/raghuram.rajan/research/papers/
     Parliamentary%20note.pdf
33. Raghuram G. Rajan, *I Do What I Do* (HarperCollins Publishers, 2017),
     p. xiii.
34. Ibid., p. 10.
35. Ibid., p. xi.
36. https://timesofindia.indiatimes.com/india/Raghuram-Rajan-mentally-
     not-fully-Indian-sack-him-Subramanian-Swamy-writes-to-PM-Modi/
     articleshow/52305377.cms
37. Raghuram G. Rajan, *I Do What I Do* (HarperCollins Publishers, 2017), p. 178.
38. https://timesofindia.indiatimes.com/business/india-business/Nirmala-
     Sitharaman-critical-of-RBI-governor-Raghuram-Rajans-one-eyed-king-
     phrase/articleshow/51884324.cms
39. Raghuram G. Rajan, *I Do What I Do* (HarperCollins Publishers, 2017),
     pp. 177–78.
40. https://www.thehindu.com/news/national/Govt.-backing-for-Rajan-
     %E2%80%98lacked-assertiveness%E2%80%99/article14578770.ece
41. https://www.livemint.com/Politics/NDvum3IHZE7BXtYJfkUiXN/
     Advani-calls-Manmohan-Singh-the-weakest-PM-ever.html
42. https://economictimes.indiatimes.com/news/politics-and-
     nation/bjp-attacks-pm-manmohan-singh-says-he-is-no-leader/
     articleshow/20218988.cms
43. Ibid.
44. Raghuram G. Rajan, *I Do What I Do* (HarperCollins Publishers, 2017), pp.
     170, 228; https://www.thehindu.com/news/national/Raghuram-Rajan-
     not-to-seek-second-term-as-RBI-Governor/article14430002.ece
45. https://in.reuters.com/article/rbi-chief-rajan-quit-idINKCN0Z50N2
46. https://www.thehindu.com/business/Economy/The-penny-drops-
     Govt.-wanted-continuity-chose-Urjit-Patel/article14580581.ece
47. https://www.thehindu.com/news/national/Govt.-backing-for-Rajan-
     %E2%80%98lacked-assertiveness%E2%80%99/article14578770.ece
48. Ibid.
49. Interview of the IAS officer by the author on 27 August 2018.
50. https://faculty.chicagobooth.edu/raghuram.rajan/research/papers/
     Parliamentary%20note.pdf
51. https://rbi.org.in/Scripts/BS_SpeechesView.aspx?Id=1055
52. https://www.bloombergquint.com/markets/india-s-60-billion-bad-bank-
     mistake#gs.Mf8uJaM
53. https://www.thehindu.com/opinion/op-ed/Why-a-%E2%80%98bad-
     bank%E2%80%99-is-tricky/article15477841.ece
54. https://ibbi.gov.in/BLRCReportVol1_04112015.pdf
55. https://www.business-standard.com/article/opinion/how-solvent-is-
     india-s-new-insolvency-law-119012000630_1.html

56. https://www.livemint.com/Politics/NFVNqE8lvABU5ZSylAMLfJ/
     Stalling-rate-in-private-sector-projects-hits-52quarter-hig.html

57. https://faculty.chicagobooth.edu/raghuram.rajan/research/papers/
     Parliamentary%20note.pdf

58. https://www.livemint.com/Opinion/ezuknR43SqrSFoZODanwQO/
     NPA-resolution-Lets-try-again.html

59. Para   8,   https://rbidocs.rbi.org.in/rdocs/Speeches/PDFs/
     GCIB190820172DE65550F56F4DFF88A22BDF2C0FADC1.PDF

60. https://www.livemint.com/Opinion/ezuknR43SqrSFoZODanwQO/
     NPA-resolution-Lets-try-again.html

61. https://www.business-standard.com/article/opinion/how-solvent-is-
     india-s-new-insolvency-law-119012000630_1.html

62. https://www.economist.com/leaders/2018/04/21/the-humbling-of-
     indias-tycoons

63. https://frontline.thehindu.com/cover-story/article25036443.ece

64. https://frontline.thehindu.com/cover-story/article25036443.ece

65. https://frontline.thehindu.com/cover-story/article25036443.ece

66. https://rbi.org.in/Scripts/PublicationReportDetails.
     aspx?UrlPage=&ID=902

67. Ibid.

68. The global financial crisis had demonstrated the need for a framework for
     effective financial crisis management and an effective resolution mechanism
     to handle systemic financial institutions. Under the Prompt Corrective
     Action framework, a resolution mechanism is put in place by the RBI
     when a financial institution has weakened substantially, but a framework
     of preventive as well as early intervention measures could potentially arrest
     the deterioration in financial institutions in the first place. The RBI had
     initiated a scheme of Prompt Corrective Action (PCA) in 2002 for banks
     which hit certain regulatory trigger points in terms of capital to risk weighted
     assets ratio (CRAR), net non-performing assets (NNPA), and return on
     assets (RoA). The scheme was revised in April 2017. Under the Revised
     PCA framework, apart from the capital, asset quality and profitability,
     leverage is monitored additionally. Under PCA, banks face restrictions
     on distributing dividends, remitting profits and even on accepting certain
     kinds of deposits. Besides, there are restrictions on the expansion of branch
     network, and the lenders need to maintain higher provisions, along with
     caps on management compensation and directors' fees. In other words, the
     entire thrust of the current PCA framework is to prevent further capital
     erosion and more importantly, to strengthen them to the point of resilience
     so that they can, as soon as possible, restart their normal operations. Eleven
     PSBs were placed under this PCA framework. Three of which exited the
     framework in February 2019. Impairment in the asset quality of the eleven
     banks had been high, necessitating sizeable provisioning and deleveraging,
     thereby constraining not only their capacity to lend but also the desirability

of their lending and acceptance of public deposits. Profitability and capital position of the eleven banks had seen erosion; https://rbi.org.in/Scripts/PublicationReportDetails.aspx?UrlPage=&ID=902

69. https://indianexpress.com/article/india/niti-aayog-vc-rajiv-kumar-npas-growth-decline-demonetisation-raghuram-rajan-policies-5337942/

70. https://faculty.chicagobooth.edu/raghuram.rajan/research/papers/Parliamentary%20note.pdf

71. https://rbidocs.rbi.org.in/rdocs/PublicationReport/Pdfs/BCF090514FR.pdf

72. https://economictimes.indiatimes.com/industry/banking/finance/banking/top-executives-of-dena-bank-and-vijaya-bank-kept-in-dark-about-the-merger-with-bank-of-baroda/articleshow/65847533.cms; https://economictimes.indiatimes.com/industry/banking/finance/banking/bank-merger-how-government-worked-out-the-marriage/articleshow/65864814.cms?from=mdr

73. Chapter VI Regulation, Supervision and Financial Stability; Para 11: https://rbi.org.in/scripts/AnnualReportPublications.aspx?Id=1124

74. https://www.thehindu.com/business/Economy/us-feds-taper-will-imply-that-funding-for-infrastructure-will-have-to-be-domestic-rbi/article6551356.ece

75. https://www.livemint.com/Politics/NFVNqE8lvABU5ZSylAMLfJ/Stalling-rate-in-private-sector-projects-hits-52quarter-hig.html

76. https://www.livemint.com/Politics/qkDQmArPJV65vk8Eycx5pN/As-India-struggles-to-cut-down-corporate-debt-the-economy-s.html

77. https://www.livemint.com/Politics/qkDQmArPJV65vk8Eycx5pN/As-India-struggles-to-cut-down-corporate-debt-the-economy-s.html

78. https://www.thehindu.com/opinion/op-ed/need-for-corrective-action/article18718848.ece

79. https://www.thehindu.com/news/national/Fall-in-exports-projected-to-be-worst-since-1952-53/article13975586.ece

80. https://www.thehindubusinessline.com/economy/exports-dip-imports-grow-715-per-cent-in-march/article23528903.ece

81. https://www.thehindubusinessline.com/economy/india-misses-2013-14-export-target/article20752287.ece1

82. https://www.thehindu.com/business/Economy/rupees-dancing-to-more-tunes-this-year/article23794789.ece

83. Ibid.

84. I.G. Patel, *Of Economics, Policy and Development: An Intellectual Journey* (Oxford University Press, 2012), p. 92.

85. Press Information Bureau, Government of India, Prime Minister's Office, 'Text of Prime Minister's Address to the Nation', 8 November 2016, http://pib.nic.in/newsite/PrintRelease.aspx?relid=153404.

86. https://www.thehindu.com/news/national/Demonetisation-of-Rs.-500-and-Rs.-1000-notes-RBI-explains/article16440296.ece

87. https://beta.indiatvnews.com/business/india-no-proposal-to-seal-bank-lockers-confiscate-jewellery-finance-ministry-357193

88. https://www.business-standard.com/article/opinion/demonetisation-dear-pm-please-don-t-mock-the-people-waiting-in-long-queues-116111400095_1.html

89. https://www.financialexpress.com/india-news/currency-demonetisation-rbi-releases-soiled-rs-100-notes-as-demand-surges/444349/;   https://www.thehindu.com/news/national/Recalibration-of-ATMs-will-take-up-to-three-weeks-says-Jaitley/article16443730.ece

90. https://www.thehindu.com/news/national/Recalibration-of-ATMs-will-take-up-to-three-weeks-says-Jaitley/article16443730.ece

91. https://www.firstpost.com/politics/narendra-modi-in-goa-full-text-once-we-get-clean-we-need-not-worry-about-even-one-corrupt-mosquito-3103608.html

92. https://indianexpress.com/article/india/india-news-india/demonetisation-manmohan-singhs-full-speech-in-rajya-sabha-4392829/

93. https://timesofindia.indiatimes.com/india/90-of-scrapped-notes-back-in-system-big-dividend-unlikely/articleshow/56210235.cms

94. https://www.thehindu.com/news/national/Supreme-Court-refuses-to-stay-demonetisation-notification/article16448531.ece

95. Ibid.

96. Ibid.

97. Ibid.

98. Ibid.

99. https://www.hindustantimes.com/india-news/sc-refuses-to-stay-demonetisationmove-govt-hopeful-of-recovering-rs-10l-cr/story-6w7uzKFZ2UkrY863aFONUO.html

100. https://www.thehindu.com/news/national/Supreme-Court-refuses-to-stay-demonetisation-notification/article16448531.ece

101. https://economictimes.indiatimes.com/news/economy/finance/after-almost-two-years-of-counting-rbi-says-99-3-of-demonetised-notes-returned/articleshow/65589904.cms

102. https://www.thehindu.com/opinion/op-ed/diary-of-an-unusual-year/article19576668.ece

103. https://www.thehindu.com/opinion/columns/Fifty-days-later/article17024053.ece

104. https://indianexpress.com/article/india/india-news-india/demonetisation-surgical-strikes-modi-manohar-parrikar-4398447/

105. https://www.thehindu.com/opinion/columns/Fifty-days-later/article17024053.ece

106. https://www.hindustantimes.com/india-news/rbi-says-ban-on-rs-1000-500-notes-proposed-hours-before-telecast-of-pm-s-speech/story-N5BQMs2RHkYUXMqzcvm44K.html

107. Ibid.

108. https://www.hindustantimes.com/india-news/rbi-says-ban-on-rs-
      1000-500-notes-proposed-hours-before-telecast-of-pm-s-speech/story-
      N5BQMs2RHkYUXMqzcvm44K.html

109. Arvind Subramanian, *Of Counsel: The Challenges of the Modi–Jaitley Economy*
      (Penguin Random House India, 2018), p. 94.

110. https://indianexpress.com/article/india/india-news-india/india-has-
      demonetised-high-value-currency-before-in-1978-4364851/

111. https://indianexpress.com/article/india/india-news-india/india-has-
      demonetised-high-value-currency-before-in-1978-4364851/

112. Author's interview with the former governor on 11 October 2018.

113. https://www.thehindu.com/news/national/centre-relaxes-fdi-norms-in-
      15-sectors/article7865451.ece

114. https://rbidocs.rbi.org.in/rdocs/AnnualReport/PDFs/RBIAR201617_
      FE1DA2F97D61249B1B21C4EA66250841F.PDF

115. https://rbidocs.rbi.org.in/rdocs/AnnualReport/
      PDFs/0ANREPORT201718077745EC9A874DB38C991F580ED14242.
      PDF

116. Page 181, Income Statement for the Year ended June 2017, https://
      rbidocs.rbi.org.in/rdocs/AnnualReport/PDFs/RBIAR201617_
      FE1DA2F97D61249B1B21C4EA66250841F.PDF

117. Ibid.

118. Ibid.

119. https://economictimes.indiatimes.com/news/economy/finance/after-
      almost-two-years-of-counting-rbi-says-99-3-of-demonetised-notes-
      returned/articleshow/65589904.cms

120. Ibid.

121. Ibid.

122. http://www.asianage.com/opinion/interview-of-the-week/020918/data-
      confirms-economic-cost-of-demo-was-higher-than-benefits.html

123. https://www.hindustantimes.com/india-news/sc-refuses-to-stay-
      demonetisationmove-govt-hopeful-of-recovering-rs-10l-cr/story-
      6w7uzKFZ2UkrY863aFONUO.html

124. http://www.asianage.com/opinion/interview-of-the-week/020918/data-
      confirms-economic-cost-of-demo-was-higher-than-benefits.html

125. https://www.thehindu.com/news/national/objective-of-demonetisation-
      was-not-confiscation-of-money-says-arun-jaitley/article19588738.ece

126. https://www.business-standard.com/article/economy-policy/day-after-
      demonetisation-jolt-govt-steps-up-defence-117083101282_1.html

127. Ibid.

128. https://www.thehindu.com/opinion/op-ed/diary-of-an-unusual-year/
      article19576668.ece

129. Interview of the former governor to the author on 7 January 2019.

130. Ibid.

131. Y.V. Reddy, *Advice & Dissent* (HarperCollins Publishers India, 2017),
      pp. 243–44.

132. Ibid.
133. https://indianexpress.com/article/business/banking-and-finance/manmohan-singh-saves-rbi-governor-urjti-patel-from-grilling-over-demonetisation/
134. Raghuram G. Rajan, *I Do What I Do* (HarperCollins Publishers, 2017), p. xiv–xv.
135. Ibid.
136. Ibid.
137. Ibid.
138. Ibid.
139. https://www.thehindu.com/news/national/key-reform-moves-on-the-back-burner/article6884263.ece
140. https://timesofindia.indiatimes.com/india/Rahul-Gandhi-tears-into-Modis-suit-boot-ki-sarkar/articleshow/46993611.cms
141. https://www.thehindu.com/business/Economy/make-in-india-campaign-industry-lines-up-behind-narendra-modis-pitch/article6447490.ece
142. https://www.narendramodi.in/text-of-prime-minister-shri-narendra-modi-s-address-in-hindi-to-the-nation-from-the-ramparts-of-the-red-fort-on-the-69th-independence-day-211475
143. http://pib.nic.in/newsite/PrintRelease.aspx?relid=135935
144. https://www.thehindu.com/elections/bihar2015/resurgent-opposition-will-have-a-say-in-reforms/article7858672.ece
145. Private conversation of the economist with the author sometime in the second half of 2015.
146. https://indianexpress.com/article/india/india-news-india/pm-modi-invites-sonia-gandhi-manmohan-singh-for-tea-gst-issue-may-come-up/
147. https://www.livemint.com/Politics/ZljtqwxyIdvaBPsmltFtUK/Arun-Jaitley-open-to-meet-Rahul-Gandhi-to-end-GST-impasse.html; https://timesofindia.indiatimes.com/india/Finance-minister-Arun-Jaitley-invites-Rahul-Gandhi-for-wedding-meet-sets-off-GST-buzz/articleshow/49838166.cms
148. https://www.thehinducentre.com/the-arena/current-issues/article24012281.ece
149. https://www.thehindu.com/news/national/anniversary-gifts-coming-on-may-26/article7228864.ece
150. Table 1.4, https://www.incometaxindia.gov.in/Documents/Direct%20Tax%20Data/time-series-data-2017-18.pdf
151. https://www.thehindu.com/sunday-anchor/sunday-anchor-steering-towards-reforms/article6751894.ece
152. https://www.thehindu.com/business/Economy/rupees-dancing-to-more-tunes-this-year/article23794789.ece
153. https://www.thehindu.com/opinion/op-ed/need-for-corrective-action/article18718848.ece
154. https://www.thehindu.com/opinion/op-ed/going-by-the-numbers-shortfall-in-gst-revenue-collection/article24636373.ece

155. Page 67 in https://fincomindia.nic.in/writereaddata/html_en_files/
     oldcommission_html/fincom13/tfc/Chapter5.pdf

156. https://www.thehindu.com/news/national/With-Congress-on-
     board-GST-Bill-may-be-passed-next-week/article14516993.
     ece#comments_14516993

157. https://www.thehindu.com/news/national/In-bid-to-push-GST-Jaitley-
     meets-Opposition-leaders/article14513330.ece

158. https://www.thehindu.com/news/national/In-bid-to-push-GST-Jaitley-
     meets-Opposition-leaders/article14513330.ece

159. https://www.thehindu.com/opinion/interview/%E2%80%98A-higher-
     rate-will-be-inflationary%E2%80%99/article14556968.ece

160. https://www.thehindu.com/opinion/interview/%E2%80%98A-higher-
     rate-will-be-inflationary%E2%80%99/article14556968.ece

161. https://www.thehindu.com/opinion/interview/%E2%80%98A-higher-
     rate-will-be-inflationary%E2%80%99/article14556968.ece

162. https://www.thehindu.com/news/national/With-Congress-on-
     board-GST-Bill-may-be-passed-next-week/article14516993.
     ece#comments_14516993

163. https://www.thehindu.com/news/national/In-bid-to-push-GST-Jaitley-
     meets-Opposition-leaders/article14513330.ece

164. https://www.thehindu.com/news/national/Amended-GST-Bill-gets-
     Parliament-green-signal/article14560332.ece

165. https://www.thehindu.com/news/national/Amended-GST-Bill-gets-
     Parliament-green-signal/article14560332.ece

166. https://www.thehindu.com/news/national/Amended-GST-Bill-gets-
     Parliament-green-signal/article14560332.ece

167. https://www.thehindu.com/news/national/Amended-GST-Bill-gets-
     Parliament-green-signal/article14560332.ece

168. http://pib.nic.in/newsite/mbErel.aspx?relid=167058

169. https://www.thehindu.com/opinion/op-ed/an-old-new-tax/
     article19150683.ece

170. Page 19, http://www.bjp.org/images/pdf/election_manifesto_english.pdf

171. https://www.thehindu.com/opinion/op-ed/an-old-new-tax/
     article19150683.ece

172. http://pib.nic.in/newsite/PrintRelease.aspx?relid=169792

173. Page 46, Chapter 2, Economic Survey 2016–17.

174. Vijay Kelkar, The Shankar Aiyar Memorial Lecture: 'Fiscal Reforms in a
     Federal Framework', Chennai, 22 October 2016.

175. Ibid.

176. https://www.thehindu.com/opinion/op-ed/going-by-the-numbers-
     shortfall-in-gst-revenue-collection/article24636373.ece

177. https://www.financialexpress.com/economy/gst-return-filing-why-
     are-central-staff-lagging-states-asks-union-finance-secretary-hasmukh-
     adhia/1196560/

178. https://economictimes.indiatimes.com/news/economy/policy/finance-ministry-crafting-strategy-to-boost-gst-revenues/articleshow/65739912.cms

179. https://special.ndtv.com/goods-and-services-tax-20/video-detail/no-pilot-project-done-now-confusion-over-gst-amit-mitra-488308

180. Meeting conducted under Chatham House Rule in Delhi on 23 October 2018.

181. https://www.business-standard.com/article/economy-policy/gst-councils-rush-job-angers-some-fms-of-opposition-ruled-states-118072300031_1.html

182. Ibid.

183. http://www.bjp.org/en/media-resources/press-releases/english-political-resolution-passed-in-bjp-national-executive-meeting-at-dr-ambedkar-international-centre-15-janpath-new-delhi

184. https://www.thehinducentre.com/the-arena/current-issues/article24012281.ece

185. https://www.thehinducentre.com/the-arena/current-issues/article9864899.ece

186. Ibid.

187. https://www.narendramodi.in/text-of-prime-ministers-remarks-at-the-inaugural-session-of-rbi-conference-on-financial-inclusion-2968

188. https://www.thehindu.com/business/Economy/cea-arvind-subramanian-reviews-oneyear-of-modi-govt/article7247733.ece

189. https://www.thehindu.com/opinion/interview/%E2%80%98A-higher-rate-will-be-inflationary%E2%80%99/article14556968.ece

190. https://in.reuters.com/article/india-farmers-politics/insight-as-election-looms-modis-popularity-wanes-in-rural-india-idINKCN1J00C5

191. https://www.hindustantimes.com/india-news/six-farmers-were-killed-in-the-june-6-police-firing-in-mandsaur-mp-govt/story-oXPWt7C0PP9PrHNc1sDvlO.html

192. https://indianexpress.com/article/india/tamil-nadu-farmers-protesting-at-jantar-mantar-to-drink-their-own-urine-4623327/; https://www.hindustantimes.com/delhi-news/tamil-nadu-farmers-return-to-jantar-mantar-with-17-skulls-and-chains/story-zqRCAUXZr2AITae2GLLoFO.html; https://www.thehindu.com/news/national/tamil-nadu-protesting-tn-farmers-drink-urine/article18192439.ece

193. https://www.thehindu.com/news/national/other-states/farmers-rally-in-maharashtra-maximum-march/article23280967.ece/photo/1/; https://www.hindustantimes.com/mumbai-news/maharashtra-farmers-protest-the-men-behind-the-long-march/story-5ZlffJgCqzv51UTTTfewaP.html

194. https://in.reuters.com/article/india-farmers-politics/insight-as-election-looms-modis-popularity-wanes-in-rural-india-idINKCN1IZ03J

195. https://www.livemint.com/Politics/iJcX5R7JftePlTZmlFhxML/Dairy-farmers-protest-in-Delhi-as-milk-prices-crash.html

196. https://www.ndtv.com/india-news/kisan-kranti-padyatra-tear-gas-water-cannons-used-as-thousands-of-protesting-farmers-try-to-enter-de-1925438

197. https://www.livemint.com/Opinion/h7Zmim3PJHrkaDRh0Z3CXN/Why-are-farmers-restless.html

198. https://www.epw.in/engage/article/jats-patels-and-marathas-want-quotas-but-do-they-deserve-them

199. https://www.thehindu.com/opinion/lead/a-vote-of-no-confidence-from-the-farmers/article24464628.ece?homepage=true

200. Ibid.

201. https://www.thehindu.com/opinion/op-ed/agriculture-needs-a-reforms-package/article22406693.ece

202. https://www.thehindu.com/opinion/op-ed/target-incomes-not-prices/article24281952.ece

203. This subsection, The Farm Crisis, draws heavily from the EPW article: https://www.epw.in/journal/2018/9/budget-2018%E2%80%9319/too-little-too-late.html

204. https://www.hindustantimes.com/india-news/govt-set-to-open-secondary-earning-avenues-to-double-farmers-incomes/story-I5H1oYTZM2RAW3OJMPyWwI.html

205. https://www.thehindu.com/opinion/op-ed/target-incomes-not-prices/article24281952.ece

206. https://www.thehindu.com/opinion/lead/a-vote-of-no-confidence-from-the-farmers/article24464628.ece?homepage=true

207. https://www.epw.in/journal/2018/9/budget-2018%E2%80%9319/too-little-too-late.html

208. https://www.hindustantimes.com/india-news/govt-set-to-open-secondary-earning-avenues-to-double-farmers-incomes/story-I5H1oYTZM2RAW3OJMPyWwI.html

209. https://www.epw.in/journal/2018/9/budget-2018%E2%80%9319/too-little-too-late.html

210. Ibid.

211. Ibid.

212. Ibid.

213. Ibid.

214. Ibid.

215. Ibid.

216. Ibid.

217. Ibid.

218. Ibid.

219. Ibid.

220. Ibid.

221. https://in.reuters.com/article/india-farmers-politics/insight-as-election-looms-modis-popularity-wanes-in-rural-india-idINKCN1J00C5

222. file:///C:/Users/win7/Downloads/Himanshu-Too-LIttle-Too-Late-EPW.pdf

223. https://timesofindia.indiatimes.com/business/india-business/sugar-industry-bailout-will-clear-only-40-of-cane-arrears-crisil-says/articleshow/64496050.cms

224. https://economictimes.indiatimes.com/blogs/cursor/the-bitter-truth-about-sugar-that-subsidy-cannot-sweeten/

225. https://www.thehindu.com/opinion/lead/a-vote-of-no-confidence-from-the-farmers/article24464628.ece?homepage=true

226. https://www.thehindu.com/opinion/op-ed/target-incomes-not-prices/article24281952.ece

227. https://www.indiabudget.gov.in/ub2019-20/bs/bs.pdf

228. https://www.thehindu.com/opinion/op-ed/agriculture-needs-a-reforms-package/article22406693.ece

229. Ashok Gulati and Shweta Saini, 'Twenty-five Years of Policy Tinkering in Agriculture', from Rakesh Mohan (ed.), *India Transformed, 25 Years of Economic Reforms,* (Penguin Viking).

230. https://www.thehindu.com/opinion/op-ed/target-incomes-not-prices/article24281952.ece

231. https://www.thehindu.com/opinion/op-ed/agriculture-needs-a-reforms-package/article22406693.ece

232. Ashok Gulati and Shweta Saini, 'Twenty-five Years of Policy Tinkering in Agriculture', from Rakesh Mohan (ed.), *India Transformed, 25 Years of Economic Reforms,* (Penguin Viking).

233. Ibid.

234. http://web.worldbank.org/WBSITE/EXTERNAL/EXTDEC/EXTRESEARCH/EXTWDRS/0,,contentMDK:23062293~pagePK:478093~piPK:477627~theSitePK:477624,00.html

235. https://rbi.org.in/scripts/BS_PressReleaseDisplay.aspx?prid=44710

236. https://www.reuters.com/article/us-india-cenbank-gurumurthy-newsmaker/maverick-accountant-gurumurthy-shaking-up-indias-central-bank-idUSKCN1NZ0IE

237. https://economictimes.indiatimes.com/industry/banking/finance/banking/rbi-member-s-gurumurthy-complains-to-governor-on-viral-acharya-speech/articleshow/66438643.cms

238. https://www.economist.com/finance-and-economics/2018/11/24/the-person-who-is-doing-most-to-undermine-the-reserve-bank-of-india

239. https://economictimes.indiatimes.com/industry/banking/finance/banking/nachiket-mors-2nd-tenure-on-rbi-board-cut-short/articleshow/66022164.cms; https://economictimes.indiatimes.com/industry/banking/finance/banking/rbi-member-s-gurumurthy-complains-to-governor-on-viral-acharya-speech/articleshow/66438643.cms

240. https://www.livemint.com/Industry/lQteyfZmGtn3XdwNoeL5iN/Swaminathan-Gurumurthy-stirs-debate-as-RBI-board-meeting.html

241. https://m.rbi.org.in/Scripts/AnnualReportPublications.aspx?Id=1239
242. Ibid.
243. https://thewire.in/political-economy/narendra-modi-government-rbi-reserves
244. Raghuram G. Rajan, *I Do What I Do* (HarperCollins Publishers, 2017), p. 221–22.
245. https://www.business-standard.com/article/economy-policy/day-after-demonetisation-jolt-govt-steps-up-defence-117083101282_1.html
246. https://www.businesstoday.in/current/economy-politics/fm-arun-jaitley-admits-section-7-of-rbi-act-was-invoked-govt-crossing-no-red-line/story/296092.html; https://economictimes.indiatimes.com/news/economy/policy/section-7-invoked-only-after-rbi-ignored-government-wish-list/articleshow/66504582.cms; https://www.livemint.com/Industry/kfSY5iaO5ltj6mFReVr72L/Govt-refuses-to-yield-on-Section-7-of-RBI-Act.html
247. https://rbi.org.in/scriptS/BS_SpeechesView.aspx?Id=1066
248. https://indianexpress.com/article/india/rbi-centre-rift-arun-jaitley-urjit-patel-viral-acharya-5425134/
249. https://economictimes.indiatimes.com/news/politics-and-nation/in-india-politicians-are-accountable-but-regulators-are-not-says-arun-jaitley/articleshow/63053677.cms?from=mdr
250. https://economictimes.indiatimes.com/industry/banking/finance/banking/rbi-member-s-gurumurthy-complains-to-governor-on-viral-acharya-speech/articleshow/66438643.cms
251. https://indianexpress.com/article/india/rbi-officials-should-exercise-restraint-or-resign-swadeshi-jagran-manch-5428165/
252. https://www.economist.com/finance-and-economics/2018/12/15/urjit-patel-the-head-of-the-reserve-bank-of-india-resigns
253. https://www.thehindu.com/business/Economy/govt-rbi-call-truce-after-a-marathon-board-meeting/article25541229.ece
254. https://economictimes.indiatimes.com/news/economy/policy/urjit-patel-met-pm-modi-on-november-9-possibly-to-thrash-out-issues/articleshow/66594873.cms
255. https://rbi.org.in/scripts/bs_viewcontent.aspx?Id=3606
256. https://www.economist.com/finance-and-economics/2018/12/15/urjit-patel-the-head-of-the-reserve-bank-of-india-resigns
257. https://www.rbi.org.in/Scripts/BS_PressReleaseDisplay.aspx?prid=45720
258. https://rbi.org.in/Scripts/governors.aspx#manmohan
259. Daman Singh, *Strictly Personal: Manmohan & Gursharan* (HarperCollins Publishers India, 2014, 2017), p. 314.
260. https://indianexpress.com/article/opinion/columns/because-data-is-a-public-good-nsc-p-c-mohanan-employment-survey-5578946/
261. http://eaindustry.nic.in/key_economic_indicators/Key_Economic_Indicators.pdf

262. Ibid.

263. https://www.thehindu.com/opinion/op-ed/need-for-corrective-action/article18718848.ece

264. https://www.thehinducentre.com/the-arena/current-issues/article24012281.ece

265. Ibid.

266. https://www.indiabudget.gov.in/ub2019-20/bs/bs.pdf

267. https://www.thehindu.com/business/Economy/government-to-infuse-rs-211-lakh-crore-into-psu-banks-over-two-years/article19912555.ece

268. https://www.livemint.com/Politics/pHwvWayyATNQjen4ckJj6O/CAG-indicts-Modi-govt-for-masking-fiscal-revenue-deficits.html

269. https://m.rbi.org.in/Scripts/BS_ViewBulletin.aspx?Id=17994

270. https://www.livemint.com/Politics/AqqOXCpYURO1ZLasIaZ3EK/Budget-2018-Arun-Jaitley-highlights-disinvestment-says-wil.html

271. https://economictimes.indiatimes.com/industry/transportation/airlines-/-aviation/government-bites-the-bullet-on-air-india-gives-in-principle-approval-for-disinvestment/articleshow/59355761.cms

272. Comment made in a private conversation with the author by senior banking journalist Raghu Mohan.

273. http://www.newindianexpress.com/opinions/columns/shankkar-aiyar/2019/jan/27/bjp-budgets-omissions-and-expectations-1930560.html

274. https://www.thehindu.com/opinion/interview/full-transcript-of-the-arun-jaitley-interview/article7117317.ece

275. https://www.thehindu.com/news/national/interview-with-columbia-economist-and-niti-aayog-vicechairman-arvind-panagariya/article7608979.ece

276. https://www.thehindu.com/news/national/the-hindu-explains-what-is-an-electoral-bond-and-how-do-we-get-one/article22367124.ece

277. https://economictimes.indiatimes.com/news/economy/policy/niti-poverty-elimination-task-force-submits-report-to-modi/articleshow/58964858.cms; https://economictimes.indiatimes.com/news/economy/indicators/india-has-100-million-more-poor-c-rangarajan-committee/articleshow/37912837.cms

278. https://www.thehinducentre.com/the-arena/current-issues/article24012281.ece

279. Interview of Yashwant Sinha to the author on 6 July 2018.

280. Amidst growing criticism of his government's inability to deliver on his 2014 electoral campaign promise of jobs-generating economic growth, Modi drew widespread flak from the opposition when in an interview in January 2018 he said selling pakoras (a variety of fried Indian snacks) should count as employment. https://www.dnaindia.com/india/report-pm-modi-interview-with-zee-news-top-10-key-takeaways-2576913

281. The official GDP growth projection for 2018–19, 7.2 per cent, suggests
a rebound once again (http://www.mospi.nic.in/sites/default/files/press_
release/FRE%20of%20National%20Income%2C%20Consumption%20
Expenditure%2C%20Saving%20and%20Capital%20Formation%20For%20
2017-18_0.pdf). Further, revisions of past years' estimates suggest that the
growth recovery Modi government inherited from the Singh government
sustained till the demonetization year when growth hit 8.2 per cent. After
which, growth was disrupted once again. These revised estimates show
faster growth rates, although the trend does not change. No significant
pickup can be seen in exports, manufacturing, agriculture and investments.

All links accessed last on 31 December 2018, except for the links for Chapter 4,
endnote 261 onwards, which were last accessed on 15 February 2019.